AF881320

ESSENTIALS OF TCP/IP

By

G. SHANMUGARATHINAM

M.E., (Ph.D.)

H.O.D. Department of Information Technology

Sudharsan Engineering College Sythyamangalam

Pudukottai (TN)

UNIVERSITY SCIENCE PRESS

(An Imprint of Laxmi Publications Pvt. Ltd.)

An ISO 9001:2015 Company

BENGALURU • CHENNAI • GUWAHATI • HYDERABAD
KOCHI • KOLKATA • LUCKNOW • RANCHI
NEW DELHI

PREFACE

This book has been written with the sole aim that the students of Engineering and other disciplines can easily understand the concepts of TCP/IP.

Author begins the introduction of the subject with a fundamental section containing essential background information, and a complete discussion of the OSI Reference Model. This is followed by the TCP/IP protocol suite. The core protocol, the backbone of TCP/IP internet work to function and classical application of TCP/IP are discussed extensively for the best understanding of the "Essentials of TCP/IP". Detailed explanations have been included to absorb the phases of development of each of the protocols and other role in the TCP/IP suite.

Author, using the experience gained through teaching of latest trends in networking to undergraduate and postgraduate students and also his research work on mobile computing, has made the whole concept appear very simple and very easy to understand. Following are the topics covered in the book extensively for a very clear understanding of the subject by every beginner.

Networking Fundamentals: Basic knowledge required for learning about network has been provided through a detailed discussion of important background materials. This also includes the essentials of networking, its benefits as well as disadvantages. A review of network types, sizes and their characteristics provides an insight into the basic ideas. Basic knowledge of mathematics namely computer mathematics, required for understanding networking concepts, has been provided. (including octal and hexadecimal numbers, conversions and bit masking.)

OSI Reference Model: A complete description of the ISO, Open System Interconnection (OSI) reference model. This reference model for networking has been explained thoroughly under this head. This section covers reasons for learning OSI model and its importance, essential concepts involved and terminology, and describes each model layer individually.

TCP/IP Overview: A high level overview of TCP/IP suite covering the history, architecture, client/server model and its operation, summary table of protocol and their layers have been all provided for reader's benefit.

TCP/IP Address Resolution Protocols: Detailed analysis of the importance of address resolution, a complete picture of the address resolution protocol (ARP) and a brief explanation of reverse address resolution protocol (RARP) are all included. While covering the address resolution protocol, discussion on caching and proxying has also been provided.

Internet Protocol (IP): An overview and history, addressing datagram encapsulation, fragmentation and reassembly, and routing are major topics covered for a clear understanding of the Internet protocol.

IP Addressing: The concept and structures of addressing, addressing types, IPV4 address classes, multicast addressing, subnet addressing, and classless addressing are all covered extensively. The details of step by step procedure to subnet a network have been provided through illustrative examples.

Internet Protocol Version 6 (IPV6): One of the most comprehensive descriptions of the new and essential version 6 of the Internet Protocol. This section discusses why IPV6 is important, and covers all the key changes between IPV4 and IPV6. It extensively discusses IPV6 addressing types and issues, IPV6 datagram formatting, IPV6 extension headers and options, and how datagrams are fragmented and routed in IPV6.

IP Support Protocols: A full discussion of two protocols that support the operation of IP. The Internet Control Message Protocol has been described fully for both IP and IPV6 (ICMP and ICMPV6), including a description of each of the ICMP message types.

TCP/IP Routing Protocols: While not specifically devoted to routing, The TCP/IP Guide provides a fairly detailed discussion of routing protocol issues.

TCP/IP Transport Protocols: A description of transport layer addressing (ports and sockets) and the two TCP/IP transport layer protocols: the User Datagram Protocol (UDP) and Transmission Control Protocol (TCP). This includes a discussion of TCP functions and characteristics, and a fully-illustrated explanation of sliding windows, TCP streams and segments, TCP connection establishment and management, message formatting, retransmission mechanisms, flow control, window size adjustment, and congestion avoidance.

TCP/IP General File Transfer Protocols: A section describing the operation of the File Transfer Protocol (FTP) and Trivial File Transfer Protocol (TFTP). The FTP section covers the FTP operational model, control and data connections, port usage, communication and transfer modes, and command and reply codes.

Socket Programming and Application: This section discusses the client and server socket in TCP and UDP. This includes a discussion of Ping and FTP using socket programming.

There are 'Choose the Best Answer' and frequently asked two marks questions, which will be much useful to the students from the exam point of view.

Organization

Chapter 1, reviews the basic concepts of seven layers and some popular networks.

Chapter 2, discusses the IP address. Chapter 3, 4 review ARP and RARP.

Subnet and Super net have been fully described in Chapter 5. Chapter 6, 7 are detailed descriptions of IP routing and ICMP. Chapter 8 discusses IPV6. TCP and UDP are fully described in Chapter 9. Chapter 10 and 11 give a brief review of the socket programming and application.

—Author

Acknowledgement

I express my deep sense of gratitude and my profound thanks to our college Chairman, Mr. V.K. Sundaram, Sudharsan Engineering college for his kind support and encouragement.

I am extremely grateful to our beloved Vice Chairman Shri. K. Ajay Kumar and Shri. K. Vijay Kumar for their constant encouragement during the preparation of this book.

I am very much grateful to Dr. R. Raghavan M.E., Ph.D Principal of Sudharsan Engineering college Sathyamanglam, Pudukkottai, Tamilnadu. He has been my source of inspiration and also my well wisher.

I am also very much grateful to Prof. Dr. N.P. Gopalan P.G Department, NIT Trichy. He has been encouraging me throughout my career and particularly in this attempt to bring this book—Essentials of TCP/IP.

I thank my parents, my wife, friends and other kind hearts that motivated me all the time.

—Author

CHAPTER 1

INTRODUCTION

1.1 INTRODUCTION TO NETWORKING

A basic understanding of computer networks is requisite in order to understand the principles of network security. In this section, we'll cover some of the foundations of computer networking, then move on to an overview of some popular networks. Following that, we'll take a more in-depth look at TCP/IP, the network protocol suite that is used to run the Internet and many intranets.

Network

A network is a group of connected, communicating devices such as computer and printer. An Internet is two or more networks that can communicate with each other. This definition suits our purpose well: a computer network is simply a system of interconnected computers.

OSI Model

Established in 1947, the International Standards Organization (ISO) is multinational body dedicated to world wide agreement on international standards. An ISO standard that covers all aspect of network communication is the open system interconnection (OSI) model. The purpose of the OSI model is to show how to facilitate communication between different system without requiring changes to the logic of the underlying hardware and software. It consists of seven separate but related layer each of which defines a part of layered architecture.

The process of moving information across a network

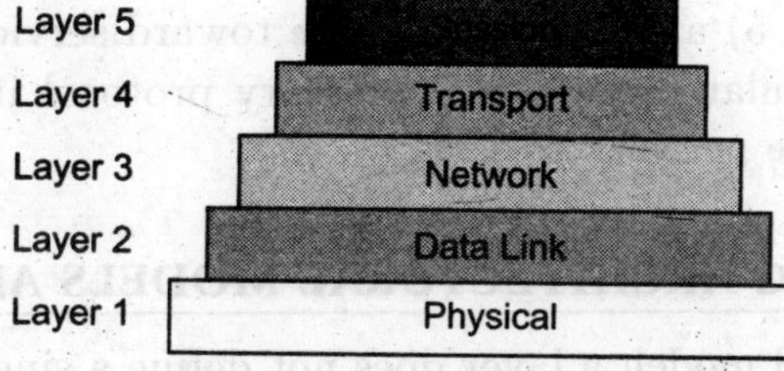

Fig. 1.1 *The OSI model.*

The OSI model is composed of seven ordered layer: physical layer 1, data link layer 2, network layer 3. transpor t layer 4. session layer 5. presentation layer 6. application layer 7.

- The model was developed by the International Standards Organization: (ISO) in 1984. It is now considered the primary Architectural model for intercomputer communications.
- The Open System Interconnection (OSI) reference model is a descriptive network scheme. It ensures greater compatibility and interoperability between various types of network technologies.
- The OSI model describes how information or data makes its way from application programmes (such as spreadsheets) through a network medium (such as wire) to another application programme located on another network.
- The OSI reference model divides the problem of moving information between computers over a network medium into SEVEN smaller and more manageable problems.
- This separation into smaller more manageable functions is known as layering.

1.2 A LAYERED NETWORK MODEL

- The OSI Reference Model is composed of seven layers, each specifying particular network functions.
- The process of breaking up the functions or tasks of networking into layers reduces complexity.
- Each layer provides a service to the layer above it in the protocol specification.
- Each layer communicates with the same layer's software or hardware on other computers.

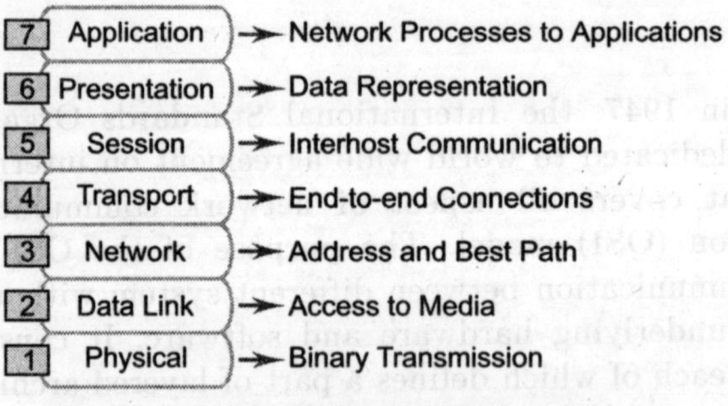

Fig. 1.2. *Seven OSI reference model layer.*

- The lower 4 layers (transport, network, data link and physical—Layers 4, 3, 2 and 1) are concerned with the flow of data from end to end through the network.
- The upper 4 layers of the OSI model (application, presentation and session—Layers 7, 6 and 5) are orientated more toward services to the applications.
- Data is Encapsulated with the necessary protocol information as it moves down the layers before network transit.

1.3 UNDERSTANDING ARCHITECTURAL MODELS AND PROTOCOLS

In an architectural model, a layer does not define a single protocol—it defines a data communication function that may be performed by any number of protocols. Because each layer defines a function, it can contain multiple protocols, each of which provides a service suitable to the function of that layer.

Every protocol communicates with its peer. A *peer* is an implementation of the same protocol in the equivalent layer on a remote computer. Peer-level communications are standardized to ensure that successful communications take place. Theoretically, each protocol is only concerned with communicating to its peer—it does not care about the layers above or below it.

A dependency, however, exists between the layers. Because every layer is involved in sending data from a local application to an equivalent remote application, the layers must agree on how to pass data among themselves on a single computer. The upper layers rely on the lower layers to transfer the data across the underlying network.

How a Protocol Stack Works

As the reference model indicates, protocols (which compose the various layers) are like a pile of building blocks stacked one upon another. Because of this structure, groups of related protocols are often called *stacks* or *protocol stacks.*

Data is passed down the stack from one layer to the next, until it is transmitted over the network by the network access layer protocols. The 4 layers in this reference model are crafted to distinguish between the different ways that the data is handled as it passes down the protocol stack from the application layer to the underlying physical network.

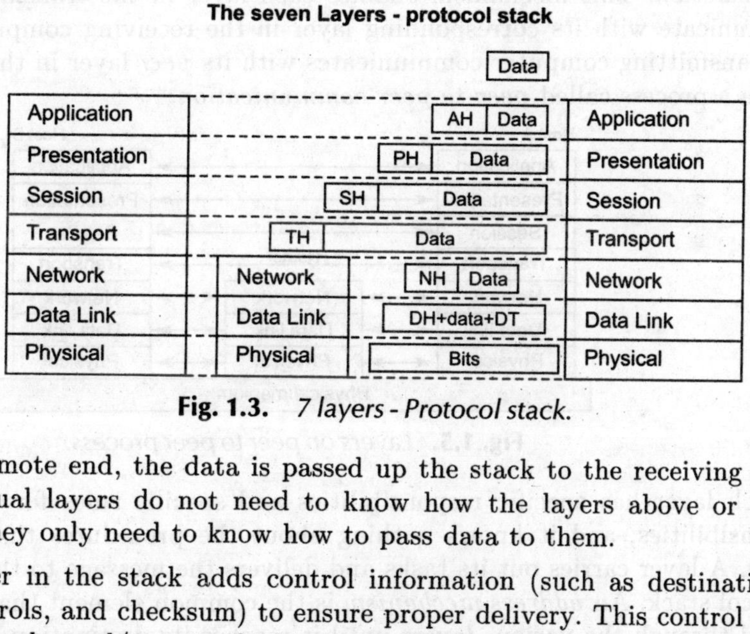

Fig. 1.3. *7 layers - Protocol stack.*

At the remote end, the data is passed up the stack to the receiving application. The individual layers do not need to know how the layers above or below them function ; they only need to know how to pass data to them.

Each layer in the stack adds control information (such as destination address, routing controls, and checksum) to ensure proper delivery. This control information is called a *header* and/or a *trailer* because it is placed in front of or behind the data to be transmitted. Each layer treats all of the information that it receives from the layer above it as data, and it places its own header and/or trailer around that information.

These wrapped messages are then passed into the layer below along with additional control information, some of which may be forwarded or derived from the higher layer. By the time a message exits the system on a physical link (such as a wire), the original message is enveloped in multiple, nested wrappers—one for each layer of protocol through which the data passed. When a protocol uses headers or trailers to package the data from another protocol, the process is called *encapsulation.* This process is illustrated in Figure 1.4.

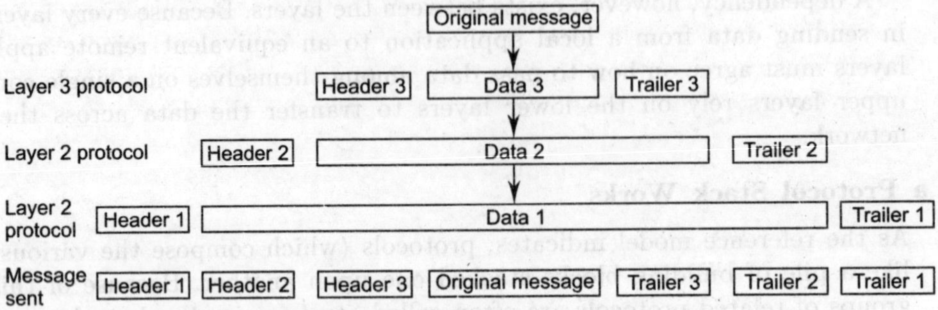

Fig. 1.4. *Encapsulation of data for network delivery.*

When data is received, the opposite happens. Each layer strips off its header and/or trailer before passing the data up to the layer above. As information flows up the stack, the information received from a lower layer is interpreted as both a header/trailer and data. The process of removing headers and trailers from data is called *decapsulation.* This mechanism enables each layer in the transmitting computer to communicate with its corresponding layer in the receiving computer. Each layer in the transmitting computer communicates with its *peer* layer in the receiving computer via a process called *peer-to-peer communication.*

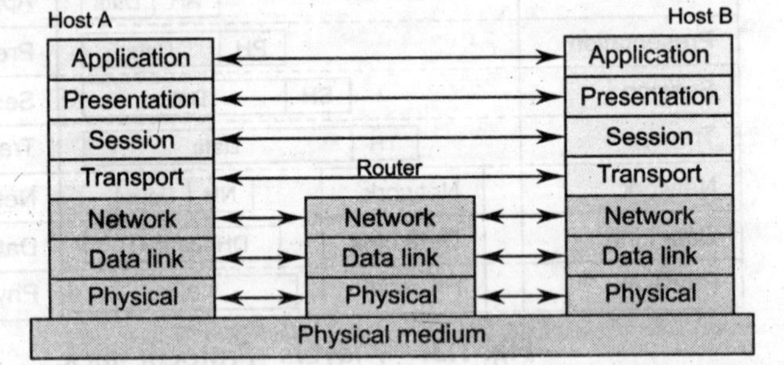

Fig. 1.5. *Layers on peer to peer process.*

Each layer has specific responsibilities and specific rules for carrying out those responsibilities, and it knows nothing about the procedures that the other layers follow. A layer carries out its tasks and delivers the message to the next layer in the protocol stack. An *address mechanism* is the common element that allows data to be routed through the various layers until it reaches its destination.

Each layer also has its own independent data structures. Conceptually, a layer is unaware of the data structures used by the layers above and below it. In reality, the data structures of a layer are designed to be compatible with the structures used by the surrounding layers for the sake of more efficient data transmission. Still, each layer has its own data structures and its own terminology to describe those structures.

1.4 LAYER IN THE OSI MODEL

Physical Layer

The physical layer coordinates the function required to transmit a bit stream over a physical medium. It deals with the mechanical and electrical specification of the interface and transmission media

Physical Characteristics of Interfaces and Media

The physical character of the interfaces between the devices and the transmission media.

Representation of Bits

The physical layer data consists of stream of bits (sequences of 0s or 1s)without any interpretation.

Data Rate

The transmission rate the number of bits sent each second is also defined by the physical layer.

Line Configuration

The physical layer is concerned with connection of devices to the media. In point-to-point configuration, two devices are connected together through a dedicated link.

Physical Topology

The physical topology defines how devices are connected to make a network .

Devices can be connected using mesh topology, star topology, a ring topology, Bus topology.

Transmission Mode

The physical layer also defines the direction of transmission between two devices : Simple, half-duplex or full-duplex.

Points to Remember

- *Moves bits between physically connected end-systems*
- *Standard prescribes*
  - *coding scheme to represent a bit*
  - *shapes and sizes of connectors*
  - *bit-level synchronization*
- *Postal network*
  - *technology for moving letters from one point to another (trains, planes, vans, bicycles, ships...)*
- *Internet*
  - *technology to move bits on a wire, wireless link, satellite channel e.*

Data Link Layer

The data link layer transforms the physical layer a raw transmission facility to reliable link it makes the physical layer appear error free to the upper layer.

Framing

The data link layer divides stream of bits received from the network layer into manageable data unit called frame.

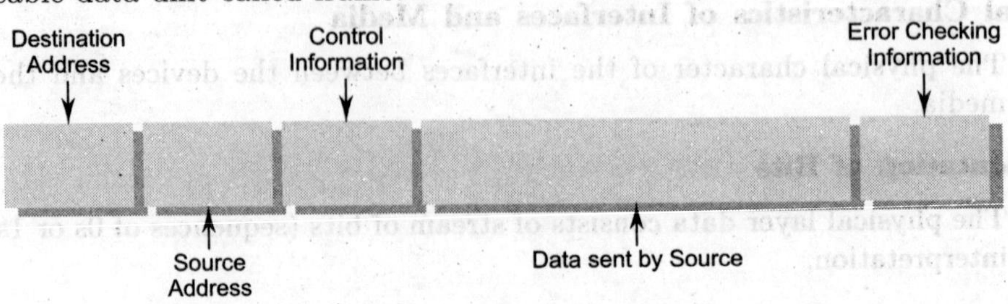

Fig. 1.6. *Frame format.*

- Structured package for moving data
- Includes raw data (or payload) along with sender's and receiver's:
  - o Network addresses
  - o Error-checking and control information.

Subdivided Data Link

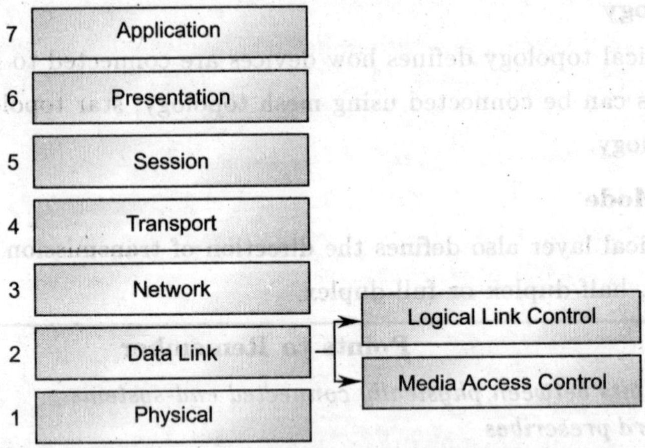

Fig. 1.7. *Subdivided data link.*

Physical Addressing

If frames are to be distributed to different system on the network the data link layer adds a header to the frame to define the sender and receiver of the frame.

Flow Control

If the rate in which the data is absorbed by the receiver is less than the rate produced in the sender the data link layer impose a flow control mechanism to prevent overwhelming the receiver.

Error Control

The data link layer adds reliability to the physical layer by adding mechanism to detect and retransmit damaged of frames. Error control is normally achieved through a trailer added to the end of the frame.

Access Control

When two or more devices are connected to the same link, data link layer protocol are necessary to determine which devices has control over link at the given time.

Points to Remember

- *Reliable communication over a single link.*
- *Introduces the notion of a frame*
  - *set of bits that belong together*
- *Idle markers tell us that a link is not carrying a frame*
- *Begin and end markers delimit a frame*
- *On a broadcast link (such as Ethernet)*
  - *end-system must receive only bits meant for it*
  - *need datalink-layer address*
  - *also need to decide who gets to speak next*
  - *these functions are provided by Medium Access Sublayer (MAS)*
- *Data link layer protocols are the first layer of software*
- *Very dependent on underlying physical link properties*
- *Usually bundle both physical and data link layer on host adaptor card*
  - *example: Ethernet*
- *Postal service*
  - *mail bag 'frames' letters*
- *Internet*
  - *a variety of data link layer protocols*
  - *most common is Ethernet*
  - *others are FDDI, SONET, HDLC*

Network Layer

The network layer is responsible for the source to destination delivery of a packet possibly across multiple network, whereas the data link layer oversees the delivery of the packet between two system on the same network the network layer ensures that each packet gets from its point of origin to its final destination.

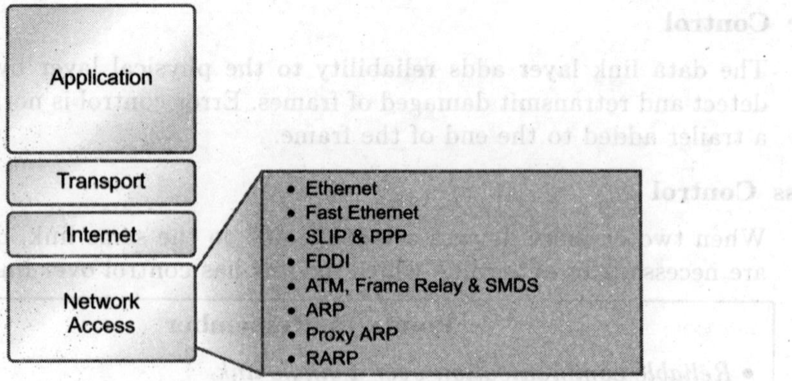

Fig. 1.8. *Network access.*

Logical Addressing

The physical addressing implemented by the data link layer handles the addressing problem locally if the packet passes the network boundary we need another addressing system to help distinguish the sources and destination system the network layer adds a header to the packet coming from the upper layer that among other things includes the logical address of the sender and receiver.

Routing

When independent network or links are connected together to create internet works.

Points to Remember

- *Carrying data from source to destination.*
- *Logically concatenates a set of links to form the abstraction of an end-to-end link*
- *Allows an end-system to communicate with any other end-system by computing a route between them*
- *Hides idiosyncrasies of data link layer*
- *Provides unique network-wide addresses*
- *Found both in end-systems and in intermediate systems*
- *At end-systems primarily hides details of data link layer*
  - o *segmentation and reassembly*
  - o *error detection*
- *At intermediate systems*
  - o *participates in routing protocol to create routing tables*
  - o *responsible for forwarding packets*
  - o *scheduling the transmission order of packets*
  - o *choosing which packets to drop*

Transport Layer

The transport layer is responsible for sources to destination (end-to-end) delivery of entire message whereas the network layer oversees end-to-end delivery of individual packet. It does not recognize any relationship between those packet. It treats each independently as through each piece belonged to a separate message.

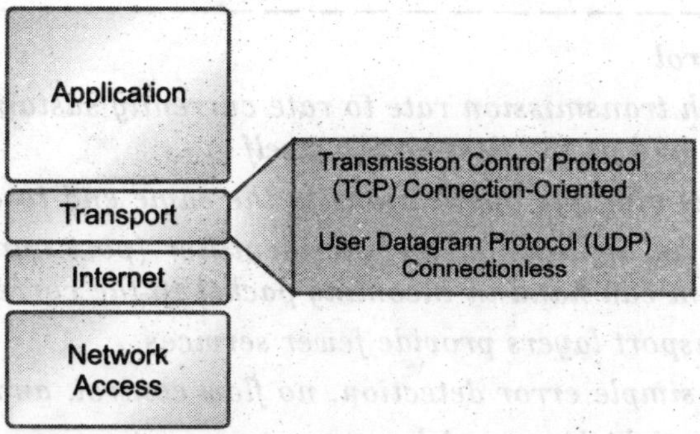

Fig. 1.9. *Above it show the transport layer.*

Services Point Addressing

Computer often run several program at the same time. The transport layer header must include type of address called service-point address (or port). The network layer gets each to the correct computer.

Segmentation and Reassembly

A message is divided into transmittable segments each segments containing a sequence number, these number enable the transport layer to reassemble the message correctly upon arriving at the destination and to identify and replace packet that were lost in the transmission.

Connection Control

The transport layer can be either connectionless or connection oriented. A connectionless transport layer treats each segment as an independent packet and delivers it to the transport layer at the destination machine. A connection oriented transport layer makes a connection with the transport layer at the destination machine first before delivery the packet.

Flow Control

Like data link layer, the transport layer is responsible for flow control.

Error Control

Like data link layer the transport layer is responsible for error control. The sending transport layer makes sure that the entire message arrives at the receiver transport layer. Without error(damage, loss OR duplication).

Points to Remember

- *Reliable end-to-end communication.*
- *Network provides a 'raw' end-to-end service*
- *Transport layer creates the abstraction of an error-controlled, flow-controlled and multiplexed end-to-end link*
- *Error control*
  - o *message will reach destination despite packet loss, corruption and duplication*
  - o *retransmit lost packets; detect, discard, and retransmit corrupted packets; detect and discard duplicated packets*

- *Flow control*
  - *match transmission rate to rate currently sustainable on the path to destination, and at the destination itself*
- *Multiplexes multiple applications to the same end-to-end connection*
  - *adds an application-specific identifier (port number) so that receiving end-system can hand in incoming packet to the correct application*
- *Some transport layers provide fewer services*
  - *e.g., simple error detection, no flow control, and no retransmission*
  - *lightweight transport layer*
- *Postal system*
  - *doesn't have a transport layer*
  - *implemented, if at all, by customers*
  - *detect lost letters (how?) and retransmit them*
- *Internet*
  - *two popular protocols are TCP and UDP*
  - *TCP provides error control, flow control, multiplexing*
  - *UDP provides only multiplexing*

Session Layer

The session layer is the network dialog controller. It established, maintains and synchronizes the interaction between communicating system.

Dialog Control

The session layer allows two system to enter in to dialog it allows the communication between two process to take place either in half duplex (one way at a time) or full duplex Mode.

Synchronization

The session layer allows a process to add checkpoint (Synchronization) intostream of data.

Points to Remember

- *Not common*
- *Provides full-duplex service, expedited data delivery, and session synchronization*
- *Token management*
- *Duplex*
  - *if transport layer is simplex, concatenates two transport endpoints together*
- *Expedited data delivery*
  - *allows some messages to skip ahead in end-system queues, by using a separate low-delay transport layer endpoint*
- *Synchronization*
  - *allows users to place marks in data stream and to roll back to a prespecified mark*

Example:

- Postal network
  - o suppose a company has separate shipping and receiving clerks
  - o chief clerk can manage both to provide abstraction of a duplex service
  - o chief clerk may also send some messages using a courier (expedited service)
  - o chief clerk can arrange to have a set of messages either delivered all at once, or not at all
- Internet
  - o doesn't have a standard session layer

Presentation Layer

The presentation is concerned with syntax and semantics of the information exchanged between two system.

Translation

The process in two system are usually exchanging information in the form of character strings number and so on the information should be changed to bit stream before being transmitted, because the different computer use different encoding system the presentation layer is responsible for interoperability between these encoding method the presentation layer at the sender changes the information from its sender dependent format into a common format. The presentation layer at the receiver machine changes the common format into its receiver machine changes the common format into its receiver dependent format.

Encryption

To carry sensitive information a system must be able to assure privacy. Encryption means that the sender transform the original information to another form and sends the resulting message out over the network decryption reverse the original to transform the message back to its original form.

Compression

Data compression reduces the number of bits contained in the information. Data compression becomes particularly important in the transmission of multimedia such as text audio and video.

Points to Remember

- *Unlike other layers which deal with headers presentation layer touches the application data*
- *Hides data representation differences between applications*

  e.g., endian-ness
  - o *characters (ASCII, unicode, EBCDIC.)*
- *Can also encrypt data*
- *Usually ad hoc*

- *Postal network*
    - *translator translates contents before giving it to chief clerk*
- *Internet*
    - *no standard presentation layer*
    - *only defines network byte order for 2- and 4-byte integers*

Application Layer

The application layer enables the user whether human or software to access the network. It provides user interfaces and support for services such as electronics mail, remote file access and transfer shared database management and other types of distributed information services.

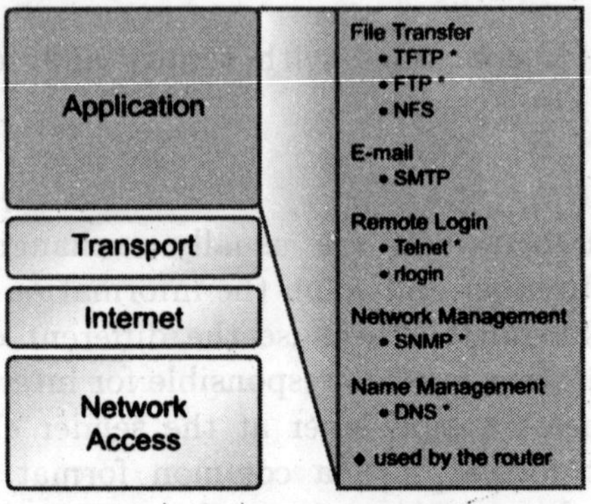

Fig. 1.10. *The application layer.*

Network Virtual Terminal

Network virtual terminal is software version of a physical terminal and allows a user to log on to remote host.

File Transfer Access and Management

This application allows a user to access files in remote host to retrieve files from remote. Computer for use in the local computer and to manage or control files in remote computer locally.

Mail Services

This application provide the basis for email forwarding and storage.

Directory Services

This application provides distributed database sources and access for global information about various objects and services.

Points to Remember

- *The set of applications that use the network*
- *Doesn't provide services to any other layer*
- *Postal network*
    - *the person who uses the postal system*

- *suppose manager wants to send a set of recall letters*
- *translator translates letters going abroad*
- *chief clerk sends some priority mail, and some by regular mail*
- *mail clerk sends a message, retransmits if not acked*
- *postal system computes a route and forwards the letters*
- *data link layer: letters carried by planes, trains, automobiles*
- *physical layer: the letter itself*

1.5 CONNECTING NETWORKS

Repeater

- Allows the connection of segments
- Extends the network beyond the maximum length of a single segment
- Functions at the Physical Layer of the OSI model
- A multi-port repeater is known as a Hub
- Connects segments of the same network, even if they use different media
- Has three basic functions
  - Receives a signal which it cleans up
  - Re-times the signal to avoid collisions
  - Transmits the signal on to the next segment

Hub

- A central point of a star topology
- Allows the multiple connection of devices
- Can be more than a basic Hub — providing additional services (Managed Hubs, Switched Hubs, Intelligent Hubs)
- In reality a Hub is a Repeater with multiple ports
- Functions in a similar manner to a Repeater
- Works at the Physical Layer of the OSI model
- Passes data no matter which device it is addressed to
- This feature adds to congestion
- Use large Hubs (24 port), or stacking them exacerbates this negative feature

Hub Features

- Type of media connection needed
- Number of ports
- Speed
- Managed or Unmanaged
- Requirement for UpLink Port ? (allows two Hubs to be connected using a patch cable — crossover cable)/
- Token Ring Hubs are known as MAUs — see last week's notes

Bridge

- Like a Repeater or Hub it connects segments
- Works at Data Layer — not Physical
- Uses Mac address to make decisions
- Acts as a 'filter', by determining whether or not to forward a packet on to another segment
- Builds a Bridging Table, keeps track of devices on each segment
- Filters packets, does not forward them, by examining their MAC address
- It forwards packets whose destination address is on a different segment from its own
- It divides a network in to multiple collision domains — so reducing the number of collisions
- Uses the Spanning Tree Protocol (STP) — to decide whether to pass a packet on to a different network segment

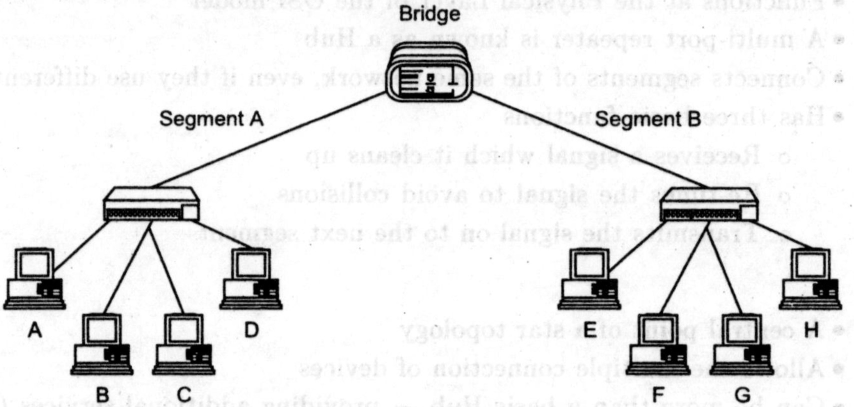

Fig. 1.11. *The bridge.*

Switch

- A multiport Bridge, functioning at the Data Link Layer
- Each port of the bridge decides whether to forward data packets to the attached network
- Keeps track of the Mac addresses of all attached devices (just like a bridge)
- Similarly priced to Hubs — making them popular
- Acts like a Hub, but filters like a Bridge
- Each port on a Switch is a collision domain

Brouter

- Functions both as Bridge and a Router — hence name
- Can work on networks using different protocols
- Can be programmed only to pass data packets using a specific protocol forward to a segment — in this case it is functioning in a similar manner to a Bridge
- If a Brouter is set to route data packets to the appropriate network with a routed protocol such as IP, it is functioning as a Router

- Works at Network Layer in an intelligent manner
- Can connect different network segments, if they are in the same building or even on the opposite side of the globe
- Work in LAN, MAN and WAN environments
- Allows access to resources by selecting the best path
- Can interconnect different networks — Ethernet with Token Ring
- Changes packet size and format to match the requirements of the destination network
- Two primary functions — to determine the 'best path' and to share details of routes with other routers
- Routing Table — a database which keeps track of the routes to networks and the associated costs
- Static Routing — routes are manually configured by a network administrator
- Dynamic Routing — adjust automatically to changes in network topology, and information it receives from other routers
- Routing Protocol — uses a special algorithm to route data across a network *e.g.*, RIP

Gateway

- Allows different networks to communicate by offering a translation service from one protocol stack to another
- They work at all levels of the OSI model — due to the type of translation service they are providing
- Address Gateway — connects networks using the same protocol, but using different directory spaces such as Message Handling Service
- Protocol Gateway — connects network using different protocols. Translates source protocol so destination can understand it
- Application Gateway — translates between applications such as from an Internet email server to a messaging server

Advantages and Disadvantages

Repeater

Advantages — Can connect different types of media, can extend a network in terms of distance, does not increase network traffic.

Disadvantages — Extends the collision domain, can not filter data, can not connect different network architectures, limited number only can be used in network.

Hub

Advantages — Cheap, can connect different media types

Disadvantages — Extends the collision domain, can not filter information, passes packets to all connected segments.

Bridge

Advantages — Limits the collision domain, can extend network distances, uses MAC address to filter traffic, eases congestion, can connect different types of media, some can connect differing architectures.

Disadvantages — Broadcast packets can not be filtered, more expensive than a repeater, slower than a repeater — due to additional processing of packets.

Switch

Advantages — Limits the collision domain, can provide bridging, can be configured to limit broadcast domain.

Disadvantages — More expensive than a hub or bridge, configuration of additional functions can be very complex.

Router

Advantages — Limits the collision domain, can function in LAN or WAN, connects differing media and architectures, can determine best path/route, can filter broadcasts.

Disadvantages — Expensive, must use routable protocols, can be difficult to configure (static routing), slower than a bridge.

1.6 SOME POPULAR NETWORKS

UUCP

UUCP (Unix-to-Unix CoPy) was originally developed to connect Unix (surprise!) hosts together. UUCP has since been ported to many different architectures, including PCs, Macs, Amigas, Apple IIs, VMS hosts, everything else we can name, and even some things we can't. Additionally, a number of systems have been developed around the same principles as UUCP.

Batch-Oriented Processing

UUCP and similar systems are *batch-oriented* systems: everything that they have to do is added to a queue, and then at some specified time, everything in the queue is processed.

Implementation Environment

UUCP networks are commonly built using *dial-up* (modem) connections. This doesn't have to be the case though: UUCP can be used over any sort of connection between two computers, including an Internet connection.

Building a UUCP network is a simple matter of configuring two hosts to recognize each other, and know how to get in touch with each other. Adding on to the network is simple; if hosts called A and B have a UUCP network between them, and C would like to join the network, then it must be configured to talk to A and/or B. Naturally, anything that C talks to must be made aware of C's existence before any connections will work. Now, to connect D to the network, a connection must be established with at least one of the hosts on the network, and so on. Figure 1.12 shows a sample UUCP network.

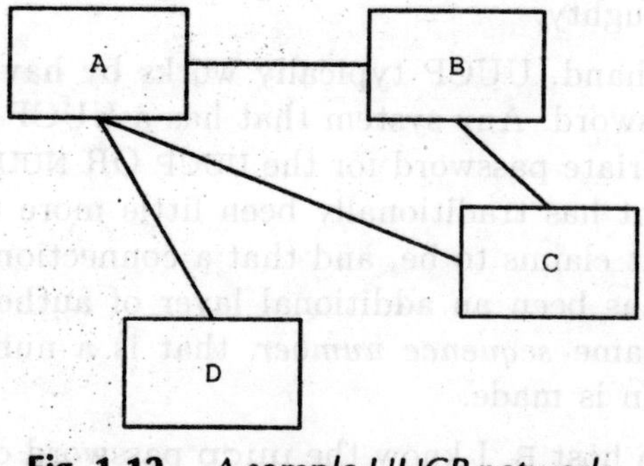

Fig. 1.12. *A sample UUCP network.*

In a UUCP network, users are identified in the format `host!userid`. The "!" character (pronounced "bang" in networking circles) is used to separate hosts and users. A `bangpath` is a string of host(s) and a userid like `A!cmcurtin` or `C!B!A!cmcurtin`. If I am a user on host `A` and you are a user on host `E`, I might be known as `A!cmcurtin` and you as `E!you`. Because there is no direct link between your host (`E`) and mine (`A`), in order for us to communicate, we need to do so through a host (or hosts!) that has connectivity to both `E` and `A`. In our sample network, `C` has the connectivity we need. So, to send me a file, or piece of email, you would address it to `C!A!cmcurtin`. Or, if you feel like taking the long way around, you can address me as `C!B!A!cmcurtin`.

The "public" UUCP network is simply a huge worldwide network of hosts connected to each other.

Popularity

The public UUCP network has been shrinking in size over the years, with the rise of the availability of inexpensive Internet connections. Additionally, since UUCP connections are typically made hourly, daily, or weekly, there is a fair bit of delay in getting data from one user on a UUCP network to a user on the other end of the network. UUCP isn't very flexible, as it's used for simply copying files (which can be netnews, email, documents, etc.) Interactive protocols (that make applications such as the World Wide Web possible) have become much more the norm, and are preferred in most cases.

However, there are still many people whose needs for email and netnews are served quite well by UUCP, and its integration into the Internet has greatly reduced the amount of cumbersome addressing that had to be accomplished in times past.

Security

UUCP, like any other application, has security tradeoffs. Some strong points for its security is that it is fairly limited in what it can do, and it's therefore more difficult to trick into doing something it shouldn't; it's been around a *long* time, and most its bugs have been discovered, analyzed, and fixed; and because UUCP networks are made up of occasional connections to other hosts, it isn't possible for someone on host E to directly make contact with host B, and take advantage of that connection to do something naughty.

On the other hand, UUCP typically works by having a system-wide UUCP user account and password. Any system that has a UUCP connection with another must know the appropriate password for the UUCP OR NUUCP account. Identifying a host beyond that point has traditionally been little more than a matter of trusting that the host is who it claims to be, and that a connection is allowed at that time. More recently, there has been an additional layer of authentication, whereby both hosts must have the same *sequence number*, that is a number that is incremented each time a connection is made.

Hence, if I run host B, I know the uucp password on host A. If, though, I want to impersonate host C, I'll need to connect, identify myself as C, hope that I've done so at a time that A will allow it, and try to guess the correct sequence number for the session. While this might not be a trivial attack, it isn't considered very secure.

The Internet

Internet: This is a word that is heard too often in the last few years. Movies, books, newspapers, magazines, television programs, and practically every other sort of media imaginable has dealt with the Internet recently.

What is the Internet?

The Internet is the world's largest network of *networks*. When we want to access the resources offered by the Internet, we don't really connect to *the Internet;* we connect to a network that is eventually connected to the *Internet backbone,* a network of extremely fast (and incredibly overloaded!) network components. This is an important point: the Internet is a network of *networks* — not a network of hosts.

A simple network can be constructed using the same protocols and such that the Internet uses without actually *connecting* it to anything else. Such a basic network is shown in Figure 1.13.

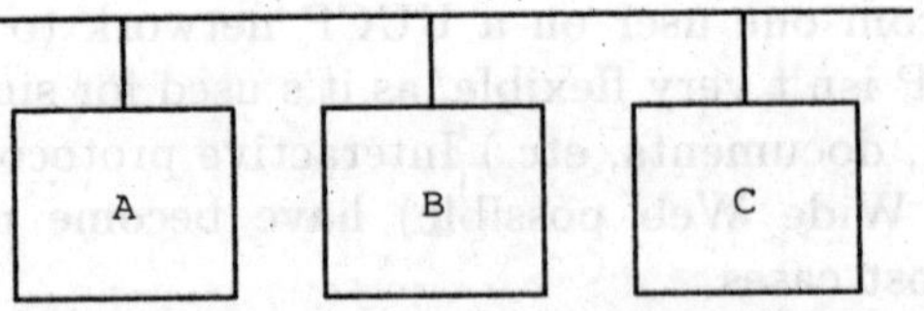

Fig. 1.13. *A simple local area network.*

We have a number of networks, which are all connected together on a *backbone,* that is a network of our networks. Our backbone is then connected to other networks, one of which is to an *Internet Service Provider* (ISP) whose backbone is connected to other networks, one of which is the Internet backbone.

If we have a connection "to the Internet" through a local ISP, we are actually connecting we computer to one of the networks, which is connected to another, and so on. To use a service from a host, such as a web server. Underlying services and protocols would send *packets* (small datagrams) with your query to our ISP's network, and then a network they're connected to, and so on, until it found a path to my employer's backbone, and to the exact network my host is on. Our host would then respond appropriately, and the same would happen in reverse: packets would traverse all of the connections until they found their way back to our computer, and we were looking atour web page.

In Figure 1.14 the network shown in Figure 1.13 is designated "LAN 1" and shown in the bottom-right of the picture. This shows how the hosts on that network are provided connectivity to other hosts on the same LAN, within the same company, outside the company, but in the same ISP *cloud*, and then from another ISP somewhere on the Inter.

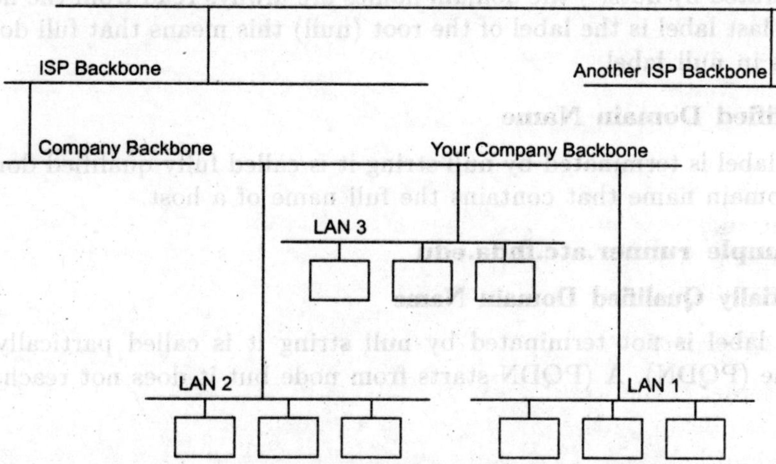

Fig. 1.14. *Wider view of internet-connected network.*

The Internet is made up of a wide variety of hosts, from supercomputers to personal computers, including every imaginable type of hardware and software.

The Domain Name Service

Name Space

A name space that maps each address to unique name can organization in two ways are flat and hierarchical.

Flat Name Space

In flat name space a name is assigned to an address. A name in this space is a sequence of characters without structure. The main disadvantage of flat name space is that it cannot be used in a large system such as the Internet because it must be centrally controlled to avoid ambiguity and duplication.

Hierarchical Name Space

In a hierarchical name space each name is made of several parts. The first part can be define the nature of the organization the second part can define the name of an organization, third part can define departments in the organization.

Domain Name Space

Domain name space are defined in inverted tree structure with root at the top the tree can have only 128 levels level 0 (root) to level 127.

Label

Each node in the tree has label which is string with the maximum of 63 characters the root label is a null string (empty string). DNS require that children of a node have different labels which guarantees the uniqueness of the domain names.

Domain Name

Each node in the tree has domain name. A full domain name is sequence of label separated by dots(.) the domain names are always read from the node up to the root. The last label is the label of the root (null) this means that full domain name always ends in null label.

Fully Qualified Domain Name

If a label is terminated by null string it is called fully qualified domain space. FQDN is domain name that contains the full name of a host.

Example runner.atc.fhda.edu

Partially Qualified Domain Name

If a label is not terminated by null string it is called partically qualified domain name (PQDN). A (PQDN starts from node but it does not reach the root

Domain

A domain is subtree of the domain space. The name of the domain is the domain name of the node at the top of the subtree.

Server

DNS defines two types of server: primary server and secondry.

A primary server loads all the information from the disk file, the secondry server loads all information from the primary server when primary downloads information from the secondry it is called zone transfer.

DNS in the Internet

DNS is a protocol that can be used in different platforms in the Internet the domain space (tree) is divided into three sections : generic domains, country domain and inverse domain.

Generic Domain

The generic domains define registered hosts according to their generic behavior. Each mode in the tree defines a domain which is an index name space database.

Generic Domain Labels

- Com commercial organization
- Edu educational institutions
- Gov government institutions
- Int international organization
- Mil military groups
- Net network support centers
- Org Nonprofit organization

Country Domain

The country domains sections follows the same format as the generic domain but uses two character country abbreviations (*e.g.*, us for united state) in place of the three character organization abbreviation at the level. Second level labels can be organization or they can be more specific national designations.

Inverse Domain

The inverse domain is used to map an address to name this may happen for example, when server has received a request from the client to do task. To determine if the client is on the authorized list it can ask its resolver to send aquery to the DNS server and ask for mapping of address to name.

DNS Message

DNS has a two type of message query and response. Both type are same format. The query message consists of header and the question record, the response message consists of header question record answer record authoritative records and additional record.

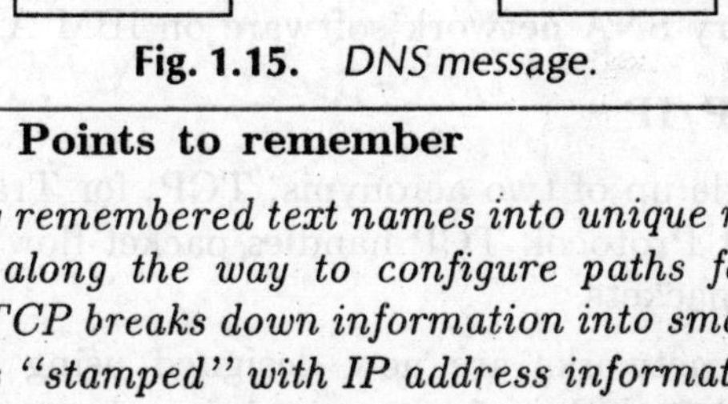

Fig. 1.15. *DNS message.*

Points to remember

1. *DNS translates easily remembered text names into unique numerical IP addresses. This allows routers along the way to configure paths for information to flow between computers. TCP breaks down information into small packets for transmission, each of which is "stamped" with IP address information.*
2. *When you set up networking for someone, you need to tell their computer where the next-level DNS server is. If you don't, they won't be able to find anything using a text-based address. If the DNS service fails, or something along the way fails and renders it unreachable, the effect is the same. This is because everything about an address must be translated into numbers.*

3. *Ditto for the gateway (sometimes called "router") address. No sending or receiving takes place external to the local network without a gateway. Even if you use numerical IP addresses.*
4. Almost everywhere *we use Bear Access to go to has a text-based address. The post office we get our email from Telnet services. Various web sites around campus. You name it. If DNS isn't properly set up and operative on both ends, nothing happens. Nothing at all.*

1.7 INTRODUCTION TO TCP/IP NETWORKING

History

The strength of Unix is the built-in networking provided under Unix. In the early 1980, the Universiy of California at Berkeley (Berkeley), had taken the original System 7 version of Unix developed at AT&T and made substantial modifications to that version of Unix. Key additions, were support for virtual memory and the initial release of TCP/IP for Unix. This release from Berkeley was known as 4.2 BSD. In 1986, Berkeley released a new version of Unix, BSD 4.3, with substantial improvements to the TCP/IP networking code.

Whether a system uses a System V or a BSD based kernel all versions of Unix now ship with 4.3 BSD networking software. Since this software was developed at Berkeley, under a US government grant, it has been available to any vendor or university at minimal cost. The TCP/IP code developed at Berkely has been ported to other operating systems, such as the DEC VMS, Macintosh, DOS, Windows, IBM CMS, IBM MVS, and many other systems.

Unix has been the platform for TCP/IP development. While Berkeley has been the main contributor, this work has produced a system for networking that has proven itself over the years. Presently, there are estimated to be over 5 million systems running the TCP/IP software suite, the overwhelming majority are microcomputers. Unix has evolved as the platform to use for integrating these many different systems into something useful.

Many vendors have provided other network on Unix systems other than (or in addition too) TCP/IP. DEC has offered a version of its ÕS DECNET software for systems running its ÕS version of Unix, named Ultrix. IBM also offers a version of their propreitary SNA network software on IBM AIX machines.

Introduction to TCP/IP

TCP/IP is made up of two acronyms, TCP, for Transmission Control Protocol, and IP, for Internet Protocol. TCP handles packet flow between systems and IP handles the routing of packets.

All modern networks are now designed using a layered approach. Each layer presents a predefined interface to the layer above it. By doing so, a modular design can be developed so as to minimize problems in the development of new applications or in adding new interfaces.

The ISO/OSI protocol with seven layers is the usual reference model. Since TCP/IP was designed before the ISO model was developed it has four layers; however the differences between the two are mostly minor. Below, is a comparison of the TCP/IP and OSI protocol stacks:

```
         OSI Protocol Stack
7. Application    -- End user services such as email.
6. Presentation   -- Data problems and data compression
5. Session     --  Authentication and authorization
4. Transport   --  Guarantee end-to-end delivery of packets
3. Network     --  Packet routing
2. Data Link   --  Transmit and receive packets
1. Physical    --  The cable or physical connection itself.
   TCP/IP Protocol Stack.
4. Application --  Authentication, compression, and end user ser-
                   vices.
3. Transport   --  Handles the flow of data between systems and
                   provides access to the network for applications
                   via the (BSD socket library)
2. Network     --  Packet routing
1. Link        --  Kernel OS/device driver interface to the network
                   interface on the computer.
```

Below are the major difference between the OSI and TCP/IP:

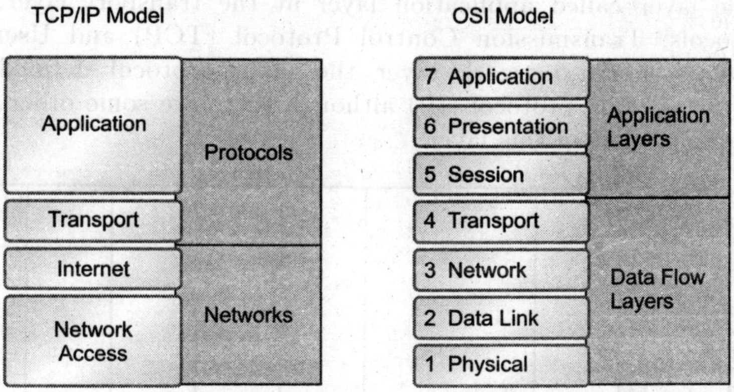

Fig. 1.16. *TCP/IP vs OSI model.*

- The application layer in TCP/IP handles the responsibilities of layers 5, 6, and 7 in the OSI model.
- The transport layer in TCP/IP does not always guarantee reliable delivery of packets as the transport layer in the OSI model does. TCP/IP offers an option called UDP that does not guarantee reliable packet delivery.

Software Componets of TCP/IP

Application Layer

Some of the applications we will cover are SMTP (mail), Telnet, FTP, Rlogin, NFS, NIS, and LPD.

Transport Layer

The transport uses two protocols, UDP and TCP. UDP which stands for User Datagram protocol does not guarantee packet delivery and applications which use this must provide their own means of verifying delivery. TCP does guarantee delivery of packets to the applications which use it.

Network Layer

The network layer is concerned with packet routing and used low level protocols such as ICMP, IP, and IGMP.

Link Layer

The link layer is concerned with the actual transmission packets as well as IP to ethernet address translation. This layer is concerned with Arp, the device driver, and Rarp.

1.8 TCP/IP PROTOCOL SUITE

The TCP/IP protocol suite was developed prior to the OSI model therefore the layer in the TCP/IP protocol suite donot match exactly with those in the OSI model. The TCP/IP protocol suite is made of 5 layer: physical, data link network, transport and application. The first 4 layer provide physical standard, network interface, internetworking and the transport function that correspond to the first 4 layers of the model. The 3 topmost layer in the OSI model however are represented in TCP/IP by single layer called application layer at the transport layer. TCP/IP define two protocols: Transmission Control Protocol (TCP) and User Datagram Protocol (UDP). At the network layer the main protocol defined by TCP/IP is the Internetworking protocol (IP) although there are some other protocol that support data movement in this layer.

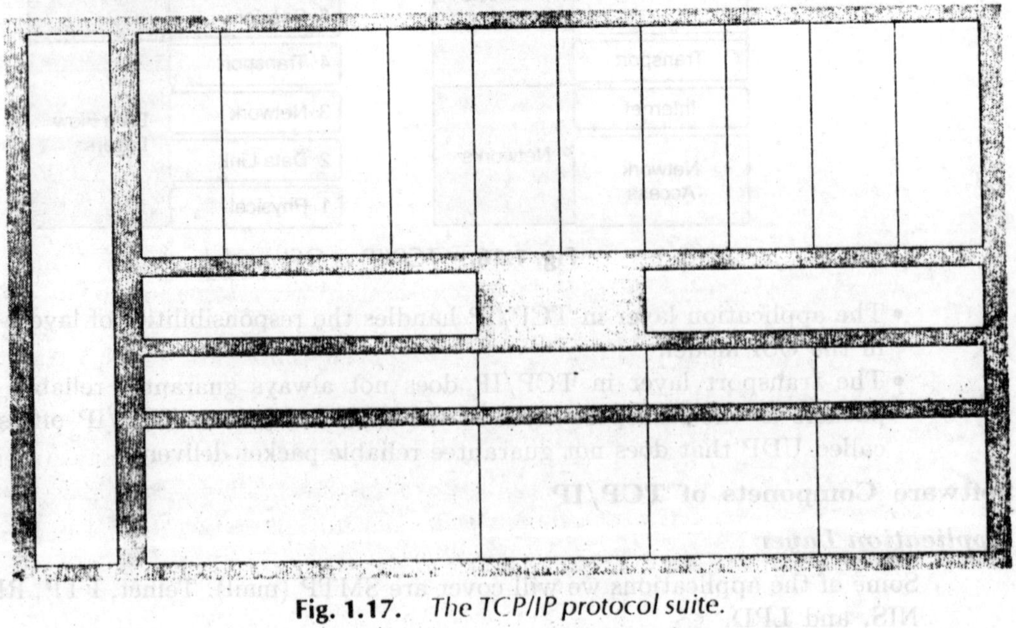

Fig. 1.17. *The TCP/IP protocol suite.*

Physical and Datalink Layer

At the physical layer and data link layer, TCP/IP does not define any specific protocol. It support all of the standard and Properly protocol. A network in TCP/IP internetwork can be Local Area Network (LAN), a Metropolitan Area Network (MAN) or a Wide Area Network (WAN).

Network Layer

At the network layer TCP/IP support the internetworking protocol (IP). IP in turn contains four supporting protocol: ARP, RARP, ICMP.

Internetwork Layer

The best known TCP/IP protocol at the internetwork layer is the *Internet Protocol* (IP), which provides the basic packet delivery service for all TCP/IP networks.

In addition to the physical node addresses used at the network access layer, the IP protocol implements a system of logical host addresses called IP addresses.

The IP addresses are used by the internetwork and higher layers to identify devices and to perform internetwork routing. The Address Resolution Protocol (ARP) enables IP to identify the physical address that matches a given IP address.

IP is used by all protocols in the layers above and below it to deliver data, which means all TCP/IP data flows through IP when it is sent and received, regardless of its final destination.

Internet Protocol

IP is a *connectionless protocol,* which means that IP does not exchange control information (called a *handshake*) to establish an end-to-end connection before transmitting data. In contrast, a *connection-oriented protocol* exchanges control information with the remote computer to verify that it is ready to receive data before sending it. When the handshaking is successful, the computers are said to have established a connection. IP relies on protocols in other layers to establish the connection if connection-oriented services are required.

IP also relies on protocols in another layer to provide error detection and error recovery. Because it contains no error detection or recovery code, IP is sometimes called an *unreliable protocol.*

The functions performed at this layer are as follows:

- **Define the datagram, which is the basic unit of transmission in the Internet.** The TCP/IP protocols were built to transmit data over the ARPANET, which was a *packet switching network.* A *packet* is a block of data that carries with it the information necessary to deliver it—in a manner similar to a postal letter that has an address written on its envelope. A packet switching network uses the addressing information in the packets to switch packets from one physical network to another, moving them toward their final destination. Each packet travels the network independently of any other packet. The *datagram* is the packet format defined by IP.

- **Define the internet addressing scheme.** IP delivers the datagram by checking the destination address in the header. If the destination address is the address of a host on the directly attached network, the packet is delivered directly to the destination. If the destination address is not on the local network, the packet is passed to a gateway for delivery. *Gateways* and *routers* are devices that switch packets between the different physical networks. Deciding which gateway to use is called *routing*. IP makes the routing decision for each individual packet.
- **Move data between the network access layer and the host-to-host transport Layer.** When IP receives a datagram that is addressed to the local host, it must pass the data portion of the datagram to the correct host-to-host transport layer protocol. This selection is done by using the *protocol number* in the datagram header. Each host-to-host transport layer protocol has a unique protocol number that identifies it to IP.
- **Route datagrams to remote hosts.** Internet gateways are commonly (and perhaps more accurately) referred to as IP routers because they use IP to route packets between networks. In traditional TCP/IP jargon, there are only two types of network devices: gateways and hosts. Gateways forward packets between networks and hosts do not. However, if a host is connected to more than one network (called a *multi-homed host*), it can forward packets between the networks. When a multi-homed host forwards packets, it acts like any other gateway and is considered to be a gateway.
- **Fragment and reassemble datagrams.** As a datagram is routed through different networks, it may be necessary for the IP module in a gateway to divide the datagram into smaller pieces. A datagram received from one network may be too large to be transmitted in a single packet on a different network. This condition only occurs when a gateway interconnects dissimilar physical networks.

  Each type of network has a *maximum transmission unit (MTU)*, which is the largest packet it can transfer. If the datagram received from one network is longer than the other network's MTU, it is necessary to divide the datagram into smaller fragments for transmission. This division process is called *fragmentation*.

Internet Control Message Protocol

The *Internet Control Message Protocol* (ICMP) is part of the internetwork layer and uses the IP datagram delivery facility to send its messages. ICMP sends messages that perform the following control, error reporting, and informational functions for the TCP/IP protocol suite:

- **Flow control.** When datagrams arrive too quickly for processing, the destination host or an intermediate gateway sends an ICMP *source quench message* back to the sender. This message instructs the source to stop sending datagrams temporarily.
- **Detect unreachable destinations.** When a destination is unreachable, the computer detecting the problem sends a *destination unreachable message* to the datagram's source. If the unreachable destination is a network or host, the message is sent by an intermediate gateway. But if the destination is an unreachable port, the destination host sends the message.

- **Redirect routes.** A gateway sends the ICMP *redirect message* to tell a host to use another gateway, presumably because the other gateway is a better choice. This message can only be used when the source host is on the same network as both gateways.
- **Check remote hosts.** A host can send the ICMP *echo message* to see if a remote computer's IP is up and operational. When a computer receives an echo message, it sends the same packet back to the source host.

Host-to-Host Transport Layer

The protocol layer just above the internetwork layer is the *host-to-host layer.* It is responsible for end-to-end data integrity. The two most important protocols employed at this layer are the *Transmission Control Protocol* (TCP) and *User Datagram Protocol* (UDP).

TCP provides reliable, full-duplex connections and reliable service by ensuring that data is resubmitted when transmission results in an error (end-to-end error detection and correction). Also, TCP enables hosts to maintain multiple, simultaneous connections. When error correction is not required, UDP provides unreliable datagram service (connectionless) that enhances network throughput at the host-to-host transport layer.

Both protocols deliver data between the *application layer* and the *internetwork layer.* Applications programmers can choose the service that is most appropriate for their specific applications.

User Datagram Protocol

The *User Datagram Protocol* gives application programs direct access to a datagram delivery service, like the delivery service that IP provides. This direct access allows applications to exchange messages over the network with a minimum of protocol overhead.

UDP is an unreliable, connectionless datagram protocol. "Unreliable" merely means that the protocol has no technique for verifying that the data reached the other end of the network correctly. Within your computer, UDP will deliver data correctly.

Why do applications programmers choose UDP as a data transport service? A number of good reasons exist. If the amount of data being transmitted is small, the overhead of creating connections and ensuring reliable delivery may be greater than the work of retransmitting the entire data set. In this case, UDP is the most efficient choice for a host-to-host transport layer protocol.

Applications that fit a "query-response" model are also excellent candidates for using UDP. The response can be used as a positive acknowledgment to the query. If a response is not received within a certain time period, the application just sends another query. Still other applications provide their own techniques for reliable data delivery and do not require that service from the transport layer protocol. Imposing another layer of acknowledgment on any of these types of applications is redundant.

Transmission Control Protocol

Applications that require the host-to-host transport protocol to provide reliable data delivery use TCP because it verifies that data is delivered across the network accurately and in the proper sequence. TCP is a *reliable, connection-oriented, byte-stream* protocol.

Application Layer

The most widely known and implemented TCP/IP application layer protocols are listed below:

- **File Transfer Protocol (FTP).** Performs basic interactive file transfers between hosts.3
- **Telnet.** Enables users to execute terminal sessions with remote hosts.
- **Simple Mail Transfer Protocol (SMTP).** Supports basic message delivery services.
- **HyperText Transfer Protocol (HTTP).** Supports the low-overhead transport of files consisting of a mixture of text and graphics. It uses a stateless, connection- and object-oriented protocol with simple commands that support selection and transport of objects between the client and the server.

In addition to widely known protocols, the application layer includes the following protocols:

- **Domain Name Service (DNS).** Also called *name service*; this application maps IP addresses to the names assigned to network devices.
- **Routing Information Protocol (RIP).** Routing is central to the way TCP/IP works. RIP is used by network devices to exchange routing information.
- **Simple Network Management Protocol (SNMP).** A protocol that is used to collect management information from network devices.
- **Network File System (NFS).** A system developed by Sun Microsystems that enables computers to mount drives on remote hosts and operate them as if they were local drives.

Some protocols, such as Telnet and FTP, can only be used if the user has some knowledge of the network. Other protocols, like RIP, run without the user even knowing that they exist.

CHAPTER 2

IP ADDRESSES

2.1 INTRODUCTION

The identifier used in the IP layer of the TCP/IP protocol suite to identify each device connected to the Internet is called the Internet address or IP address. An IP address is a 32 bit binary address that uniquely and universally identifies a device

IP addresses are unique in the sense that each address defines one and only connection to the Internet.

Address Space

A protocol like IP that defines an address space. An address space is the total number of addresses used by the protocol. If a protocol uses N bits to define an address the address space 2 power of N because each bit can have two different values (0 and 1) and N bits can have 2 power of N.

Notation

There are three common notations to show an IP address : binary notation, dotted decimal notation and hexadecimal notation.

Binary Notation

In binary notation the IP address is displayed as 32 bits to make the address more readable. One or more space is usually inserted between each octed (8 bits). Each octet is often referred to as a byte. So it is common to hear an IP address referred to as 32 bit address or 4 octed address or 4 byte address.

Dotted Decimal Notation

To make the IP address more compact and easier to read Internet addresses are usally written in decimal form with decimal point (dot) separating the byte.

2.2 IP ADDRESSES

Internet Protocol (IP)

The Internet Protocol (IP) is a network-layer (Layer 3) protocol that contains addressing information and some control information that enables packets to be routed. IP is documented in RFC 791 and is the primary network-layer protocol in the Internet protocol suite. Along with the Transmission Control Protocol (TCP), IP represents the heart of the Internet protocols. IP has two primary responsibilities: providing connectionless, best-effort delivery of datagrams through an internetwork ; and providing fragmentation and reassembly of datagrams to support data links with different maximum-transmission unit (MTU) sizes.

IP Packet Format

An IP packet contains several types of information, as illustrated in Figure 2.1.

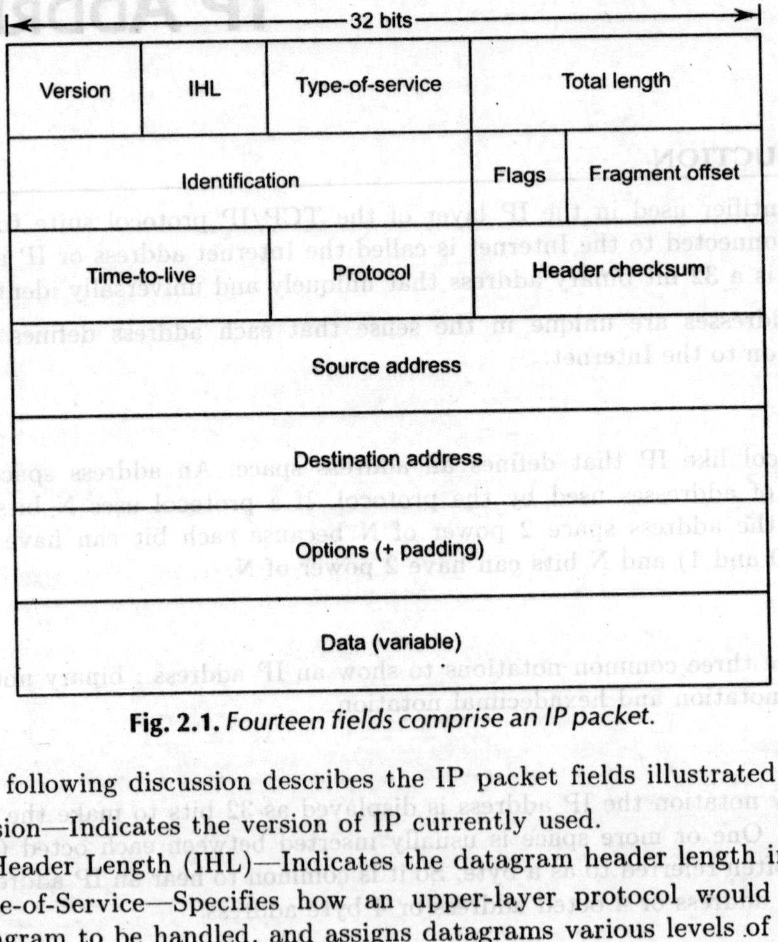

Fig. 2.1. *Fourteen fields comprise an IP packet.*

The following discussion describes the IP packet fields illustrated in:

- Version—Indicates the version of IP currently used.
- IP Header Length (IHL)—Indicates the datagram header length in 32 bit words.
- Type-of-Service—Specifies how an upper-layer protocol would like a current datagram to be handled, and assigns datagrams various levels of importance.
- Total Length—Specifies the length, in bytes, of the entire IP packet, including the data and header.

- Identification—Contains an integer that identifies the current datagram. This field is used to help place together datagram fragments.
- Flags—Consist of a 3 bit field of which the two low-order (least significant) bits control fragmentation. The low-order bit specifies whether the packet can be fragmented. The middle bit specifies whether the packet is the last fragment in a series of fragmented packets. The third or high-order bit is not used.
- Fragment Offset—Indicates the position of the fragment's data relative to the beginning of the data in the original datagram, which allows the destination IP process to properly reconstruct the original datagram.
- Time-to-Live—Maintains a counter that gradually decrements down to zero, at which point the datagram is discarded. This keeps packets from looping endlessly.
- Protocol—Indicates which upper-layer protocol receives incoming packets after IP processing is complete.
- Header Checksum—Helps ensure IP header integrity.
- Source Address—Specifies the sending node.
- Destination Address—Specifies the receiving node.
- Options—Allows IP to support various options, such as security.
- Data—Contains upper-layer information.

2.3 IP ADDRESSING BASICS

- In keeping with the layered nature of network models, it makes sense to associate the MAC layer address with the data link layer (or TCP/IP network access layer, if you prefer to think in terms of that model), and to associate IP addresses with the Network layer (or the TCP/IP Internet layer).
- As data moves through intermediate hosts between the original sender and the ultimate receiver, it does so between pairs of machines, where each pair resides on the same physical network.
- At the network layer, the original sender's address is represented in the IP source address field in the IP packet header, and the ultimate recipient's address is represented in the IP destination address field in the same IP packet header.
- The IP destination address value, in fact, is what drives the sometimes-long series of intermediate transfers, or hops, which occur as data makes its way across a network from sender to receiver.
- Numeric IP addresses use dotted decimal notation when expressed in decimal numbers, and take the form n.n.n.n., in which n is guaranteed to be between zero and 255 for each and every value.
- The numeric values in dotted decimal representations of numeric IP addresses are usually decimal values, but may occasionally appear in hexadecimal (base 16) or binary (base 2) notation.
- Duplication of numeric IP addresses is not allowed because that would lead to confusion.
- Also, there is a notion of "neighborhood" when it comes to interpreting numeric IP addresses.

Proximity between two numeric IP addresses (especially if the difference is only in the rightmost one or two octets) can sometimes indicate that the machines to which those addresses correspond reside close enough together to be on the same general network, if not on the same physical cable segment.

IP Address Format

The 32 bit IP address is grouped 8 bits at a time, separated by dots, and represented in decimal format (known as dotted decimal notation). Each bit in the octet has a binary weight (128, 64, 32, 16, 8, 4, 2, 1). The minimum value for an octet is 0, and the maximum value for an octet is 255. Illustrates the basic format of an IP address.

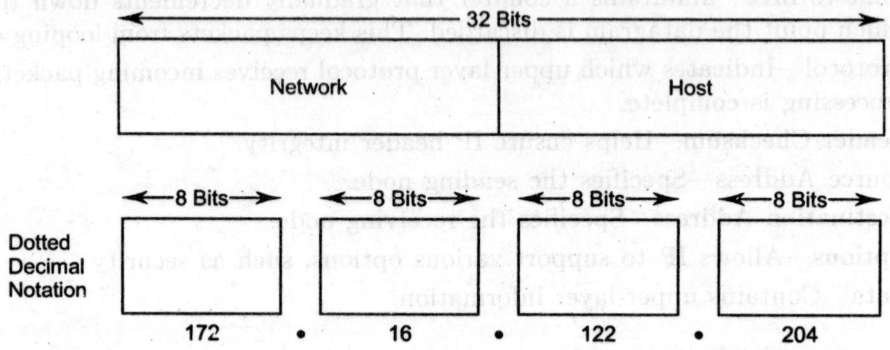

Fig. 2.2. *An IP address consists of 32 bits, grouped into four octets.*

IP Address Classes

IP addressing supports five different address classes: A, B, C, D, and E. Only classes A, B, and C are available for commercial use. The left-most (high-order) bits indicate the network class and provide reference information about the five IP address classes.

Class formats

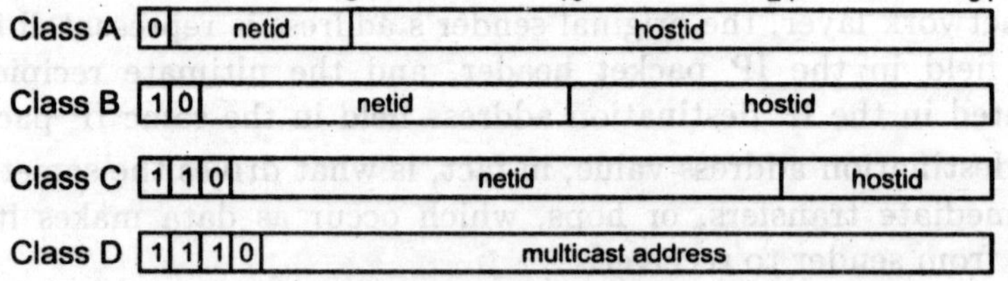

Fig. 2.3. *Class format.*

- Initially, these addresses were further subdivided into five classes, from Class A to Class E.
- For the first three classes of addresses, divide the octets as follows to understand how they behave:

Class A	n	h.h.h
Class B	n.n	h.h
Class C	n.n.n	h

- If more than one octet is part of the network or host portion of the address, then the bits are simply concentrated to determine the numeric address.
- The network portion of that address is 10, whereas the host portion is 12.120.2, treated as a three-octet number.
- Address Classes D and E are for special uses.
- Class D addresses are used for multicast communications, in which a single address may be associated with more than one network host machine.

  This is useful only when information is broadcast to more than one recipient at a time so it should come as no surprise that video and teleconferencing applications, for example, use multicast addresses.

More about Class A Addresses

- Expressed in binary form (ones and zeroes only), Class A addresses always take the form:

  0bbbbbbb.bbbbbbbb.bbbbbbbb.bbbbbbbb
- The leading digit is always zero, and all other digits can be either ones or zeroes.
- On any IP network, addresses consisting of all zeroes and all ones are reserved for special uses, so of those 128 possible network addresses, only those from 00000001 to 01111110 (or 1 to 126, in decimal terms) are considered usable.
- The address for network 10 is reserved for private network use.
- Also, by convention, the address 127.n.n.n is reserved for loopback testing (or checking the integrity and usability of a TCP/IP protocol stack installed on any computer.

Class A Address Facts and Figures

Maximum networks	$2^7 - 2$	126
Maximum usable networks	$2^7 - 4$	124
Hosts per network	$2^{24} - 2$	16,777,214
Private IP Address	10.0.0.0.0	1
Address range	1.0.0.0	126.0.0.0

Fig. 2.4. *Class A address.*

Class B Addresses Always Take the Form

10bbbbbb.bbbbbbbb.bbbbbbbb.bbbbbbbb

- The leading two digits are 10, and the remaining digits can be either ones or zeroes.
- RFC 1918 stipulates that 16 Class B addresses, from 172.16.0.0 to 172.32.255.255, are reserved for private use
- This means that the maximum number of public IP addresses for Class B is 16,382-16, or 16,366.

Class B Address Facts and Figures

Maximum networks	$2^{14} - 2$	16,382
Maximum usable networks	$2^{14} - 18$	16,366
Hosts per network	$2^{14} - 2$	65,534
Private IP Address	172.16.0.0 to 172.32.255.255	16
Address range	128.0.0.0	191.255.0.0

Fig. 2.5. *The ClassB address.*

More about Class C Addresses

- Class C addresses always take the form :
  110bbbbb.bbbbbbbb.bbbbbbbb.bbbbbbbb
- The leading three digits are 110, and the remaining digits can be either ones or zeroes.
- Note that this scheme reduces the total number of networks possible by the most significant three bits.

Class C Address Facts and Figures

Maximum networks	$2^{21} - 2$	2,097,150
Maximum usable networks	$2^{12} - 258$	2,096,894
Hosts per network	$2^{8} - 2$	254
Private IP Address	192.168.0.0 to 192.168.255.255	256
Address range	192.0.1.0	223.255.255.255

Fig. 2.6. *The Class C Address.*

Address Classes D and E

- Class D addresses always take the form :
  1110bbbb.bbbbbbbb.bbbbbbbb.bbbbbbbb
- Class E addresses always take the form :
  11110bbb.bbbbbbbb.bbbbbbbb.bbbbbbbbb
- Class D is used for multicast addresses so that multiple users can "share" a single IP address and receive the same broadcast across a network from a single transmission.

  Network, Broadcast, Multicast, and Other Special IP Addresses
- When an IP packet moves from its sender to its receiver, the network portion of the address directs that traffic from the sender's network to the receiver's network.
- The only time the host portion of the address comes into play is when the sender and receiver both reside on the same physical network or subnet.
- The broadcast address represents a network address that all hosts on a network must read.
- Although broadcasts still have some valid uses on modern networks, they originated in an era when networks were small and of limited scope, in which a sort of

"all hands on deck" message represented a convenient way to ask for services when a specific server could not be explicitly identified.

Broadcast Packet Structures

- IP broadcast packets have two destination address fields—one Data Link layer destination address field, and one destination network address field. Multicast Packet and Address Structures
- When a host uses a service that employs a multicast address (such as the 224. 0.0.9 address used for RIPv2 router updates), it registers itself to "listen" on that address, as well as on its own unique host address.
- That host must also inform its IP gateway (the router or other device that will forward traffic to the host's physical network) that it is registering for this service so that device will forward such multicast traffic to that network (otherwise, it will never appear there).

Multicast Packet and Address Structures

- The Internet Corporation for Assigned Names and Numbers (ICANN) allocates multicast addresses on a controlled basis.
- Formerly, addresses were under the auspices of IANA, the Internet Assigned Numbers Authority.

Table. 2.1. Reference Information about the Five IP Address Classes

IP Address Class	*Format*	*Purpose*	*High-Order Bit(s)*	*Address Range*	*No. Bits Network/Host*	*Max. Hosts*
A	N.H.H.H[1]	Few large organizations	0	1.0.0.0 to 126.0.0.0	7/24	16,777, 214[2] (2^{24} – 2)
B	N.N.H.H	Medium-size organizations	1, 0	128.1.0.0 to 191.254.0.0	14/16	65, 543 (2^{16} – 2)
C	N.N.N.H	Relatively small organizations	1, 1, 0	192.0.1.0 to 223.255.254.0	22/8	245 (2^8 – 2)
D	N/A	Multicast groups (RFC 1112)	1, 1, 1, 0	224.0.0.0 to 239. 255.255.255	N/A (not for commercial use)	N/A
E	N/A	Experimental	1, 1, 1, 1	240.0.0.0 to 254. 255.255.255	N/A	N/A

The class of address can be determined easily by examining the first octet of the address and mapping that value to a class range in the following table. In an IP address of 172.31.1.2, for example, the first octet is 172. Because 172 falls between 128 and 191, 172.31.1.2 is a Class B address. Table 2.1 Summarizes the range of possible values for the first octet of each address class.

CHAPTER 3

ARP

3.1 ADDRESS RESOLUTION PROTOCOL (ARP) OVERVIEW

The two machines on a given network to communicate, they must know the other machine's physical (or MAC) addresses. By broadcasting Address Resolution Protocols (ARPs), a host can dynamically discover the MAC-layer address corresponding to a particular IP network-layer address.

After receiving a MAC-layer address, IP devices create an ARP cache to store the recently acquired IP-to-MAC address mapping, Encapsulation of ARP message in a physical frame.

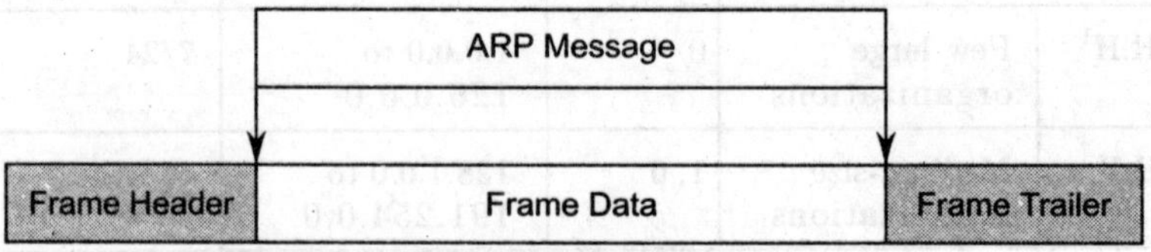

Fig. 3.1. *Encapsulation of ARP message.*

ARP Process

1. ARP requestor sends a broadcast frame with the destination IP address, its source IP address and MAC address, asking for the destination MAC address.
2. Host with destination IP address sends a directed frame back to ARP requestor filling in its MAC address and storing the MAC address of the sender in an ARP table (or cache).

Optionally, all other hosts within the same broadcast domain add the sender's MAC and IP addresses to its ARP cache.

3.2 ARP MESSAGE

There are four types of ARP messages that may be sent by the ARP protocol. These are identified by four values in the "operation" field of an ARP message. The types of message are:

1. ARP request
2. ARP reply
3. RARP request
4. RARP reply

The format of an ARP message is shown in Figure 3.2

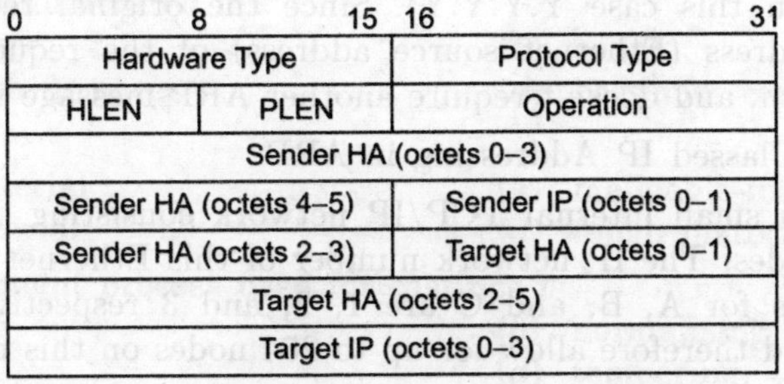

Fig. 3.2. *ARP format.*

Format of an ARP message used to resolve the remote MAC Hardware Address (HA).

To reduce the number of address resolution requests, a client normally caches resolved addresses for a (short) period of time. The ARP cache is of a finite size, and would become full of incomplete and obsolete entries for computers that are not in use if it was allowed to grow without check. The ARP cache is therefore periodically flushed of all entries. This deletes unused entries and frees space in the cache. It also removes any unsuccessful attempts to contact computers which are not currently running.

3.3 ADVANTAGE OF ADDRESS RESOLUTION PROTOCOL (ARP)

Example 1:

Figure 3.3 shows the use of ARP when a computer tries to contact a remote computer on the same LAN using the "ping" program. It is assumed that no previous IP datagrams have been received form this computer, and therefore arp must first be used to identify the MAC address of the remote computer.

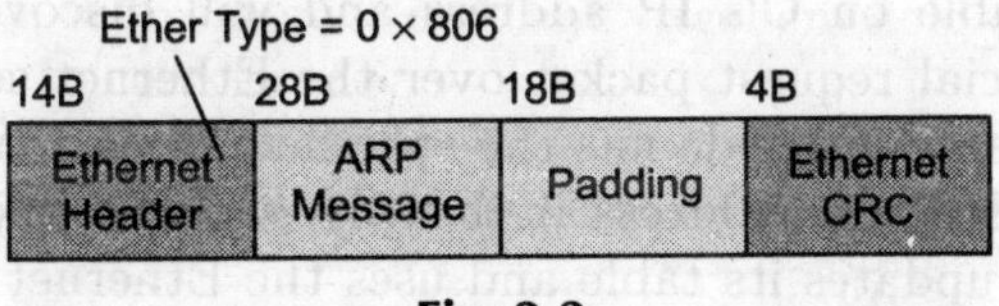

Fig. 3.3

The ARP request message ("who is X.X.X.X tell Y.Y.Y.Y", where X.X.X.X and Y.Y.Y.Y are IP addresses) is sent using the Ethernet broadcast address, and an Ethernet protocol type of value 0x806. Since it is broadcast, it is received by all systems in the same collision domain (LAN). This ensures that the target of the query is connected to the network, it will receive a copy of the query. Only this system responds. The other systems discard the packet silently.

The target system forms an arp response ("X.X.X.X is hh:hh:hh:hh:hh:hh", where hh:hh:hh:hh:hh:hh is the Ethernet source address of the computer with the IP address of X.X.X.X). This packet is unicast to the address of the computer sending the query (in this case Y.Y.Y.Y). Since the original request also included the hardware address (Ethernet source address) of the requesting computer, this is already known, and doesn't require another ARP message to find this out.

Example 2: Classed IP Addressing in ARP

Consider a small internal TCP/IP network consisting of one Ethernet segment and three nodes. The IP network number of this Ethernet segment is 200.1.2. The host numbers for A, B, and C are 1, 2, and 3 respectively. These are Class C addresses, and therefore allow for up to 254 nodes on this network segment.

Each of these nodes have corresponding Ethernet addresses, which are 6 bytes long. They are normally written in hexadecimal form separated by dashes (02-FE-87-4A-8C-A9 for example).

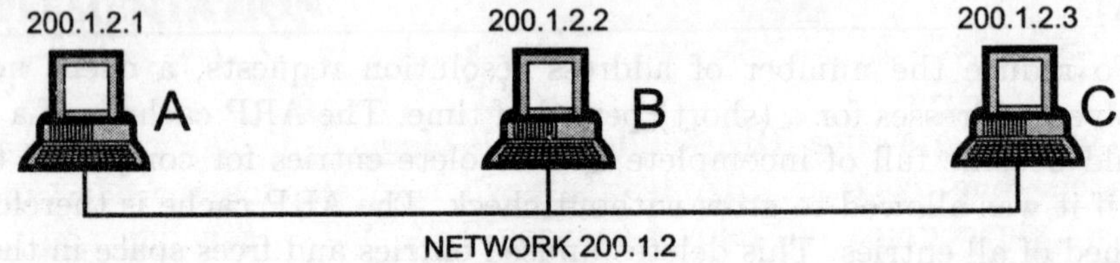

Fig. 3.4

In Figure 3.4 and subsequent diagrams, we have emphasized the network number portion of the IP address.

Suppose that A wanted to send a packet to C for the first time, and that it knows C's IP address. To send this packet over Ethernet, A would need to know C's Ethernet address. The Address Resolution Protocol (ARP) is used for the dynamic discovery of these addresses.

ARP keeps an internal table of IP address and corresponding Ethernet address. When A attempts to send the IP packet destined to C, the ARP module does a lookup in its table on C's IP address and will discover no entry. ARP will then broadcast a special request packet over the Ethernet segment, which all nodes will receive. If the receiving node has the specified IP address, which in this case is C, it will return its Ethernet address in a reply packet back to A. Once A receives this reply packet, it updates its table and uses the Ethernet address to direct A's packet to C. ARP table entries may be stored statically in some cases, or it keeps entries in its table until they are "stale" in which case they are flushed.

Source IP address = 128.192.6.7 (80 C0 06 07)
Source MAC address = 00 00 C0 8D 9C FB
Destination IP address = 128.192.6.193 (80 C0 06 C1)
Destination MAC address = 00 00 1D E5 A3 B9

PREAMBLE	FF FF FF FF FF FF	00 00 C0 8D 9C FB
08 06	HARDWARE TYPE (01)	PROTOCOL TYPE (0800)
HLEN (06)	PLEN (04)	OPERATION (01)
00 00 C0 8D 9C FB		80 C0 06 07
00 00 00 00 00 00		80 C0 06 C1
FRAME CHECK SEQUENCE		

Fig. 3.5. *ARP request.*

PREAMBLE	00 00 C0 8D 9C FB	00 00 1D E5 A3 B9
08 06	HARDWARE TYPE (01)	PROTOCOL TYPE (0800)
HLEN (06)	PLEN (04)	OPERATION (02)
00 00 1D E5 A3 B9		80 C0 06 07
00 00 C0 8D 9C FB		80 C0 06 C1
FRAME CHECK SEQUENCE		

Fig. 3.5. *ARP response.*

3.4 ARP TABLE (OR CACHE)

- To minimize broadcasts due to ARP requests, IP hosts and gateways store tables of MAC and IP addresses (called ARP tables or cashes).
- Each entry in the cache contains (IP address, MAC address, Time to Live).
- Sample ARP cache:

IP Address	*MAC Address*	*TTL*
128.192.6.111	00:00:C0:B8:A5:E3	155s
128.192.10.141	08:00:20:7C:7F:7E	246s
128.192.106.159	00:05:02:E6:48:41	626s
128.192.153.21	00:00:1B:16:F7:FF	332s
128.192.237.52	00:00:0C:4E:60:8F	185s
128.192.26.126	00:00:94:21:66:14	439s

- The Time to Live (TTL) field has either a fixed or adjustable maximum (usually a workstation or router, respectively).
- TTL is set to maximum when ARP request received, not set when communicating with another host.
- Tools to display ARP info (TTL usually not displayed) :
  - o ARP (Windows 9x/NT/2000)
  - o ARP (Unix)

Proxy ARP

- Some devices (such as routers) respond to ARP requests for IP addresses connected to other networks by providing their MAC address in an ARP reply.
- This behavior is called proxy (or promiscuous) ARP.
- Proxy ARP example:

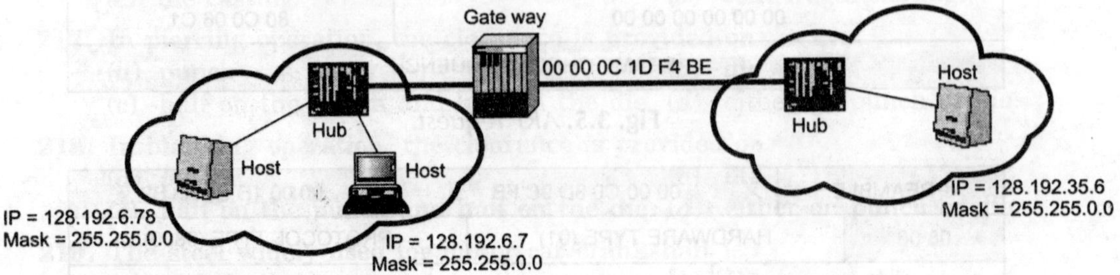

3.5 ARP IMPLEMENTATION

ARP Package

In this section we give an example of a simplified ARP software package the purpose is to show the components of a hypothetical ARP package and the relationship between the components. This ARP package involes five components : a cache table queues, an output module, an input module and cache-control module. The package receives an IP datagram that needs to be encapsulated in a frame that needs the destination physical (hardware) address. If the ARP package finds this address it delivers the ip packet and the physical address to the data link layer for transmission.

Cache Table

A sender usually has more than one IP datagram to send to the same destination. It is inefficient to use the ARP protocol for each datagram destined for the same host or router. The solution is the cache table when a host or router receives the corresponding physical address for an IP datagram the address can be saved in the cache table. This address can be used for the datagrams destined for the same receiver within the next few minutes. However as space in the cable table is very limited mappings in the cache are not retained for an unlimited time.

The cache table is implemented as an array of entries. In our pacakage each entry contains the following fields:

State. This column shows the state of the entry. It can have one of three values : **Free pending or resolved.** The Free state means that the time-to-live for this entry has expired. The space can be used for a new entry.

Pending. State means a request for this entry has been sent but the reply has not yet been received.

Resolved. State means that the entry is complete. The entry now has the physical (hardware) address of the destination. The packets waiting to be sent to this destination can use information in this entry.

Hardware type. This field is the same as the corresponding field in the ARP packet.

Protocol type. This field is the same as the corresponding field in the ARP packet.

Hardware length. This field is the same as the corresponding field in the ARP packet.

Protocol length. This field is the same as the corresponding field in the ARP packet.

Interface number. A router (or a multihomed host) can be connected to different networks each with a different interface number. Each network can have different hardware and protocol types.

Queue number. ARP uses numbered queues to enqueue the packets waiting for address resolution. Packets for the same destination are usually enqueued in the same queue.

Attempts. This column shows the number of times an ARP request is sent out for this entry.

Time-out. This column shows the lifetime of an entry inseconds.

Hardware address. This column shows the destination hardware address. It remains empty until resolved by ARP reply.

Protocol address. This column shows the destination IP address.

Queues

Our ARP package maintains a set of queues one for each destination to hold the IP packets while ARP tries to resolve the hardware address. The output module sends unresolved packets into the corresponding queue. The input module removes a packet from a queue and sends it with resolved physical address to the data link layer for transmission.

Output Module

The output module waits for an IP software. The output module checks the cache table to find an entry corresponding IP address of this packet. The destination IP address of the IP packet must match the protocol address of the entry.

If the entry is found and the state of the entry is RESOLVED, the packet along with the destination hardware address is passed to the data link layer for transmission.

If the entry is found and the state of the entry is PENDING the packet waits until the destination hardware address is found. Because the state is PENDING there is a queue already created for this destination. The module sends the packet to this queue.

If no entry is found the module creates a queue and enqueues the packet. A new entry with the state of PENDING is created for this destination and the value of the ATTEMPTS field is set to 1. An ARP request packet is then broadcast.

Input Module

The input module waits until an ARP packet (request or reply) arrives. The input modules checks the cache table to find an entry corresponding to this ARP packet. The target protocol address should match the protocol address of the entry.

If the entry is found and the state of the entry is PENDING the module updates the entry by copying the target hardware address in the packet to the hardware address field of the entry and changing the state to RESOLVED. The module also sets the value of the TIME-OUT for this entry. It then dequeues the packets from the corresponding queue one by one and delivers them along with the hardware address to the data link layer for transmission.

If the entry is found and the state is RESOLVED, The module still updates the entry. This is because the target hardware address could have been changed. The value of the TIME-OUT field is also reset.

If the entry is not found the module creates a new entry and adds it to the table. The protocol requires that any information received is added to the table for future use. The state is set to RESOLVED and TIME-OUT is set.

Now the module checks to see if the arrived ARP packet is request. If it is the module immediately creates an ARP reply message and sends it to the sender. The ARP reply packet is created by changing the value of the operation field from request to reply and filling in the target hardware address.

Cache-Control Module

The cache control module is responsible for maintaining the cache table. It periodically checks the cache table entry by entry.

If the state of the entry is FREE, it continues to the next entry. If the state is PENDING,

The module increments the value of the attempts field buy 1. It then checks the value of the attempts field. If this value is greater than the maximum number of attempts allowed. The state is changed to FREE and the corresponding queue is destroyed. However, if the number of attempts is less than the maximum the module creates and sends another ARP request.

If the state of the entry is RESOLVED the module decrements the value of the time-out field by the amount of the time elapsed since the last check. If this value is less than or equal to zero, the state is changed to FREE and the queue is destroyed.

Step by Step Implementation

Output Module

Step 1. *Sleep untilan IP packet is received from software.*

Step 2. *Check cache table for an entry corresponding to the destination of this IP pocket.*

Step 3. *If found:*

Step 3.1. *If the state is resolved:*

Step 3.1.1. *Extract the value of the hardware address from the entry.*

Step 3.1.2. *Send the packet and the hardware address to data link layer.*

Step 3.1.3. *Return.*

Step 3.2. *If the state is pending:*

Step 3.2.1. *Enqueue the packet to the corresponding queue.*

Step 3.2.2. *Return.*

Step 4. *If not found:*

Step 4.1. *Create a cache entry with state with stare set to pending and attempts set to 1.*

Step 4.2. *Create a queue.*

Step 4.3. *Enqueue the packet.*

Step 4.4. *Send an ARP request.*

Step 5. *Return.*

Input Module

Step 1. *Sleep until an ARP packet (request or reply) arrives.*

Step 2. *Check the cache table to find an entry corresponding to this ARP packet.*

Step 3. *If found:*

Step 3.1. *Update the entry.*

Step 3.2. *If the state is pending.*

Step 3.2.1. *While the queue is not empty:*

Step 3.2.1.1. *Dequeue one packet.*

Step 3.2.1.2. *Send the packet and the hardware address to date link.*

Step 4. *If not found:*

Step 4.1. *Create an entry.*

Step 4.2. *Add the entry to the table.*

Step 5. *If the packet is a request:*

Step 5.1. *Send an ARP reply.*

Step 6. *Return.*

Cache-Control Module

Step 1. *Sleep until the periodic timer matures.*

Step 2. *For every entry in the cache tavle:*

Step 2.1. *If the state is free:*

Step 2.1.1. *Continue.*

Step 2.2. *If the state is pending:*

Step 2.2.1. *Increment the value of attempts by 1.*

Step 2.2.2. *If attempts greater than maximum:*

Step 2.2.2.1. *Change the state to free.*

Step 2.2.2.2. *Destroy the corresponding queue.*

Step 2.2.3. *Else:*

Step 2.2.3.1. *Send an arp request.*

Step 2.2.4. *Continue.*

Step 2.3. *If the state is resolved:*

Step 2.3.1. *Decrement the value of time-out by the value of elapsed time.*

Step 2.3.2. *If time-out less than or equal to zero:*

Step 2.3.2.1. *Change the state to free.*

Step 2.3.2.2. *Destroy the corresponding queue.*

Step 3. *Return.*

CHAPTER 4

RARP

4.1 INTRODUCTION TO REVERSE ADDRESS RESOLUTION PROTOCOL (R AR P)

The Ethernet address, is the physical address and it is 48 bit, and we also know that ARP provides a mapping from the 32 bit IP address to the 48 bit physical address. The RARP does it reverse order. *i.e.*, RARP is used by systems without a disk drive (normally diskless workstations). Figure 4.1 shows the two protocols.

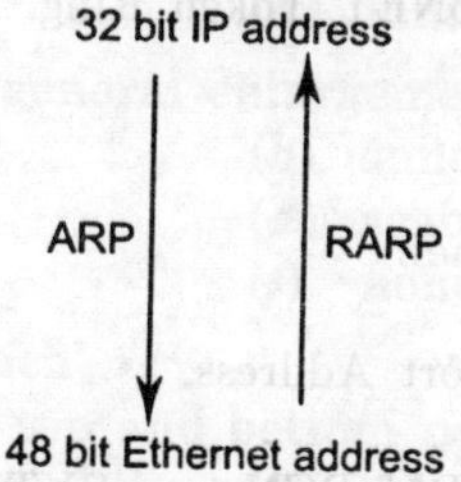

Fig. 4.1. *Address resolution protocols ARP and RARP.*

Application programs always use the IP address when specifying a destination. Because hosts and routers must use a physical address to transmit a datagram across an underlying hardware network, they rely on address resolution schemes like ARP to map between an IP address and an equivalent hardware address.

Usually, a computer's IP address is stored in its hard disk drive, where the Operating System reads when starting up. So how a diskless node can get its IP address ? The idea is simple. The machine that needs to know its IP address sends a request along with the physical address, to a server running on the other machine, and waits until the server sends a response. We assume that the server has access to a disk, where it keeps a database of Internet address. The server finds the correct IP address for the physical address and sends a reply to the machine. Actually the physical address of the machine will be the unique identification of the machine. But how does the requester know the physical address of the server ? Usually, the requester broadcast the request to the entire machines on the network. One or more servers respond.

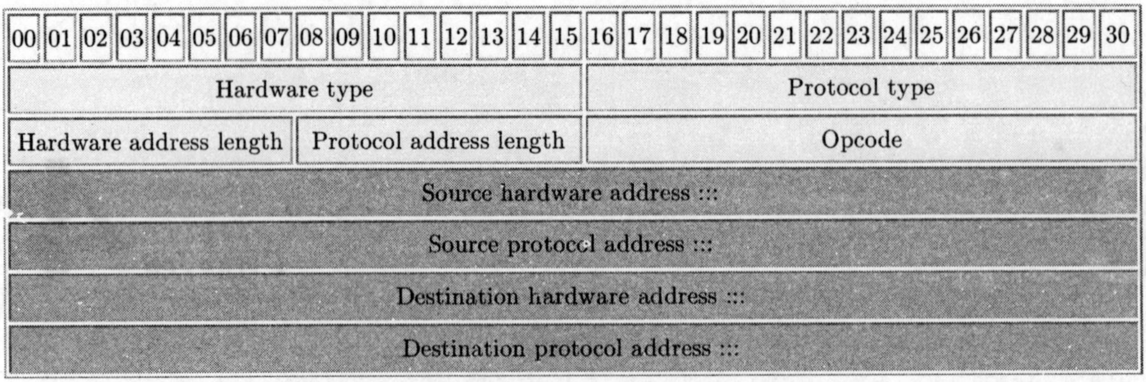

Fig. 4.2. *RARP packet.*

Hardware type. 16 bits

Table. 4.1. Rarp Description

Type	***Description***
1	Ethernet.
2	Experimental Ethernet.
3	Amateur Radio AX.25.
4	Proteon ProNET Token Ring.
5	Chaos.
6	IEEE 802.
7	ARCNET.
8	Hyperchannel.
9	Lanstar.
10	Autonet Short Address.
11	LocalTalk.
12	LocalNet (IBM PCNet or SYTEK LocalNET).
13	Ultra link.
14	SMDS.
15	Frame Relay.
16	ATM, Asynchronous Transmission Mode.
17	HDLC.
18	Fibre Channel.
19	ATM, Asynchronous Transmission Mode.
20	Serial Line.
21	ATM, Asynchronous Transmission Mode.
22	MIL-STD-188-220.
23	Metricom.
24	IEEE 1394.1995.
25	MAPOS.
26	Twinaxial.
27	EUI-64.
28	HIPARP.

Protocol type. 16 bits.

Protocol	*Description*
0x800	*IP.*

Hardware address length. 8 bits.

Length of the hardware address in bytes.

Protocol address length. 8 bits.

Length of the protocol address in bytes.

Opcode. 8 bits.

Opcode	*Description*	*References*
3	*Request Reverse.*	*RFC 903*
4	*Reply Reverse.*	*RFC 903*

Source hardware address. Variable length.

Source protocol address. Variable length.

Destination hardware address. Variable length.

Destination protocol address. Variable length.

CHAPTER 5

SUBNET AND SUPERNET

5.1 INTRODUCTION

Subnet

IP networks can be divided into smaller networks called subnetworks (or subnets). Subnetting provides the network administrator with several benefits, including extra flexibility, more efficient use of network addresses, and the capability to contain broadcast traffic (a broadcast will not cross a router).

Subnets are under local administration. As such, the outside world see an organization as a single network and has no detailed knowledge of the organization's internal structure.

A given network address can be broken up into many subnetworks. For example, 172.16.1.0, 172.16.2.0, 172.16.3.0, and 172.16.4.0 are all subnets within network 171.16.0.0. (All 0s in the host portion of an address specifies the entire network.)

IP Subnet Mask

Subnetting is a technique that allows the network administrator to divide a network into smaller networks by using the same network number assignment. The advantages of subnetting are given below:

- **Simplified administration.** With the help of routers networks can be broken up into smaller subnets that can be managed more independently and efficiently.
- **Restructuring of the internal network without affecting external networks.** A organization can continue to use it's allocated IP addresses without having to obtain additional IP blocks.
- **Improved security.** Subnetting will allow an organization to separate internal networks on the internetwork but will not be visible to external networks.
- **Isolation of network traffic.** With the help of routers and subnetting, network traffic can be kept to a minimum.

  Subnetted IP Appearance on the Internetwork

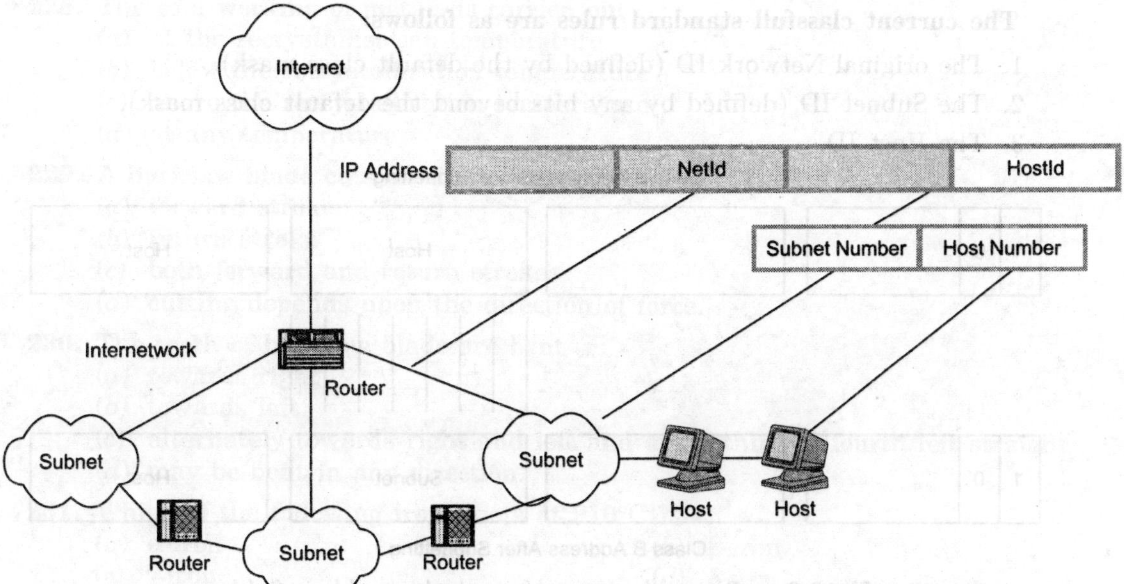

Fig. 5.1

In Figure 5.1 illustrates how a subnetted IP appears on an internal Intra-Net and the Internet. The Internet only reads the **NetId** and the routers on the Internet are only concerned with routing the IP packet to the Intra-Net external router. When the IP packet reaches the external router, which has been configured for subnet routing reads the **HostId**. The router then forwards the packet to appropriate subnet where it is delivered to the host.

5.2 DETERMINING THE SUBNET MASK TO USE

Figure 5.2 shows that when subnetting an IP address the NetId remains unchanged but the HostId is further sectioned or divided up.

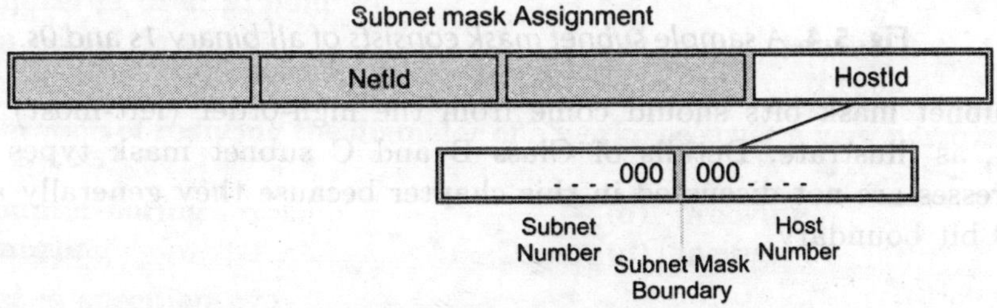

Fig. 5.2. *Subnet mark alignment.*

The Current Classfull Standard

There are a number of different ways to define the available range of IP addresses. Some network equipment may follow a more current addressing scheme called CIDR. To date, CIDR has not been adopted as the standard.

The current classfull standard rules are as follows:

1. The original Network ID (defined by the default class mask).
2. The Subnet ID (defined by any bits beyond the default class mask).
3. The Host ID.

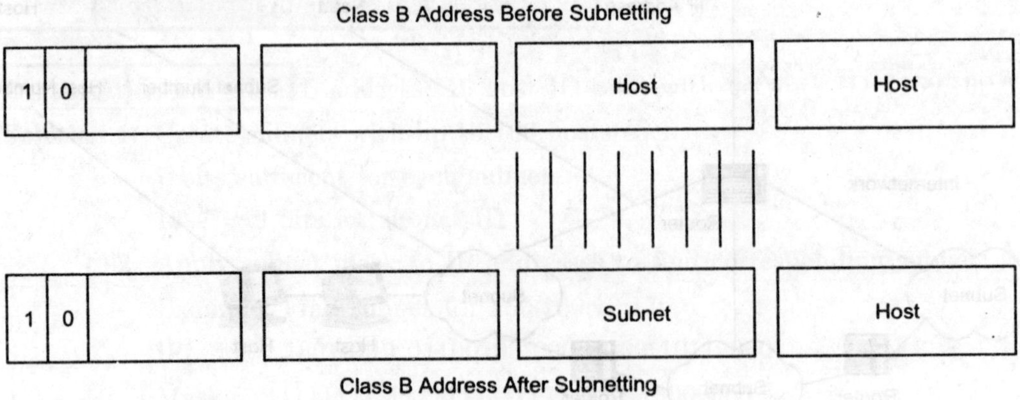

Fig. 5.3. *Bits are borrowed from the host address field to create the subnet address field.*

Subnet masks use the same format and representation technique as IP addresses. The subnet mask, however, has binary 1s in all bits specifying the network and subnetwork fields, and binary 0s in all bits specifying the host field. Illustrates a sample subnet mask.

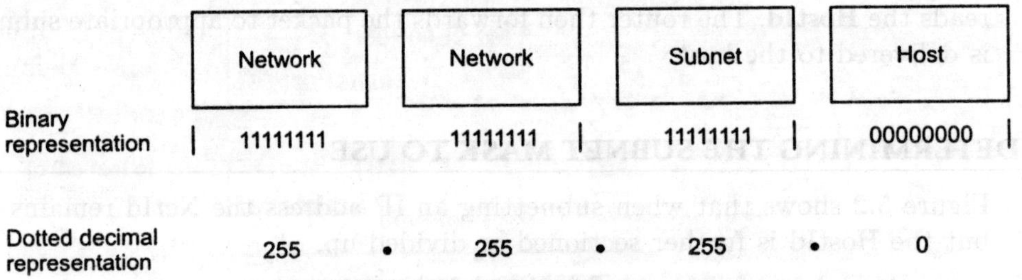

Fig. 5.4. *A sample subnet mask consists of all binary 1s and 0s.*

Subnet mask bits should come from the high-order (left-most) bits of the host field, as illustrate. Details of Class B and C subnet mask types follow. Class A addresses are not discussed in this chapter because they generally are subnetted on an 8 bit boundary.

5.3 SOME ADDRESSING RULES

- Each octet can range from 0 to 255.
- Network IDs range from 1 to 223.
- The network ID cannot be 127. This ID is reserved for loopback and diagnostic functions.

- The network and the host ID bits cannot all be 1's (255.255.255.255). This address is interpreted as a broadcast address.
- The network and the host ID bits cannot all be 0's (0.0.0.0). This address is interpreted to mean "this network only."
- In any class IP address you cannot have 0 as the first octet (this network only) or 255 as the last octet (broadcast).
- The host ID must be unique to the local network ID.
- Networks connected by routers need unique network IDs.
- Networks connected to the Internet need to have unique network ID portions assigned by the InterNIC.

5.4 FIND THE SUBNET ADDRESS

We use binary notation for both the address and the mask and then apply AND operation to find the subnet address.

Short Method

(*a*) If the byte in the mask is 255 copy the byte in the address.

(*b*) If the byte in the mask is 0, replace the byte in the address with 0.

(*c*) If the byte in the mask is neither 255 nor 0, we write the mask and the address in binary and apply the AND operation.

Default Mask and Subnet Mask

The number of 1s in a default mask is predetermined 8,16,24, in subnet mask the number of 1s is more than the number of 1s in the corresponding default mask.

Number of Subnetworks

The number of subnetworks can be found out by counting the extra 1s that are added to the default mask to make the subnet mask.

Example: It is 2 the number of subnet is 2*2 or 4.

Number of Address as Per Subnet

The number of address as per subnetwork can be found by counting the number of 0s in the subnet mask.

5.5 DESIGNING SUBNET

1. Determine the number of subnet needed for the organization.
2. Find the number of 1s in the default mask.
3. Find the number of 1s that defines the subnets.
4. Add the number of 1s in step 2 and 3.
5. Find the number of 0s by subtracting the number of 1s in step 4 from 32.
6. Find the range of address in each subnet.

6.1 *First method*—The first address in the first subnet is the first address in the block we then add the number of addresses in each subnet to get the last address.

6.2 *Second method*—We start with the last subnet the last address in the last subnet is the last address in the block we then apply mask to obtain the first address in this subnet.

Example Subnet

Organization has Class B address (16 host ID bits) with network ID : 150.100.0.0.

Solution 1. Create subnets with up to 100 hosts each

7 bits sufficient for each subnet

16–7 = 9 bits for subnet ID

2. Apply subnet mask to IP addresses to find corresponding subnet

Example: Find subnet for 150.100.12.176

IP add = 10010110 01100100 00001100 10110000

Mask = 11111111 11111111 11111111 10000000

AND = 10010110 01100100 00001100 10000000

Subnet = 150.100.12.128

Subnet address used by routers within organization

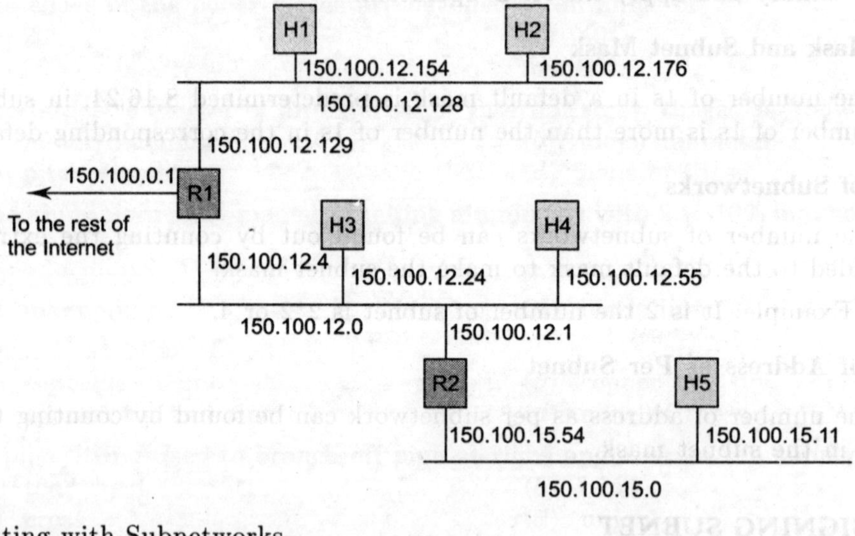

Routing with Subnetworks.

IP layer in hosts and routers maintain a routing table.

Originating host: To send an IP packet, consult routing table.

If destination host is in same network, send packet directly using appropriate network interface. Otherwise, send packet indirectly; typically, routing table indicates a default router.

Router: Examine IP destination address in arriving packet.

If destination IP address not own, router consults routing table to determine next-hop and associated network interface and forwards packet.

Routing Table

Each row in routing table contains:

Destination IP address.

IP address of next-hop router.

Physical address.

Statistics information.

Flags

H=1 (0) indicates route is to a host (network).

G=1 (0) indicates route is to a router (directly connected destination).

Routing table search order & action.

Complete destination address; send as per next-hop & G flag.

Destination network ID; send as per next-hop & G flag.

Default router entry; send as per next-hop.

Declare packet undeliverable; send ICMP "host unreachable error" packet to originating host.

Example: Host H5 sends packet to host H2

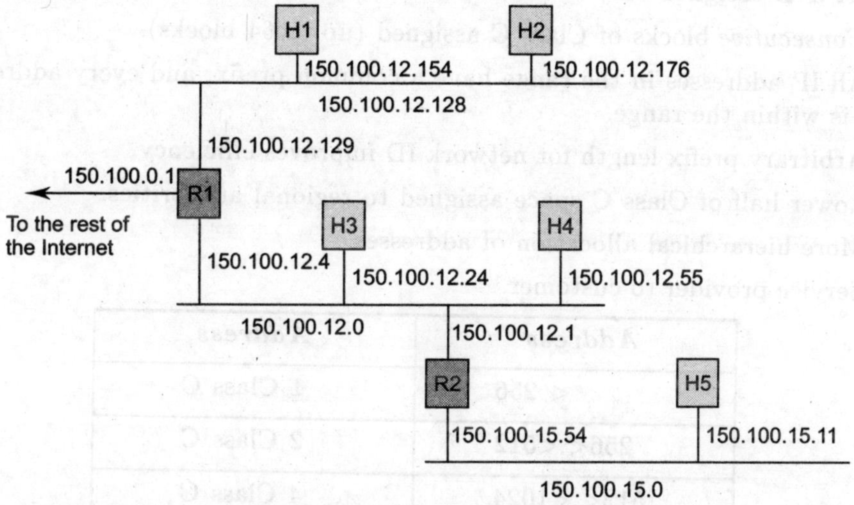

Destination	*Next-Hop*	*Flags*	*Net I/F*
127.0.0.1	127.0.0.1	H	lo0
default	150.100.15.54	G	emd0
150.100.15.0	150.100.15.11		emd0

IP address problems:

1. IP addresses were being exhausted.
2. IP routing tables were growing very large.
3. IP Address Exhaustion.
4. Class A, B, and C address structure inefficient.
5. Class B too large for most organizations, but future proof.
6. Class C too small.
7. Rate of Class B allocation implied exhaustion by 1994.
8. IP routing table size.
9. Growth in number of networks in Internet reflected in no of table entries.
10. From 1991 to 1995, routing tables doubled in size every 10 months.
11. Stress on router processing power and memory allocation.
12. Short-term solution.
13. Classless Inter domain Routing (CIDR), RFC 1518.
14. New allocation policy (RFC 2050).
15. Private IP Addresses set aside for intranets.
16. Long-term solution: IPv6 with much bigger address space.

New Address Allocation Policy

Class A & B assigned only for clearly demonstrated need.

Consecutive blocks of Class C assigned (up to 64 blocks).

All IP addresses in the range have a common prefix, and every address with that prefix is within the range.

Arbitrary prefix length for network ID improves efficiency.

Lower half of Class C space assigned to regional authorities.

More hierarchical allocation of addresses.

Service provider to customer.

Address	***Address***
< 256	1 Class C
256<,<512	2 Class C
512<,<1024	4 Class C
1024<,<2048	8 Class C
2048<,<4096	16 Class C
4096<,<8192	32 Class C
8192<,<16384	64 Class C

5.6 SUPERNETTING

As the Internet is growing with millions of computers connected with it, the address space of the IP is going to be exhausted. To accommodate the growth, a new version of IP would have to be defined, but we can have the temporary solution, which is called as classless addressing, supernetting or supernet addressing. CIDR (Classless Inter Domain Routing) is an interim solution to the address problem.

While the Internet protocol's 32 bit address space can in theory provide up to two billion addresses, the class system makes inefficient use of the addresses. The class networks are already assigned, and most organizations are too large for Class C networks. So that Class B networks are taken, because they fit the profile of most organization. However, many host addresses go unused by organizations that have Class B address. This is where IP addresses are wasted by the class system.

We know that, in every IP address there are two parts, one for networkId and the other for hostId. If only Class A addressing were used there would be 126 networks in the routing scheme and each router would only need to keep track of the location of these networks. But Class C networks are rapidly being assigned, creating an Internet with millions of networks. This introduces one problem : every Class C networks require a routing table entry. CIDR is a way to prevent this explosion in the size of the Internet routing tables.

To understand how supernetting works, consider a medium sized organization that joints the Internet. Such an organization would prefer to use a single Class B address for two reasons: a Class C address cannot accommodate more than 254 hosts and a Class B address has sufficient bits to make subnetting convenient. To conserve Class B numbers the supernetting scheme assigns an organization a block of Class C address instead of using a single Class B number.

The block must be large enough to number all the networks the organization will finally connect to the Internet. For example, suppose an organization requests a Class B address and intends to subnet using the third octet as a subnet field. Instead of a single Class B number, supernetting assigns the organization a block of 256 contiguous Class C numbers that the organization can then assign to physical networks.

Allocating many Class C addresses in place of a single Class B address conserves Class B numbers and solves the immediate problem of address space exhaustion. However, it creates a new problem: the information that routers store and exchange increases dramatically. For example, assigning an organization 256 Class C addresses instead of a Class B address requires 265 routerinstead of one.

The CIDR technique solves the problem. Conceptually CIDR collapses a block of contiguous Class C addresses into a single entry represented by a pair: (network address, count)

where network address is the smallest address in the block and count specifies the total number of network addresses in the block. For example, the pair (192.5.48.0, 3) is used to specify the three network addresses 192.5.48.0, 192.5.49.0 and 192.5.50.0. The benefit of supernetting is the routing tables are much smaller.

Supernetting, as might be guessed, is more or less the opposite of subnetting. Rather than making additional subnets, one takes a group of subnets and combines them into one. Again, It's actually a little easier than subnetting, because, as will be explained below, rather than a formula of 2^n–2, one simply uses 2^n.

The subnets must be contiguous. For instance, three subnets of 192.168.1.0, 192.168.2.0 and 192.168.3.0. Note that the third octets are consecutive, 1, 2 and 3. So, rather than take (in binary) 0's from the host portion of the address and making them ones, we're taking 1's and making them zeros.

The formula in this case, rather than 2^n–2 is simply 2^n. We need to combine three subnets. If we needed to MAKE three subnets, we'd try 2^2–2. 4–2=2, not enough, we'd have to go to 2^3=8. 8–2=6, and therefore, we would have changed 3 0's in the last octet to 1's, changing our subnet mask from 255.255.255.0 to 255.255.255.224.

However, we're COMBINING 3 subnets into one this time. So,we have three subnets, 192.168.1.0, 192.168.2.0 and 192.168.3.0, all of which have a subnet mask of 255.255.255.0. 2^1=2. Nope, not enough. 2^2=4. 4 is larger than 3, so that gives us enough. We have to change 2 1's in the third octect to 0's. So, in binary, we have 11111111.11111111.11111111.00000000. We are changing 2 of those ones in the third octet to 0's. So, we have 11111111.11111111.11111100.00000000. Our new subnet mask is 255.255.252.0.

Suppose we have 8 subnets that we want to combine. First, what power of 2 equals or is greater than 8? 2^3=8. Ok, we need to knock off 3 1's from the third octet. So, a subnet mask of 255.255.248.0 will enable us to combine the 8 subnets into one.

The points to remember here. Instead of changing 0's to ones, beginning at the left side of an octet, we are changing ones to 0's, beginning at the right side of the octet. The subnets that are being combined must be contiguous, such as 192.168.1.0, 192.168.2.0, etc. At least for test purposes, we can't combine 192.168.1.0, 192.168.6.0 and 192.168.11.0. Figure out how many subnets you are combining. Figure out which power of 2 is equal or greater to that number, *e.g.,* if it's 8 subnets that you're combining, what is n in 2^n=8. If it was just two subnets being combined, then it would be 2^1=2. If three subnets, then 2^2=4, if 5 subnets then 2^3=8, etc. Whatever n turns out to be, that's how many 1's you are taking away—from the RIGHT side of the octet, and changing them to 0's.

You probably have either memorized, or have your own method by now for remembering that 10000000 is 128, 11000000 is 192, 11100000 is 224, etc. So, if we change the last 2 1's of 255.255.255.0 to 0's that will be 252. If we change three 1's to 0 it will be 248, etc.

You can of course, simply memorize tables again, but it probably isn't necessary. At least in the practice tests I've seen, there were never more than 16 subnets to be combined, meaning that if you simply remember 240, 248, 252 and 254, you'll be fine. (For 16 subnets to be combined we would go 2^n=16. n=4. Take the last 4 1's of the third octet and make them 0's. This gives us 11110000 in binary, or 240 in decimal.

Hopefully, the above will simplify subnetting and supernetting enough for the reader to not only be able to use this knowledge on the exam but also in the real world, assuming that they can't find a freeware subnet calculator.

CHAPTER 6

IP ROUTING

6.1 INTRODUCTION

Internet Routing

Internet routing devices traditionally have been called gateways. In today's terminology, however, the term gateway refers specifically to a device that performs application-layer protocol translation between devices. Interior gateways refer to devices that perform these protocol functions between machines or networks under the same administrative control or authority, such as a corporation's internal network. These are known as autonomous systems. Exterior gateways perform protocol functions between independent networks.

Routers within the Internet are organized hierarchically. Routers used for information exchange within autonomous systems are called interior routers, which use a variety of Interior Gateway Protocols (IGPs) to accomplish this purpose. The Routing Information Protocol (RIP) is an example of an IGP.

Routers that move information between autonomous systems are called exterior routers. These routers use an exterior gateway protocol to exchange information between autonomous systems. The Border Gateway Protocol (BGP) is an example of an exterior gateway protocol.

6.2 IP ROUTING

IP routing protocols are dynamic. Dynamic routing calls for routes to be calculated automatically at regular intervals by software in routing devices. This contrasts with static routing, where routers are established by the network administrator and do not change until the network administrator changes them.

An IP routing table, which consists of destination address/next hop pairs, is used to enable dynamic routing. An entry in this table, For example, would be interpreted as follows : to get to network 171.32.0.0, send the packet out Ethernet interface 0 (E0).

IP routing specifies that IP datagrams travel through internetworks one hop at a time. The entire route is not known at the onset of the journey. At each stop, the next destination is calculated by matching the destination address within the datagram with an entry in the current node's routing table.

Each node's involvement in the routing process is limited to forwarding packets based on internal information. The nodes do not monitor whether the packets get to their final destination, nor does IP provide for error reporting back to the source when routing anomalies occur. This task is left to another Internet protocol, the Internet Control-Message Protocol (ICMP), which is discussed in the following section.

Consider now two separate Ethernet networks that are joined by an IP router, C.

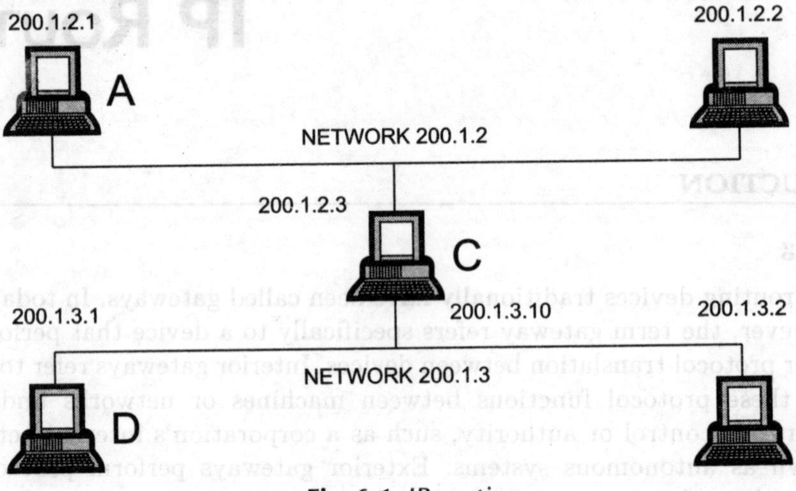

Fig. 6.1. *IP routing.*

Device C is acting as a router between these two networks. A router is a device that choose different paths for the network packets, based on the addressing of the IP frame. It is handling. Different routes connect to different networks. The router will have more than one address as each route is part of a different network.

Since there are two separate Ethernet segments, each network has its own Class C network number. This is necessary because the router must know which network interface to use to reach a specific node, and each interface is assigned a network number. If A wants to send a packet to E, it must first send it to C who can then forward the packet to E. This is accomplished by having A use C's Ethernet address, but E's IP address. C will receive a packet destined to E and will then forward it using E's Ethernet address. These Ethernet addresses are obtained using ARP as described earlier.

If E was assigned the same network number as A, 200.1.2, A would then try to reach E in the same way it reached C in the previous example — by sending an ARP request and hoping for a reply. However, because E is on a different physical wire, it will never see the ARP request and so the packet cannot be delivered. By specifying that E is on a different network, the IP module in A will know that E cannot be reached without having it forwarded by some node on the same network as A.

6.3 DIRECT VS. INDIRECT ROUTING

Direct routing was observed in the first example when A communicated with C. It is also used in the last example for A to communicate with B. If the packet does not need to be forwarded, *i.e.*, both the source and destination addresses have the same network number, direct routing is used.

Indirect routing is used when the network numbers of the source and destination do not match. This is the case where the packet must be forwarded by a node that knows how to reach the destination.

In the last example, A wanted to send a packet to E. For A to know how to reach E, it must be given routing information that tells it who to send the packet to in order to reach E. This special node is the "gateway" or router between the two networks. A Unix-style method for adding a routing entry to A is route add [destination_ip] [gateway] [metric]. Where the metric value is the number of hops to the destination. In this case, route add 200.1.3.2 200.1.2.3 1 will tell A to use C as the gateway to reach E. Similarly, for E to reach A, route add 200.1.2.1 200.1.3.10 1 will be used to tell E to use C as the gateway to reach A.

It is necessary that C have two IP addresses — one for each network interface. This way, A knows from C's IP address that it is on its own network, and similarly for E. Within C, the routing module will know from the network number of each interface which one to use for forwarding IP packets.

In most cases it will not be necessary to manually add this routing entry. It would normally be sufficient to set up C as the default gateway for all other nodes on both networks. The default gateway is the IP address of the machine to send all packets to that are not destined to a node on the directly-connected network. The routing table in the default gateway will be set up to forward the packets properly, which will be discussed in detail later.

Static vs. Dynamic Routing

Static routing is performed using a preconfigured routing table which remains in effect indefinitely, unless it is changed manually by the user. This is the most basic form of routing, and it usually requires that all machines have statically configured addresses, and definitely requires that all machines remain on their respective networks. Otherwise, the user must manually alter the routing tables on one or more machines to reflect the change in network topology or addressing. Usually at least one static entry exists for the network interface, and is normally created automatically when the interface is configured.

Dynamic routing uses special routing information protocols to automatically update the routing table with routes known by peer routers. These protocols are grouped according to whether they are Interior Gateway Protocols (IGPs) or Exterior Gateway Protocols. Interior gateway protocols are used to distribute routing information inside of an Autonomous System (AS). An AS is a set of routers inside the domain administered by one authority. Examples of interior gateway protocols are OSPF and RIP. Exterior gateway protocols are used for inter-AS routing, so that each AS may be aware of how to reach others throughout the Internet. Examples of exterior gateway protocols are EGP and BGP.

6.4 IMPLEMENTATION OF IP ROUTING

- Routing based on IP routing table of the form (netmask, net-address, next-hop).
- Routing algorithm :
  1. Extract destination IP address ipdest from datagram.
  2. Starting at the beginning of the routing table (and for each entry):
     (a) Calculate network portion of ipdest --> ipnet = AND(netmask, ipdest).
     (b) If ipnet equals net-address, send datagram to next-hop.
     (c) If ipnet does not equal net-address, repeat steps a. and b. for next entry.
     (d) If no table entry matches, declare a routing error.
- Routing table order:
  1. Directly connected networks (DCN)
  2. Host-specific routes (HSR)
  3. Net-specific routes (NSR)
  4. Default route (DR).
- Hosts have minimal routing tables (usually two entries — directly connected network and default route).
- Network for host routing examples.

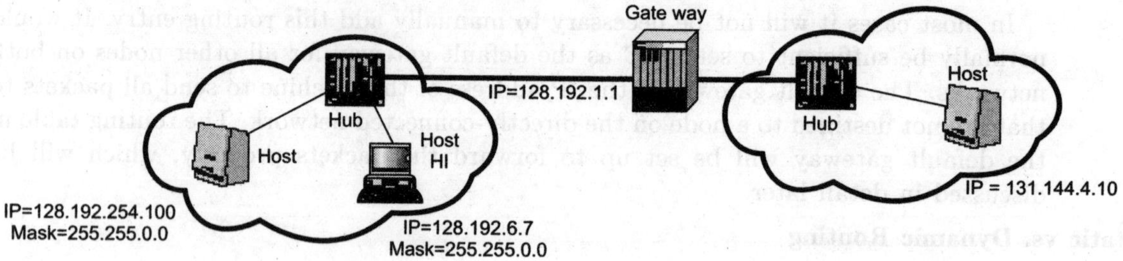

- Routing table for host H1.

entry	*netmask*	*net-address*	*next-hop*	*hop-count*	*(comments)*
1	255.255.0.0	128.192.0.0	128.192.6.7	0	DCN
2	0.0.0.0	0.0.0.0	128.192.1.1	1	DR

- Host routing example 1:
  1. Datagram ipdest=128.192.254.100
  2. Calculate network portion of ipdest using 1st routing table entry netmask :
  3. ipdest = 10000000 11000000 11111110 01100100 (128.192.254.100)
  4. netmask = 11111111 11111111 00000000 00000000 (255.255.0.0)
  5. AND operation --
  6. ipnet = 10000000 11000000 00000000 00000000 (128.192.0.0)
  7. Compare ipnet and 1st routing table entry net-address

8. 128.192.0.0 equals 128.192.0.0
9. Since they match, send it to next-hop=128.192.6.7, *i.e.*, communicate di rectly with destination host.

- Host routing example 2:

1. Datagram ipdest=131.144.4.10
2. Calculate network portion of ipdest using 1st routing table entry netmask :
3. ipdest = 10000011 10010000 00000100 00001010 (131.144.4.10)
4. netmask = 11111111 11111111 00000000 00000000 (255.255.0.0)
5. AND operation ----------------------------------
6. ipnet = 10000011 10010000 00000000 00000000 (131.144.0.0)
7. Compare ipnet with 1st routing table entry net-address
8. 128.192.0.0 does *not* equal 131.144.0.0
9. Since they don't match, calculate network portion of ipdest using 2nd routing table entry netmask:
10. ipdest = 10000011 10010000 00000100 00001010 (131.144.4.10)
11. netmask = 00000000 00000000 00000000 00000000 (0.0.0.0)
12. AND operation ----------------------------------
13. ipnet = 00000000 00000000 00000000 00000000 (0.0.0.0)
14. Compare ipnet with 2nd routing table entry net-address
15. 0.0.0.0 does equal 0.0.0.0
16. Since they match, send it to next-hop=128.192.1.1, *i.e.*, the default gateway
17. Network for gateway routing examples

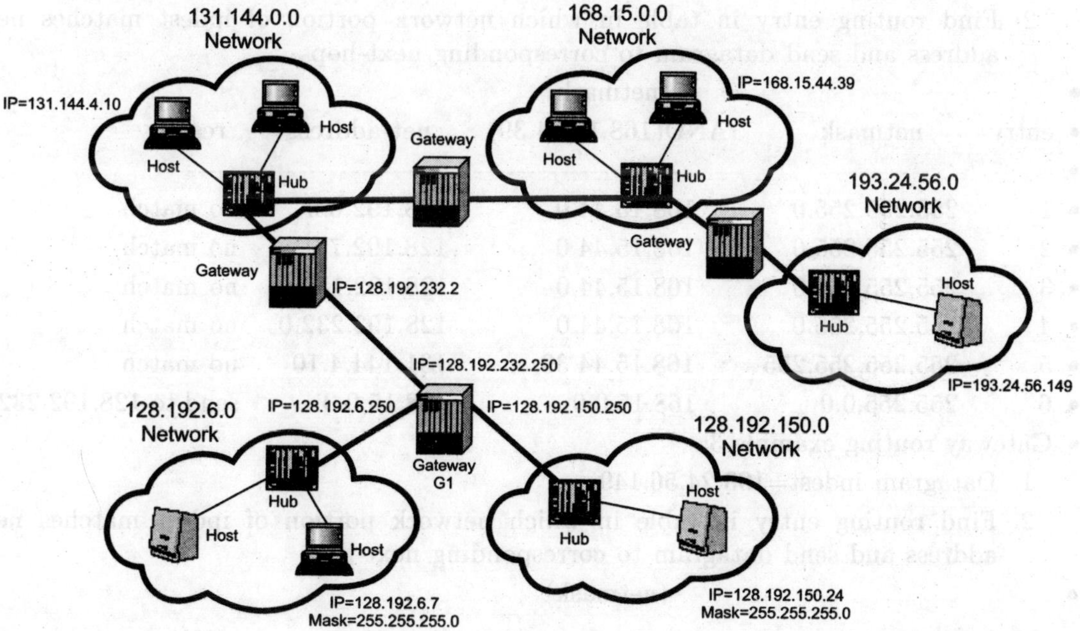

- Routing table for gateway G1

entry	*netmask*	*net-address*	*next-hop*	*hop-count*	*(comments)*
1	255.255.255.0	128.192.6.0	128.192.6.250	0	DCN
2	255.255.255.0	128.192.7.0	128.192.7.250	0	DCN
3	255.255.255.0	128.192.150.0	128.192.150.250	0	DCN
4	255.255.255.0	128.192.232.0	128.192.232.250	0	DCN
5	255.255.255.255	131.144.4.10	128.192.232.2	1	HSR
6	255.255.0.0	168.15.0.0	128.192.232.2	2	NSR
7	0.0.0.0	0.0.0.0	128.192.232.2	1	DR

- Gateway routing example 1:
  1. Datagram ipdest=128.192.150.24
  2. Find routing entry in table in which network portion of ipdest matches net-address and send datagram to corresponding next-hop

entry	netmask	(netmask) AND(128.192.150.24)	net-address	result
1	255.255.255.0	128.192.150.0	128.192.6.0	no match
2	255.255.255.0	128.192.150.0	128.192.7.0	no match
3	255.255.255.0	128.192.150.0	128.192.150.0	send directly

- Gateway routing example 2:
  1. Datagram ipdest=168.15.44.39
  2. Find routing entry in table in which network portion of ipdest matches net-address and send datagram to corresponding next-hop

entry	netmask	(netmask) AND(168.15.44.39)	net-address	result
1	255.255.255.0	168.15.44.0	128.192.6.0	no match
2	255.255.255.0	168.15.44.0	128.192.7.0	no match
3	255.255.255.0	168.15.44.0	128.192.150.0	no match
4	255.255.255.0	168.15.44.0	128.192.232.0	no match
5	255.255.255.255	168.15.44.39	131.144.4.10	no match
6	255.255.0.0	168.15.0.0	168.15.0.0	send to 128.192.232.2

- Gateway routing example 3:
  1. Datagram ipdest=193.24.56.149
  2. Find routing entry in table in which network portion of ipdest matches net-address and send datagram to corresponding next-hop

- (netmask)

entry	netmask	AND(193.24.56.149)	net-address	result
------	----------	------------------	------------	-----
1	255.255.255.0	193.24.56.0	128.192.6.0	no match
2	255.255.255.0	193.24.56.0	128.192.7.0	no match
3	255.255.255.0	193.24.56.0	128.192.150.0	no match
4	255.255.255.0	193.24.56.0	128.192.232.0	no match
5	255.255.255.255	193.24.56.149	131.144.4.10	no match
6	255.255.0.0	193.24.0.0	168.15.0.0	no match
7	0.0.0.0	0.0.0.0	0.0.0.0	send to 128.192.232.2
(default gateway)				

Routing Update Protocols

- Routing update protocols are used to modify the routing tables in gateways.
- Autonomous system - a collection of networks and gateways controlled by a single authority

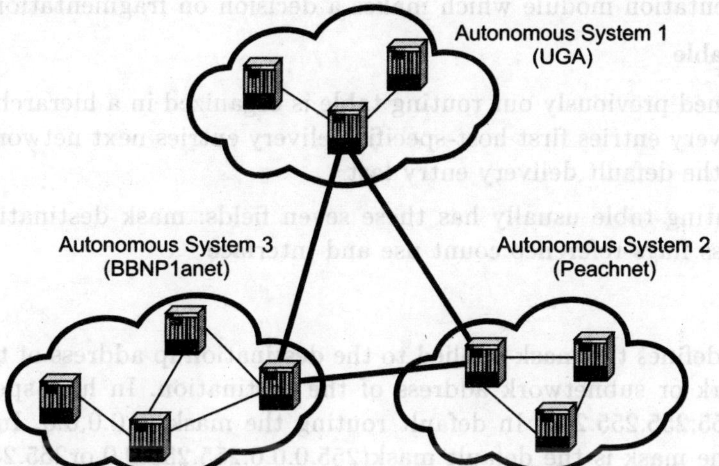

- Two general types of update protocols
  - o Interior gateway protocols - Used among gateways within an autonomous system
    - Routing Information Protocol (RIP, RIP2)
    - Open Shortest Path First (OSPF)
  - o Exterior gateway protocols - Used by gateways connecting autonomous systems
    - Exterior Gateway Protocol (EGP)
    - Border Gateway Protocol (BGP)
- OSPF & RIP used at UGA
  - o Only Foundry core routers communicate via OSPF
  - o Foundry routers broadcast RIP sometimes (don't listen)

- o RIP turned off all other routers
- o Hosts can listen to RIP but must *NOT* broadcast RIP

Step by Step Implementation

Routing table and routing module

In this section we discuss a simplified routing module. The module presented in pseudocode basically shows how the router can extract the outgoing interface for the packet and the next-hop address if the delivery is indirect When looking for the route the router must first check for direct delivery then host specific delivery then network specific delivery and finally default delivery this hierarchical stategy can be implemented in the routing module or in the routing table to make our routing module as simple as possible. We have used a routing table that is organized according to the above hierarchical scheme.

The module receives an ip packet from the ip processing module

The routing module consults the routing table to find the best route for the packet. After the route is found the packet is sent along with the next-hop address to the fragmentation module which makes a decision on fragmentation

Routing table

As mentioned previously our routing table is organized in a hierarchical scheme with direct-delivery entries first host-specific delivery entries next network-specific entries third and the default delivery entry last

The routing table usually has these seven fields: mask destination address next-hop address flags reference count use and interface

Mask

This field defines the mask applied to the destination ip address of the packet to find the network or subnetwork address of the destination. In host-specific routing the mask is 255.255.255.255. In default routing the mask is 0.0.0.0. In an unsubnetted network the mask is the default mask(255.0.0.0.255.255.0.0.or255.255.255.0 for class A,B or C respectively.)

Destination

This field defines either the destinaton host address(host-specific address) or the destination network address(network-specific) address. A host-specific destination address gives the full destination address netid and hostId. A network-specific destination address gives only the address of the network to which the destination entity is connected. The netId is specific but the host Id is all 0s.

Next-hop address

This field defines the address of the next-hop router to which the packet is delivered

Flags

This field defines up to five flags. Flags are on /off switches that signify either presence or absence. The five flags are U(up), G(gateway), H(host-specific), D(added by redirection) and M(modified by redirection).

(*a*) U (up) the U flag indicates the router is up and running. If this flag is not present it means that the router is down the packet cannot be forwarded and is discarded

(*b*) G (gateway) the G flag means that the destination is in another network. The packet should be delivered to the next-hop router for delivery(indirect delivery)when this flag is missing. It means the destination is in this network (direct delivery).

(*c*) H (host-specific)-the H flag indicates that the entry in the destination field is a host-specific address. When it is missing it means that the address is only the network address of the destination

(*d*) D (added by redirection)-the D flag indicates that routing information for this destination has been added to the host routing table by a redirection message from ICMP

(*e*) M (modified by redirection)-the M flag indicates that the routing information for this destination has been modified by a redirection and the ICMP

(*f*) Reference count this field gives the number of users that are using this route at any moment. For example if five people at the same time are connecting to the same host from this router the value of this count is 4

Use this field shows the number of packets transmitted through this router for the corresponding destination.

Interface: this field shows the name of the interface

Routing Module

The routing module receives an IP packet from the ip processing module. In our example the routing modulel goes from entry to entry trying to find a match. When it finds a match it quits because the routing table is hierarchically organized. It is guaranteed that the module first looks for a direct-delivery match, if no match is found the module looks for a host -specific delivery and so on.

Step1: *for each entry in the routing table*

Step1.1 *apply the mask to packet destination address*

Step1.2 *if the result matches the value in the destination field*

Step1.2.1 *if the G flag is present*

Step1.2.1.1 *use the next-hop entry in the table as next-hop address*

Step1.2.2 *if the G flag is missing*

Step1.2.2.1 *use packet destination address direct delivery*

Step1.3 *send packet to fragmentation module with next-hop address*

Step1.4 *stop*

Step2: *if no match is not found send an icmp error message*

Step3: *stop*

CHAPTER 7

ICMP

7.1 INTRODUCTION

Internet Control Message Protocol (ICMP) The Internet Control Message Protocol (ICMP) is a network-layer Internet protocol that provides message packets to report errors and other information regarding IP packet processing back to the source. ICMP is documented in RFC 792.

7.2 ICMP MESSAGES

The Internet Control Message Protocol (ICMP) is a network-layer Internet protocol that provides message packets to report errors and other information regarding IP packet processing back to the source. The Internet Control Message Protocol (ICMP) is classic example of a client server application. The ICMP server executes on all IP end system computers and all IP intermediate systems (*i.e.*, routers). The protocol is used to report problems with delivery of IP datagrams within an IP network. It can be ued to show when a particular End System (ES) is not responding, when an IP network is not reachable, when a node is overloaded, then an error occurs in the IP header information, etc. The protocol is also frequently used by Internet managers to verify correct operations of End Systems (ES) and to check that routers are correctly routing packets to the specified destination address. Figure 7.1 shows the problem in Network and ICMP message.

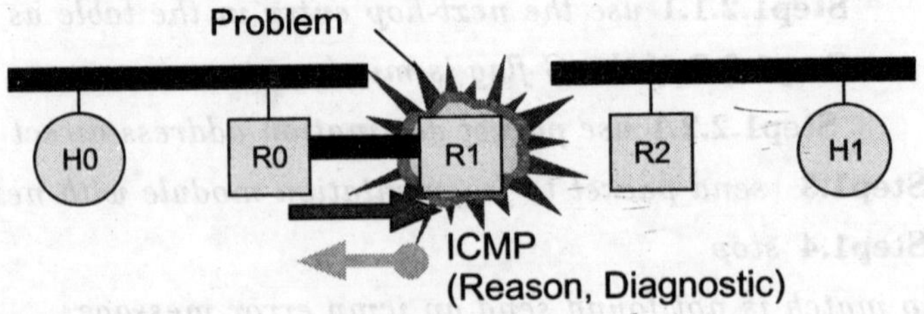

Fig. 7.1.

ICMP messages generated by router R1, in response to message sent by H0 to H1 and forwarded by R0. This message could, for instance be generated if the MTU of the link between R0 and R1 was smaller than size of the IP packet, and the packet had the Don't Fragment (DF) bit set in the IP packet header.The ICMP message is returned to H0, since this is the source address specified in the IP packet that suffered the problem.

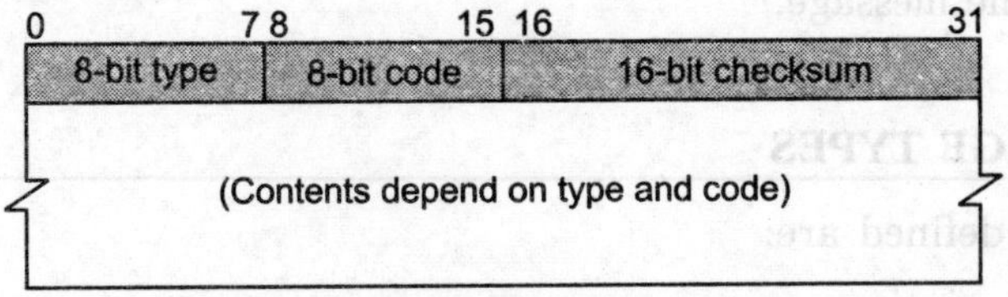

Fig. 7.2. *ICMP message format*

An ICMP message consists of 4 bytes of PCI and an optional message

The format of an ICMP message is shown in Figure 7.2. The 8-bit type code identifies the types of message. In this case two types of message are involved. The ECHO request (sent by the client) and the ECHO reply (the response by the server). Each message may contain some optional data. When data are sent by a server, the server returns the data in the reply which is generated. ICMP packets are encapsulated in IP for transmission across an internet.

It is the responsibility of the network layer (IP) protocol to ensure that the ICMP message is sent to the correct destination. This is achieved by setting the destination address of the IP packet. The source address is set to the address of the computer generating the ICMP ECHO request and the IP protocol type is set to "ICMP" to indicate that the packet is to be handled by the remote end system's ICMP server program.

Figure 7.3 shows the encapsulation over an Ethernet LAN using an IP network layer header, and a MAC link layer header and trailer containing the 32-bit checksum:

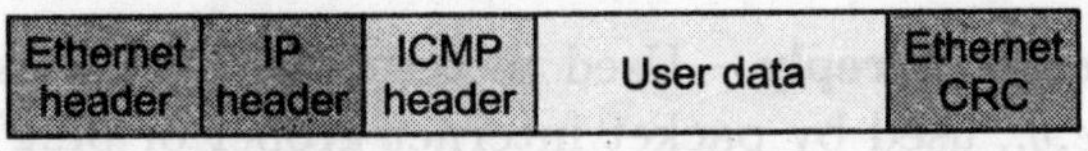

Fig. 7.3. *ICMP Format.*

For a complete ICMP packet (neglecting the Ethernet preamble)

The "ping" program contains a client interface to ICMP. It may be used by a user to verify whether an end-to-end Internet Path is operational. The ping program also collects performance statistics (*i.e.,* the measured round trip time and the number of times the remote server fails to reply. Each time an ICMP echo reply message is received, the ping program displays a single line of text. The text printed by ping shows the received sequence number, and the measured round trip time (in milliseconds). Each ICMP Echo message contains a sequence number (starting at 0) that is incremented after each transmission, and a timestamp value indicating the transmission time.

ICMPs are used by routers, intermediary devices, or hosts to communicate updates or error information to other routers, intermediary devices, or hosts.

Each ICMP message contains three fields that define its purpose and provide a checksum. They are TYPE, CODE, and CHECKSUM fields. The TYPE field identifies the ICMP message, the CODE field provides further information about the associated TYPE field, and the CHECKSUM provides a method for determining the integrity of the message.

7.3 ICMP MESSAGE TYPES

The TYPES defined are:

TYPE Description

---- -----------

0. Echo Reply
1. Destination Unreachable
2. Source Quench
3. Redirect Message
4. Echo Request
5. Time Exceeded
6. Parameter Problem
7. Timestamp Request
8. Timestamp Reply
9. Information Request (No Longer Used)
10. Information Reply (No Longer Used)
11. Address Mask Request
12. Address Mask Reply

Echo Request and Echo Reply

- **ICMP echo request/reply** – Used to test whether a destination is reachable and responding (*e.g.*, used by packet internet groper or ping).

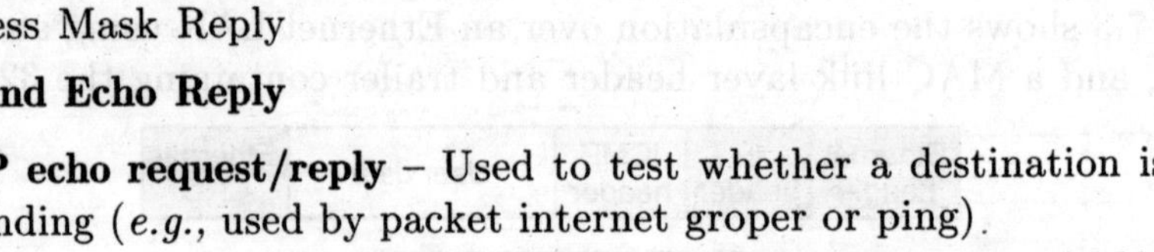

Fig. 7.4. *Echo request and echo reply*

This is the ICMP most used to test IP connectivity commonly known as PING. The Echo Request ICMP will have a Type field of 8 and a Code field of 0. Echo Replies have a Type field of 0 and a Code field of 0.

Destination Unreachable

When a packet is undeliverable, a Destination Unreachable, Type 3, ICMP is generated. Type 3 ICMPs can have a Code value of 0 to 15.

- Used by a gateway to indicate that it cannot route or deliver an IP datagram

0	8	16 24 31
TYPE (3)	CODE*	CHECKSUM
UNUSED (MUST BE ZERO)		
IP HEADER + 1ST 64 BITS OF DATAGRAM		
....		

Fig. 7.5. *Destination unreachable.*

Code

Value Description

----- -----------

0. Network Unreachable
1. Host Unreachable
2. Protocol Unreachable
3. Port Unreachable
4. Fragmentation needed and DF (Don't Fragment) set
5. Source route failed
6. Destination Network unknown
7. Destination Host unknown
8. Source Host isolated
9. Communication with Destination Network Administratively Prohibited
10. Communication with Destination Host Administratively Prohibited
11. Network Unreachable for Type Of Service
12. Host Unreachable for Type Of Service
13. Communication Administratively Prohibited by Filtering
14. Host Precedence Violation
15. Precedence Cutoff in Effect

Source Quench

- **ICMP source quench** – Used by a gateway to indicate that it is congested, source slows down the rate at which it sends datagrams

0	8	16 24 31
TYPE (4)	CODE (0)	CHECKSUM
UNUSED (MUST BE ZERO)		
IP HEADER + 1ST 64 BITS OF DATAGRAM		
....		

Fig. 7.6. *ICMP source quench.*

An ICMP Source Quench message has a Type field of 4 and Code 0. Source Quench messages are sent when the destination is unable to process traffic as fast as the source is sending it. The Source Quench ICMP tells the source to cut back the rate at which it is sending data. The destination will continue to generate Source Quench ICMPs until the source is sending at an acceptable speed.

Redirect Message

- **ICMP redirect** – Used by a gateway to tell a directly connected host that a more efficient gateway should be used for a specific IP address

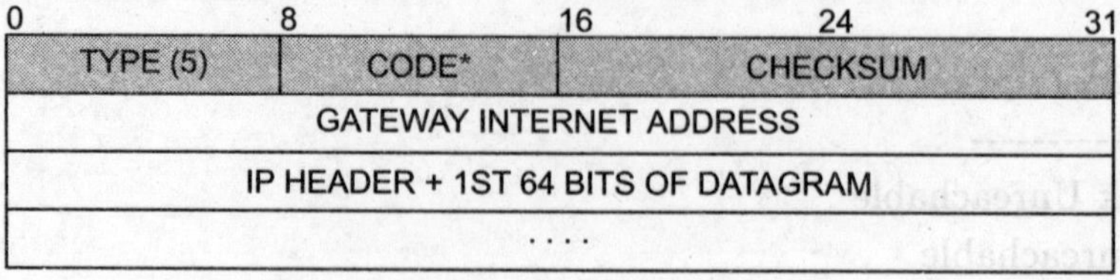

Fig. 7.7. *ICMP redirect message.*

An intermediary device will generate an ICMP Redirect Message when it determines that a route being requested can be reached either locally or through a better path. Redirect Message ICMPs are Type 5 and are further defined by the following Code field values:

Type 5

Code

Value Description

----- -----------

0. Redirect datagrams for the Network
1. Redirect datagrams for the Host
2. Redirect datagrams for the Type of Service and Network
3. Redirect datagrams for the Type of Service and Host

Time Exceeded

- **ICMP time exceeded** – Used by a gateway to indicate that a routing loop has occurred (sent when the IP TTL value reaches 0 or when segment reassembly time exceeded)

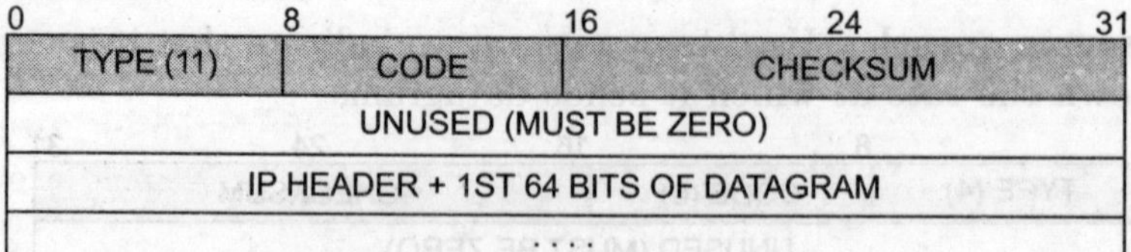

Fig. 7.8. *ICMP time exceeded*

If a router or host discards a packet due to a time-out, it will generate a Time Exceeded Type 11 ICMP. The Time Exceeded ICMP will have a Code value of either 0 or 1. A Code 0 is generated when the hop count of a datagram is exceeded and the packet is discarded. A Code 1 is generated when the reassemble of a fragmented packet exceeds the time-out value.

Parameter Problem

When an intermediary device or host discards a datagram due to inability to process, an ICMP 12 is generated. Common causes of this ICMP are corrupt header information or missing options. If the reason for the ICMP is a required missing option, the ICMP will have a Code value of 1. If the Code value is 0, the Pointer field will contain the octet of the discarded datagram's header where the error was detected.

Timestamp Request and Timestamp Reply

Timestamp Request and Timestamp Reply is a rudimentary method for synchronizing the time maintained on different devices. The Request has a Type field of 13 and the Reply is Type 14. This method for time synchronization is crude and unreliable. Therefore, it is not heavily used.

Information Request and Information Reply

These ICMP types were originally designed to allow a booting host to discover an IP address. This method is obsolete and is no longer used. Most common methods for IP address discovery are BOOTP (bootstrap protocol) and DHCP (dynamic host configuration protocol). BOOTP is defined by RFC1542, and DHCP is defined by RFC1541. For information about Microsoft's implementation of DHCP, please see the following Microsoft Knowledge Base article:

169289 DHCP (Dynamic Host Configuration Protocol) Basics

Address Mask Request and Address Mask Reply

A booting computer to determine the subnet mask in use on the local network uses the Address Mask Request ICMP Type 17. An intermediary device or computer acting as an intermediary device will reply with a Type 18 ICMP Address Mask Reply ICMP.

7.4 ICMP ROUTER-DISCOVERY PROTOCOL (IRDP)

IRDP uses Router-Advertisement and Router-Solicitation messages to discover the addresses of routers on directly attached subnets. Each router periodically multicasts Router-Advertisement messages from each of its interfaces. Hosts then discover addresses of routers on directly attached subnets by listening for these messages. Hosts can use Router-Solicitation messages to request immediate advertisements rather than waiting for unsolicited messages.

IRDP offers several advantages over other methods of discovering addresses of neighboring routers. Primarily, it does not require hosts to recognize routing protocols, nor does it require manual configuration by an administrator.

Router-Advertisement messages enable hosts to discover the existence of neighboring routers, but not which router is best to reach a particular destination. If a host uses a poor first-hop router to reach a particular destination, it receives a Redirect message identifying a better choice.

CHAPTER 8

IPV6

8.1 INTRODUCTION

The existing IP is given version number 4 and the new version of IP is given version number 6, and that is why it is called as Ipv6. But what necessitates the new invention of IP?

Version 4 of Internet Protocol (IPV4) provides the basic communication mechanism of the TCP/IP suit the global Internet; when IP was designed a 32-bit address space was more than enough. Only a few organizations had LAN, and fewer had WAN. But now most medium sized companies have multiple LANs and the number of nodes connected with Internet is growing fast. Now-a-days, the Internet is being widely used by universities, high-tech. industries, government, and other institutions. So the 32-bit address space of IPV4 is not sufficient to assign IP address for the new customers of Internet. This cannot accommodate projected growth of the global Internet beyond the year 2020.

Although the need for larger address space is the most immediate motivation, other reasons also caused the new design. In particular, using Internet for real time applications, (including security features for electronic commerce) make the entertainment industry able to use the Internet, (with multimedia support) etc, caused the invention of new IP. The IETF decided to assign the revision of IP version number 6 and to name it IPV6 to distinguish it from the current IPV4. What happened to version number 5? An experimental protocol known as the stream protocol is assigned version number 5.

Features of IPV6:

The proposed IPV6 protocol retains many of the features of IPV4. For example, IPV6 supports connectionless delivery, facilities for fragmentation, and source routing. However, there are many changes occurred in the protocol format.

The changes introduced by IPV6 can be grouped in to several categories:

- **Large addresses:** The new address size is the most noticeable change. IPV6 quadruples the size of an IPV4 address from 32 bits to 128 bits. The IPV6 address space is so large that it cannot be exhausted in the foreseeable future.

- **Extended address hierarchy:** IPV6 uses the larger address space to create additional levels of addressing hierarchy. In particular, IPV6 can define a hierarchy of ISPs as well as a hierarchical structure within a given site.
- **Flexible header format:** IPV6 uses an entirely new and incompatible datagram format. Unlike the Ipv4 fixed-format header, Ipv6 defines a set of optional headers.
- **Improved options:** Like IPV4, IPV6 allows a datagram to include optional control information. IPV6 includes new options that provide additional facilities not available in IPV4.
- **Provision for protocol extension:** Perhaps the most significant change in IPV6 is a move away from a protocol that fully specifies all details to a protocol that can permit additional features. The extension capability has the potential to allow the IETF to adapt the protocol to changes in underlying network hardware or to new applications.
- **Support for auto configuration and renumbering:** IPV6 provides facilities that allow computers on an isolated network to assign themselves addresses and begin communicating without depending on a router or manual configuration. The protocol also includes a facility that permits a manager to renumber networks dynamically.
- **Support for resource allocation:** IPV6 has two facilities that permit pre-allocation of network resources: a flow abstraction and a differentiated service specification.

8.2 THE BASE HEADER FORMAT OF IPV6

The IPV6 base header format is shown in Figure 8.1.

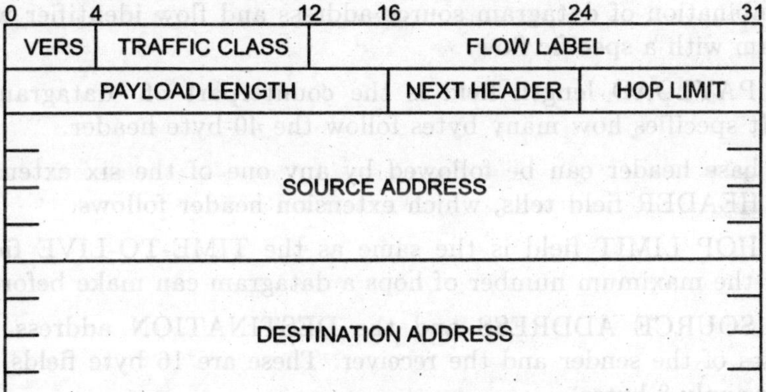

Fig. 8.1. *The base header format of IPV6.*

There are many changes in the format of IP header of IPV6 from the header format of IPV4.

- Alignment has been changed from 32 bit to 64 bit multiples.

- The header length field has been eliminated because it is fixed as 40 octets, and the datagram length field has been replaced by a PAYLOAD LENGTH field.
- The size of source and destination address fields has been increased to 16 octets each.
- Fragmentation information has been removed from the base header, and it is added to an extension header.
- The TIME-TO-LIVE field has been replaced by HOP LIMIT field.
- The SERVICE TYPE is renamed to be a TRAFFIC CLASS field, and extended with a FLOW LABEL field.
- The PROTOCOL field has been replaced by the type of the next header.

IN the IPV6 header format, the version field is always 6 for IPV6. The fields TRAFFIC CLASS and FLOW LABEL are used in making forwarding decisions. The field SERVICE TYPE in IPV4 has been renamed as TRAFFIC CLASS. In addition, a new mechanism in IPV6 supports resource reservation and allows a router to associate each datagram with a given resource allocation. The underlying abstraction, a flow consist no a path through an Internet, along with intermediate routers guarantee a specific quality of service. Field FLOW LABEL in the base header contains information that routers use to associate a datagram with a specific flow and priority. For example two applications that need to send video can establish a flow on which the delay and bandwidth is guaranteed. Alternatively, a network provider may require a subscriber to specify the quality of service desired, and then use a flow to limit the traffic a specific computer or specific application sends. Note that flows can also be used within a given organization to manage network resources and ensure that all applications receive a fair share. A router uses the combination of datagram source address and flow identifier when associating a datagram with a specific flow.

The PAYLOAD length field is the counterpart of "datagram length" field of IPV4. It specifies how many bytes follow the 40-byte header.

The base header can be followed by any one of the six extension headers. The NEXT HEADER field tells, which extension header follows.

The HOP LIMIT field is the same as the TIME-TO-LIVE field of IPV4. It is strictly the maximum number of hops a datagram can make before being discarded.

The SOURCE ADDRESS and the DESTINATION address fields specify the addresses of the sender and the receiver. These are 16 byte fields, whereas in IPV4, these are only 8 bytes.

Proposed IPV6 Address Space Assignment.

There are two central issues on partitioning the address space. (a) How to manage address assignments and (b) how to map an address to a route. The first issue focuses on the practical problem of devising a hierarchy of authority. The current IPv4 uses two level hierarchy, the network and the host, but the large address space of IPv6 permits a multilevel hierarchy. The second issue focuses on the computation efficiency of a router. A router must check each datagram and choose a path to the destination. As the Figure 8.2. shows the address space of IPV6 is divised into address classes. The address space is not partitioned into sections of equal size.

Binary Prefix	*Type Of Address*	*Part Of Address Space*
0000 0000	Reserved(IPv4 compatibility)	1/256
0000 0001	Unassigned	1/256
0000 001	NSAP Addresses	1/128
0000 010	IPX Addresses	1/128
0000 011	Unassigned	1/128
0000 1	Unassigned	1/32
0001	Unassigned	1/16
001	Aggregatable Global Unicast	1/8
010	Unassigned	1/8
011	Unassigned	1/8
100	Unassigned	1/8
101	Unassigned	1/8
110	Unassigned	1/8
1110	Unassigned	1/16
1111 0	Unassigned	1/32
1111 10	Unassigned	1/64
1111 110	Unassigned	1/128
1111 1110 0	Unassigned	1/512
1111 1110 10	Link-Local Unicast Addresses	1/1024
1111 1110 11	Site-Local Unicast Addresses	1/1024
1111 1111	Multicast Addresses	1/256

Fig. 8.2. *The proposed division of IPV6 address into types, which are analogous to IPV4 classes.*

As in IPV4, the prefix of an address determines its address type.

As the figure shows, only 15% of the address space has been assigned at present. The IETF will use the remaining portions as demand grows.

8.3. IPV6 COLON HEXADECIMAL NOTATION

The large address size of the IPV6 has the new problem of writing the address. The dotted decimal notation used for IPV4, does not make the compaction easier. A new notation has been introduced for writing 16-byte addresses. To understand the reason, consider an example of 128-bit number expressed in dotted decimal notation.

1. 104.230.140.100.92.80.200.17.0.0.8.255.255.255.10.168

This is more difficult to enter, manipulate and read. To make the address slightly compact a scheme which is called as colon hexadecimal notation or colon hex in which each 16-bit value is written in hexadecimal and separated by a colon symbol is adopted.

The equivalent colon hex notation for the above said address becomes:

2. 68E6:8C64:5C50:C811:0:8FF:FFFF:AA8

It is easy to read because, it is requiring a fewer digits and fewer separator characters than dotted decimal notation. In addition, the colon hex notation gives two techniques, that make it very handy and useful. First colon hex notation allows, zero compression in which a string of repeated zeros is replaced by a pair of colons. For example,

3. FF05:0:0:0:0:0:0:B3

Can be written as

4. FF05::B3

But, to avoid confusion, zero compression must be used only once in an address. Second, colon hex allows dotted decimal suffixes which can be used during the transition from IPv4 to IPv6. For example,

0:0:0:0:0:0:128.10.2.1

is a valid colon hex notation. Using zero compression, this can be written as

::128.10.2.1

The colon hex notation also allows the CIDR-like notation, in which an address is followed by a slash and an integer that specifies a number of bits. For example

5. 10CD::B6:0:0:0:0/60

specifies that, the first 60 bits of address or

6. 10CD00000000B6

in hexadecimal.

8.4 THE EXTENSION HEADERS

Some of the missing fields in IPV6 are still needed sometimes, so IPV6 introduced the concept of an (optional) extension header. These headers can be used with the base header to provide more information. Six types of extension headers are defined at present. Each one is optional, but if more than one is present they must follow the base header in the given order.

Extension Header	Description
Hop-by-Hop options	Miscellaneous information for routes
Routing	Full or partial route to follow
Fragmentation	Management of datagram fragments
Authentication	Verification of the sender's identity
Encrypted security payload	Information about the encrypted contents
Destination options	Additional information for the destination

Fig. 8.3. *Different types of extension headers.*

Each of the base and extension headers contains a NEXT HEADER field. The value in the NEXT HEADER field is used to parse the datagram. The following figure shows the NEXT HEADER

Field of three datagrams that contain zero, one and two extension headers.

CHAPTER 9

TCP AND UDP

The Transmission Control Protocol

It is important to understand TCP if one is to understand the historic, current and future architecture of the Internet protocols. Most applications on the Internet make use of TCP, relying upon its mechanisms that ensure safe delivery of data across an unreliable IP layer below. The fundamental concepts behind TCP and how it is used to transport data between two endpoints are discussed in detail in this section.

9.1 INTRODUCTION

The Transmission Control Protocol (TCP) standard is defined in the Request For Comment (RFC) standards document number 793 by the Internet Engineering Task Force (IETF). The original specification written in 1981 was based on earlier research and experimentation in the original ARPANET. The design of TCP was heavily influenced by what has come to be known as the "end-to-end argument"

As it applies to the Internet, the end-to-end argument says that by putting excessive intelligence in physical and link layers to handle error control, encryption or flow control the system. This is because these functions will usually need to be done at the endpoints duplicate the effort along the way. The result of an end-to-end network then, is to provide minimal functionality on a hop-by-hop basis and maximal control between end-to-end communicating systems.

The end-to-end argument helped determine how two characteristics of TCP operate; performance and error handling. TCP performance is often dependent on a subset of algorithms and techniques such as flow control and congestion control. Flow control determines the rate at which data is transmitted between a sender and receiver. Congestion control defines the methods for implicitly interpreting signals from the network in order for a sender to adjust its rate of transmission.

The term congestion control is a bit of a misnomer. Congestion avoidance would be a better term since TCP cannot control congestion . Ultimately intermediate devices, such as IP routers would only be able to control congestion.

Congestion control is currently a large area of research and concern in the network community. A companion study on congestion control examines the current state of activity in that area.

Timeouts and retransmissions handle error control in TCP. Although delay could be substantial, particularly if you were to implement real-time applications, the use of both techniques offer error detection and error correction thereby guaranteeing that data will eventually be sent successfully.

The nature of TCP and the underlying packet switched network provide formidable challenges for managers, designers and researchers of networks. Once regulated to low speed data communication applications, the Internet and in part TCP are being used to support very high speed communications of voice, video and data. It is unlikely that the Internet protocols will remain static as the applications change and expand. Understanding the current state of affairs will assist us in understanding protocol changes made to support future applications.

9.2 TRANSMISSION CONTROL PROTOCOL SERVICES

TCP is often described as a byte stream, connection-oriented, reliable delivery transport layer protocol. In turn, we will discuss the meaning for each of these descriptive terms.

Byte Stream Delivery

TCP interfaces between the application layer above and the network layer below. When an application sends data to TCP, it does so in 8-bit byte streams. It is then up to the sending TCP to segment or delineate the byte stream in order to transmit data in manageable pieces to the receiver1. It is this lack of "record boundaries" which give it the name "byte stream delivery service".

Connection-Oriented

Before two communicating TCPs can exchange data, they must first agree upon the willingness to communicate. Analogous to a telephone call, a connection must first be made before two parties exchange information.

Reliability

A number of mechanisms help provide the reliability that TCP guarantees. Each of these is described briefly below.

Checksums. All TCP segments carry a checksum, which is used by the receiver to detect errors with either the TCP header or data.

Duplicate data detection. It is possible for packets to be duplicated in packet switched network; therefore TCP keeps track of bytes received in order to discard duplicate copies of data that has already been received.

Retransmissions. In order to guarantee delivery of data, TCP must implement retransmission schemes for data that may be lost or damaged. The use of positive acknowledgements by the receiver to the sender confirms successful reception of data.

The lack of positive acknowledgements, coupled with a timeout period calls for a retransmission.

Sequencing. In packet switched networks, it is possible for packets to be delivered out of order. It is TCP's job to properly sequence segments it receives so that it can deliver the byte stream data to an application in order.

Timers. TCP maintains various static and dynamic timers on data sent. The sending TCP waits for the receiver to reply with an acknowledgement within a bounded length of time. If the timer expires before receiving an acknowledgement, the sender can retransmit the segment.

9.3 TCP HEADER FORMAT

Remember that the combination of TCP header and TCP in one packet is called a TCP segment. Figure 9.1 depicts the format of all valid TCP segments. The size of the header without options is 20 bytes. We will briefly define each field of the TCP header.

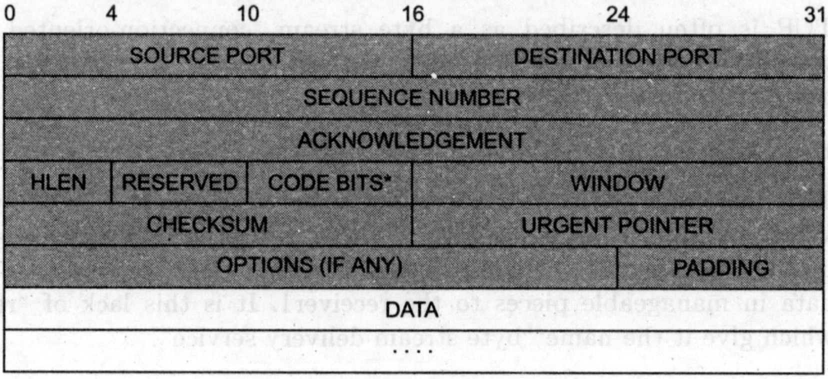

Fig. 9.1. *TCP header format.*

Source Port

A 16-bit number identifying the application the TCP segment originated from within the sending host. The port numbers are divided into three ranges, well-known ports (0 through 1023), registered ports (1024 through 49151) and private ports (49152 through 65535). Port assignments are used by TCP as an interface to the application layer. For example, the TELNET server is always assigned to the well-known port 23 by default on TCP hosts. A complete pair of IP addresses (source and destination) plus a complete pair of TCP ports (source and destination) define a single TCP connection that is globally unique.

Destination Port

A 16-bit number identifying the application the TCP segment is destined for on a receiving host. Destination ports use the same port number assignments as those set aside for source ports

Sequence Number

A 32-bit number identifying the current position of the first data byte in the segment within the entire byte stream for the TCP connection. After reaching $2^{32} - 1$, this number will wrap around to 0.

Acknowledgement Number

A 32-bit number identifying the next data byte. The sender expects from the receiver. Therefore, the number will be one greater than the most recently received data byte. This field is only used when the ACK control bit is turned on.

Header Length

A 4-bit field that specifies the total TCP header length in 32-bit words (or in multiples of 4 bytes if you prefer). Without options, a TCP header is always 20 bytes in length. The largest a TCP header may be 60 bytes. This field is required because the size of the options field(s) cannot be determined in advance. Note that this field is called "data offset" in the official TCP standard, but header length is more commonly used.

Reserved

A 6-bit field currently unused and reserved for future use.

Control Bits

Urgent Pointer (URG). If this bit field is set, the receiving TCP should interpret the urgent pointer field (see below).

Acknowledgement (ACK). If this bit field is set, the acknowledgement field described earlier is valid.

Push Function (PSH). If this bit field is set, the receiver should deliver this segment to the receiving application as soon as possible. An example of its use may be to send a Control-BREAK request to an application, which can jump ahead of queued data.

Reset the Connection (RST). If this bit is present, it signals the receiver that the sender is aborting the connection and all queued data and allocated buffers for the connection can be freely relinquished.

Synchronize (SYN). When present, this bit field signifies that sender is attempting to "synchronize" sequence numbers. This bit is used during the initial stages of connection establishment between a sender and receiver.

No More Data from Sender (FIN). If set, this bit field tells the receiver that the sender has reached the end of its byte stream for the current TCP connection.

Window

A 16-bit integer used by TCP for flow control in the form of a data transmission window size. This number tells the sender how much data the receiver is willing to accept. The maximum value for this field would limit the window size to 65,535 bytes, however a "window scale" option can be used to make use of even larger windows.

Checksum

A TCP sender computes a value based on the contents of the TCP header and data fields. This 16-bit value will be compared with the value the receiver generates using the same computation. If the values match, the receiver can be very confident that the segment has arrived intact.

Urgent Pointer

In certain circumstances, it may be necessary for a TCP sender to notify the receiver of urgent data that should be processed by the receiving application as soon as possible. This 16-bit field tells the receiver when the last byte of urgent data in the segment ends.

Options

In order to provide additional functionality, several optional parameters may be used between a TCP sender and receiver. Depending on the option(s) used, the length of this field will vary in size, but it cannot be larger than 40 bytes due to the size of the header length field (4 bits). The most common option is the maximum segment size (MSS) option. A TCP receiver tells the TCP sender the maximum segment size it is willing to accept through the use of this option. Other options are often used for various flow control and congestion control techniques.

Padding

Because options may vary in size, it may be necessary to "pad" the TCP header with zeroes so that the segment ends on a 32-bit word boundary as defined by the standard.

Data

Although not used in some circumstances (*e.g.*, acknowledgement segments with no data in the reverse direction), this variable length field carries the application data from TCP sender to receiver. This field coupled with the TCP header fields constitute a TCP segment.

9.4 USER DATAGRAM PROTOCOL (UDP)

The User Datagram Protocol (UDP) is a connectionless transport-layer protocol (Layer 4) that belongs to the Internet protocol family. UDP is basically an interface between IP and upper-layer processes. UDP protocol ports distinguish multiple applications running on a single device from one another.

Unlike the TCP, UDP adds no reliability, flow-control, or error-recovery functions to IP. Because of UDP's simplicity, UDP headers contain fewer bytes and consume less network overhead than TCP.

UDP is useful in situations where the reliability mechanisms of TCP are not necessary, such as in cases where a higher-layer protocol might provide error and flow control.

UDP is the transport protocol for several well-known application-layer protocols, including Network File System (NFS), Simple Network Management Protocol (SNMP), Domain Name System (DNS), and Trivial File Transfer Protocol (TFTP).

The UDP packet format contains four fields, as shown in Figure 9.2. These include source and destination ports, length, and checksum fields.

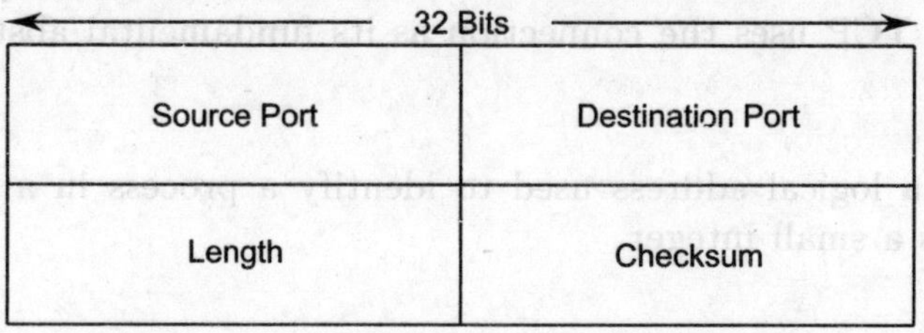

Fig. 9.2. *A UDP packet consists of four fields.*

Source and destination ports contain the 16-bit UDP protocol port numbers used to demultiplex datagrams for receiving application-layer processes. A length field specifies the length of the UDP header and data. Checksum provides an (optional) integrity check on the UDP header and

- UDP provides an unreliable, connectionless delivery
- Application programs using UDP are responsible for message loss, duplication, delay, out-of-order delivery, and loss of connectivity
- Examples of applications that use UDP transport include Network Time Protocol (NTP), Sun's Network File System (NFS), and the Simple Network Management Protocol (SNMP)
- Each UDP message is called a user datagram

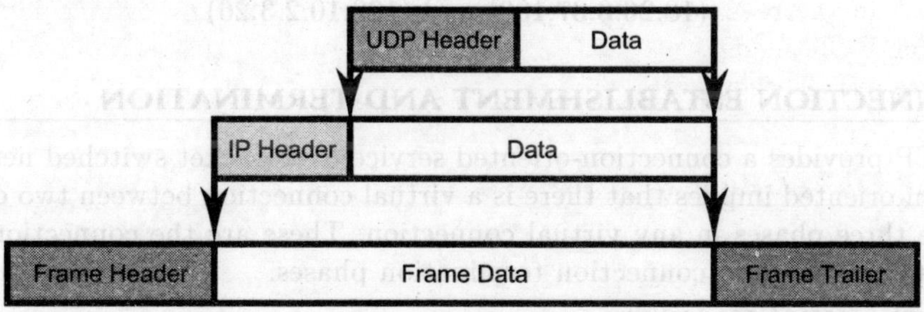

Fig. 9.3. *UDP message encapsulation.*

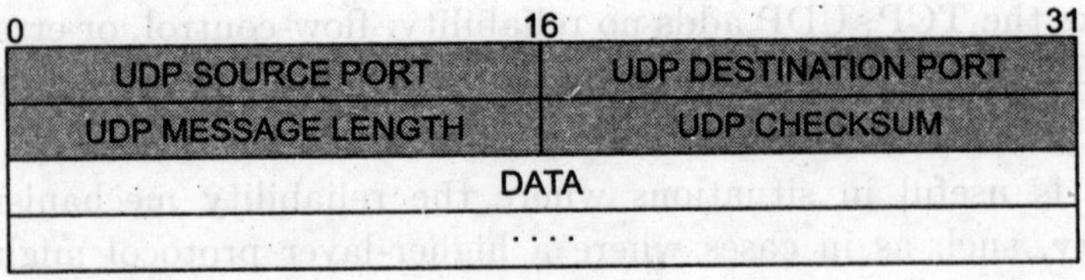

Fig. 9.4. *UDP message format.*

- UDP messages are stored in queues on destination host, one queue per destination port.

Ports, connections and endpoints

In order to establish connection, TCP makes use of ports, connection and endpoints. TCP uses the connection as its fundamental abstraction.

Port

Port is a logical address used to identify a process in a machine and is usually denoted as a small integer.

Connection

Connection is nothing but a virtual circuit between two application programs. A pair of endpoints defines every connection, so naturally an application program serves as the connection "endpoints".

Endpoint notation:

For example,

(*i*). The endpoint (128.10.2.3, 26) specifies TCP port 26 on the machine with IP address 128.10.2.3

(*ii*). If there is a connection from machine (18.26.0.37) to machine (128.10.2.3), it can be defined by the endpoints:

(18.26.0.37,109) and (128.10.2.3,26)

9.5 CONNECTION ESTABLISHMENT AND TERMINATION

TCP provides a connection-oriented service over packet switched networks. Connection-oriented implies that there is a virtual connection between two endpoints. There are three phases in any virtual connection. These are the connection establishment, data transfer and connection termination phases.

Three-Way Handshake

In order for two hosts to communicate using TCP they must first establish a connection by exchanging messages in what is known as the three-way handshake. The diagram below depicts the process of the three-way handshake.

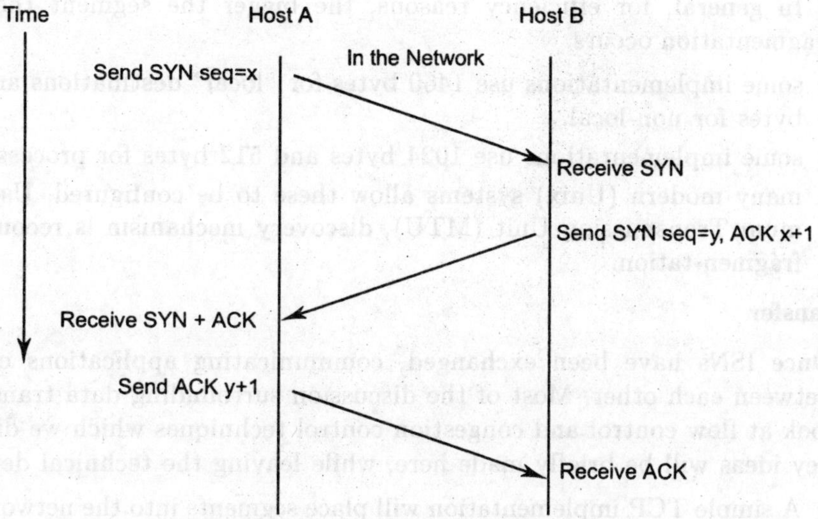

Fig. 9.5. *TCP connection establishment.*

From Figure 9.5, it can be seen that there are three TCP segments exchanged between two hosts, Host A and Host B. Reading down the diagram depicts events in time.

To start, Host A initiates the connection by sending a TCP segment with the SYN control bit set and an initial sequence number (ISN) represented as the variable x in the sequence number field.

At some moment later in time, Host B receives this SYN segment, processes it and responds with a TCP segment of its own. The response from Host B contains the SYN control bit set and its own ISN represented as variable y. Host B also sets the ACK control bit to indicate the next expected byte from Host A should contain data starting with sequence number x+1.

When Host A receives Host B's ISN and ACK, it finishes the connection establishment phase by sending a final acknowledgement segment to Host B. In this case, Host A sets the ACK control bit and indicates the next expected byte from Host B by placing acknowledgement number y+1 in the acknowledgement field.

In addition to the information shown in the diagram above, an exchange of source and destination ports to use for this connection are also included in each senders' segments.

Maximum Segment Size (MSS)

A TCP protocol data unit is called a "segment".

Each end of a TCP connection may announce in a SYN segment the maximum segment size that it is prepared to receive. If there is no announcement, the default is 536 bytes. (This is sometimes wrongly called negotiation.)

In general, for efficiency reasons, the bigger the segment the better, until IP fragmentation occurs.

- some implementations use 1460 bytes for "local" destinations and the default 536 bytes for non-local.
- some implementations use 1024 bytes and 512 bytes for processing efficiency.
- many modern (Unix) systems allow these to be configured. Use of the IP Maximum Transmission Unit (MTU), discovery mechanism is recommended to avoid fragmen-tation.

Data Transfer

Once ISNs have been exchanged, communicating applications can transmit data between each other. Most of the discussion surrounding data transfer requires us to look at flow control and congestion control techniques which we discuss later. A few key ideas will be briefly made here, while leaving the technical details aside.

A simple TCP implementation will place segments into the network for a receiver as long as there is data to send and as long as the sender does not exceed the window advertised by the receiver. As the receiver accepts and processes TCP segments, it sends back positive acknowledgements, indicating where in the byte stream it is. These acknowledgements also contain the "window" which determines how many bytes the receiver is currently willing to accept. If data is duplicated or lost, a "hole" may exist in the byte stream. A receiver will continue to acknowledge the most current contiguous place in the byte stream it has accepted.

If there is no data to send, the sending TCP will simply sit idly by waiting for the application to put data into the byte stream or to receive data from the other end of the connection.

If data queued by the sender reaches a point where data sent will exceed the receiver's advertised window size, the sender must halt transmission and wait for further acknowledgements and an advertised window size that is greater than zero before resuming.

Timers are used to avoid deadlock and unresponsive connections. Delayed transmissions are used to make more efficient use of network bandwidth by sending larger "chunks" of data at once rather than in smaller individual pieces.

Connection Termination

In order for a connection to be released, four segments are required to completely close a connection. Four segments are necessary due to the fact that TCP is a full-duplex protocol, meaning that each end must shut down independently.[6] The connection termination phase is shown in Figure 9.6.

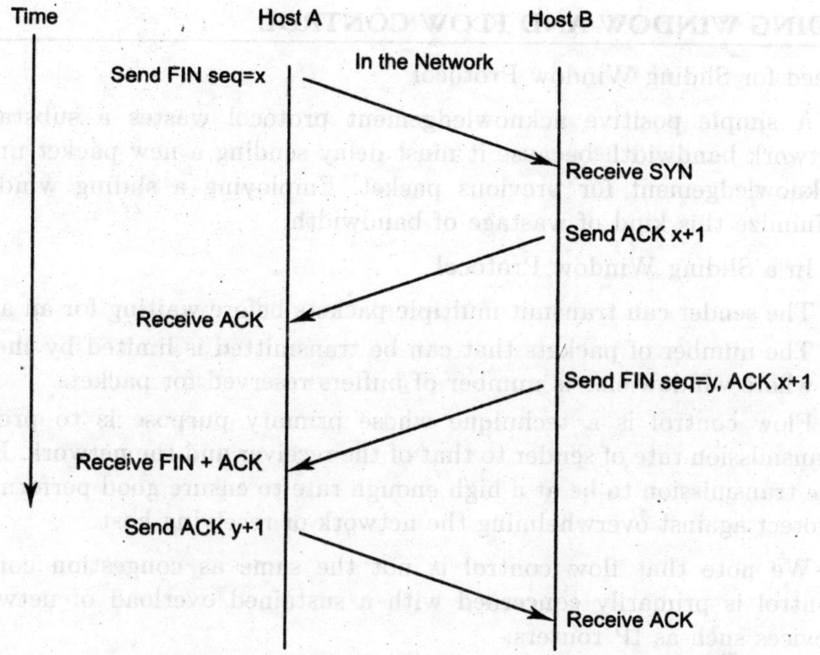

Fig. 9.6. *TCP connection termination.*

Notice that instead of SYN control bit fields, the connection termination phase uses the FIN control bit fields to signal the close of a connection.

To terminate the connection. In our example, the application running on Host A signals TCP to close the connection. This generates the first FIN segment from Host A to Host B. When Host B receives the initial FIN segment, it immediately acknowledges the segment and notifies its destination application of the termination request. Once the application on Host B also decides to shut down the connection, it then sends its own FIN segment, which Host A will process and respond with an acknowledgement.

9.6 PROBLEMS IN RELIABILITY

In a stream delivery service, reliability problem rises due to

- Duplicate packets: When there is a high delay in the network, the acknowledgements may be delayed. This makes the source to think that the packet is lost or corrupted and eventually it leads to premature retransmission causing duplicates packets. To avoid the problems of duplicate packets, the protocol assigns each packet a sequence number and makes the receiver to remember the sequence number it has received and to check for duplicates each time it receives a packet.
- Delayed / duplicated acknowledgements : To avoid the confusion caused by delayed or duplicated acknowledgements, the protocols send the sequence numbers back in acknowledgements, so the receiver can correctly associate acknowledgements with packets.

9.7 SLIDING WINDOW AND FLOW CONTROL

Need for Sliding Window Protocol

A simple positive acknowledgement protocol wastes a substantial amount of network bandwidth because it must delay sending a new packet until it receives an acknowledgement for previous packet. Employing a sliding window protocol can minimize this kind of wastage of bandwidth.

In a Sliding Window Protocol

- The sender can transmit multiple packets before waiting for an acknowledgement.
- The number of packets that can be transmitted is limited by the window size, K, where window size is number of buffers reserved for packets.

Flow control is a technique whose primary purpose is to properly match the transmission rate of sender to that of the receiver and the network. It is important for the transmission to be at a high enough rate to ensure good performance, but also to protect against overwhelming the network or receiving host.

We note that flow control is not the same as congestion control. Congestion control is primarily concerned with a sustained overload of network intermediate devices such as IP routers.

TCP uses the window field, briefly described previously, as the primary means for flow control. During the data transfer phase, the window field is used to adjust the rate of flow of the byte stream between communicating TCPs.

Figure 9.7. illustrates the concept of the sliding window.

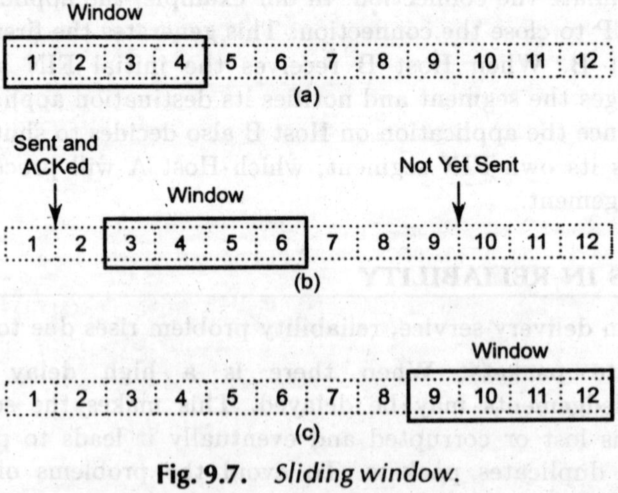

Fig. 9.7. *Sliding window.*

In this simple example, there is a 4-byte sliding window. Moving from left to right, the window "slides" as bytes in the stream are sent and acknowledged. The size of the window and how fast to increase or decrease the window size is an area of great research.

9.8 TIMEOUT AND RETRANSMISSION

Like other protocols, TCP also adopt the fundamental technique "positive acknowledgement with retransmission". But since TCP is intended to use in an internet environment, a segment traveling between two machines may traverse, a single low-delay network or it may traverse across multiple intermediate networks through multiple routers. Thus it is impossible to know previously about the time at which an acknowledgement will return to the source. Thus to accommodate the varying delays, TCP uses variant algorithm called adaptive retransmission algorithm.

Adaptive Retransmission Algorithm

- TCP monitors the performance (delay) of each connection and calculates the timeout value as a function of current Round Trip Time (RTT).

  Where

  RTT = Acknowledgement Arrival Time - Segment Sent Time

  Timeout = α* RTT (α = constant weighting factor)

- Whenever there is a new RTT, TCP adjusts the average RTT for the connection as

  RTT = (β* Old_RTT) + ((1- β) *New_RTT)

  Where

  $\beta \rightarrow$ Constant weighting factor ($0<\beta<1$)

- Problem

- • Acknowledgement ambiguity: In case of a delayed acknowledgement, TCP may timeout and retransmit the segment. Since both datagrams carry exactly the same data, when an acknowledgement arrives, the sender has no way identifying whether an acknowledgement corresponds to original or retransmitted datagram. This phenomenon is called acknowledgement ambiguity, which could be rectified using Karn's algorithm.

- Solution

- • Karn's Algorithm: Karn's algorithm makes the sender to combine the retransmission timeout with a timer backoff technique

  o The backoff technique computes an initial timeout using the formula

  Timeout = α* RTT (α = constant weighting factor)

  o After that, each time it retransmits a segment, TCP increases the timeout value by a back off value as below

  new_timeout = backoff * timeout

  o This back offing repeats until TCP can successfully transfer a segment without retransmission.

  o Finally, when an acknowledgement arrives corresponding to a segment which does not require retransmission, TCP recomputes RTT and resets the timeout accordingly.

Nagle algorithm

A general rule, known as the Nagle Algorithm says that a sender must not have more than one unacknowledged "small" segment. Any further data from the application is held by the sender until the outstanding segment is acknowledged. Here small means of size less than the maximum segment size.

This is not desirable in highly interactive environments such an X window client/server interaction or a screen based terminal session, under these circumstances Nagle can be turned off by using the TCP_NODELAY socket option. Nagle may also sometimes be turned off anyway for a connection with both hosts on the same LAN.

Many interactive applications (Telnet, Rlogin, etc.) send and echo single bytes, which can mean many 41-byte IP packets.

The Nagle Algorithm (RFC896 1984) alleviates this:

- when a "small" segment has been sent, no further small segments can be sent until the first is ACKed.

This has the effect of blocking up groups of characters on slower connections.

9.9 CONGESTION CONTROL

TCP congestion control and Internet traffic management issues in general is an active area of research and experimentation. This final section is a very brief summary of the standard congestion control algorithms widely used in TCP implementations.

Slow Start

Slow Start, a requirement for TCP software implementations is a mechanism used by the sender to control the transmission rate, otherwise known as sender-based flow control. This is accomplished through the return rate of acknowledgements from the receiver. In other words, the rate of acknowledgements returned by the receiver determine the rate at which the sender can transmit data.

When a TCP connection first begins, the Slow Start algorithm initializes a congestion window to one segment, which is the maximum segment size (MSS) initialized by the receiver during the connection establishment phase. When acknowledgements are returned by the receiver, the congestion window increases by one segment for each acknowledgement returned. Thus, the sender can transmit the minimum of the congestion window and the advertised window of the receiver, which is simply called the transmission window.

Slow Start is actually not very slow when the network is not congested and network response time is good. For example, the first successful transmission and acknowledgement of a TCP segment increases the window to two segments. After successful transmission of these two segments and acknowledgements completes, the window is increased to four segments. Then eight segments, then sixteen segments and so on, doubling from there on up to the maximum window size advertised by the receiver or until congestion finally does occur.

Congestion Avoidance

During the initial data transfer phase of a TCP connection the Slow Start algorithm is used. However, there may be a point during Slow Start that the network is forced to drop one or more packets due to overload or congestion. If this happens, Congestion Avoidance is used to slow the transmission rate. However, Slow Start is used in conjunction with Congestion Avoidance as the means to get the data transfer that so it doesn't slow down and stay slow.

In the Congestion Avoidance algorithm a retransmission timer expiring or the reception of duplicate ACKs can implicitly signal the sender that a network congestion situation is occurring. The sender immediately sets its transmission window to one half of the current window size (the minimum of the congestion window and the receiver's advertised window size), but to at least two segments. If congestion was indicated by a timeout, the congestion window is reset to one segment, which automatically puts the sender into Slow Start mode. If congestion was indicated by duplicate ACKs, the Fast Retransmit and Fast Recovery algorithms are invoked.

As data is received during Congestion Avoidance, the congestion window is increased. However, Slow Start is only used up to the halfway point where congestion originally occurred. This halfway point was recorded earlier as the new transmission window. After this halfway point, the congestion window is increased by one segment for all segments in the transmission window that are acknowledged. This mechanism will force the sender to more slowly grow its transmission rate, as it will approach the point where congestion had previously been detected.

Fast Retransmit

When a duplicate ACK is received, the sender does not know if it is because a TCP segment was lost or simply that a segment was delayed and received out of order at the receiver. If the receiver can re-order segments, it should not be long before the receiver sends the latest expected acknowledgement. Typically no more than one or two duplicate ACKs should be received when simple out of order conditions exist. If however more than two duplicate ACKs are received by the sender, it is a strong indication that at least one segment has been lost. The TCP sender will assume enough time has lapsed for all segments to be properly re-ordered by the fact that the receiver had enough time to send three duplicate ACKs.

When three or more duplicate ACKs are received, the sender does not even wait for a retran-smission timer to expire before retransmitting the segment (as indicated by the position of the duplicate ACK in the byte stream). This process is called the Fast Retransmit algorithm.

Fast Recovery

Since the Fast Retransmit algorithm is used when duplicate ACKs are being received, the TCP sender has implicit knowledge that there is data still flowing to the receiver. Why? The reason is because duplicate ACKs can only be generated when a segment is received. This is a strong indication that serious network congestion may not exist and that the lost segment was a rare event. So instead of reducing the flow of data abruptly by going all the way into Slow Start, the sender only enters Congestion Avoidance mode.

Rather than start at a window of one segment as in Slow Start mode, the sender resumes transmission with a larger window, incrementing as if in Congestion Avoidance mode. This allows for higher throughput under the condition of only moderate congestion.

Remember points

- *The word "segment" is the term used to describe TCP's data unit size transmitted to a receiver. TCP determines the appropriate use of this segment size rather than leaving it up to higher layer protocols and applications.*
- *Duplicate packets are typically caused by retransmissions, where the first packet may have been delayed and the second sent due to the lack of an acknowledgement. The receiver may then receive two identical packets.*
- *As opposed to a connectionless-oriented protocol such as that used by the user datagram protocol (UDP).*
- *There are additional details of the connection establishment, data transfer and termination phases that are beyond the scope of this book.*
- *It was discovered early on that some implementations of TCP performed poorly due to this scenario. It has been termed the silly window syndrome.*
- *Although it is possible, it is not very common for TCP to be operating in the "half-close state".*
- *We assume in this example that bytes are immediately acknowledged so that the window can move forward. In practice the sender's window shrinks and grows dynamically as acknowledgements arrive in time.*

9.10 TCP PERFORMANCE

TCP is a complex protocol that handles communication over a wide variety of underlying network technologies. In spite of accommodating a wide generality , surprisingly, the performance does not get hindered. For example,

(*i*) Experiments at Berkeley have shown that TCP can deliver 8 Mbps of through-put between two workstations on a 10 Mbps Ethernet.

(*ii*) Experiments at Cray Research Inc. have demonstrated that TCP throughput approaches a gigabit per second.

Problems Affecting TCP Performance

Silly window syndrome

Early TCP implementations exhibited a problem known as silly window syndrome in which each acknowledgement advertises a small amount of space available and each segment carries a small amount of data.

To understand the problem, let us consider the effect of each in turn.

- Acknowledgement advertising a small window size
  - Consider a case where, the sender is of high speed and receiver reads the data one octet at a time

- On connection establishment, receiving TCP allocates a buffer of K bytes and advertises the window size as K using the WINDOW field in acknowledgement segment.
- The sending TCP generates data and transmit segments with data for the entire window.
- Eventually the sender will receive an acknowledgement with window size as 0
- When the receiving application reads one octet of data, it sends an acknowledgement advertising the window size as 1.
- The sending TCP responds by transmitting one octet of data.
- Merits:
  The single-octet window advertisement works correctly to keep the receiver's buffer filled
- Demerits:
  (*i*) Results in a series of small data segments.
  (*ii*) Transferring small segments consumes unnecessary network bandwidth because each datagram carries only one octet of data: the ratio of header to data is large
  (*iii*) Transferring small segments introduces unnecessary computational overhead because TCP on both sides must process each segment.

Segment carrying a small amount of data

- Consider a case where the TCP implementation aggressively sends the data whenever available and sender generates data one octet at a time.
- After the application generates on octet of data, TCP creates and transmits a segment.
- Demerits:
  (*i*) Transferring small segments consumes unnecessary network bandwidth because each datagram carries only one octet of data: the ratio of header to data is large.
  (*ii*) Transferring small segments introduces unnecessary computational overhead because TCP on both sides must process each segment.

Avoiding Silly Window Syndrome

TCP specifications now include heuristics to prevent silly window syndrome. A heuristic used on the sending machine avoids transmitting a small amount of data in each segment. A heuristic used on the receiving machine avoids sending small increments in window advertisements that can trigger small data packets. Since TCP connection is full duplex, in practice, it must contain both sender and receiver silly window avoidance code.

Receiver-side Silly Window Avoidance

Heuristic

Before sending an updated window advertisement after advertising a zero window, wait for space to become available that is either at least 50% of the total buffer size or equal to a maximum sized segment.

Explanation

- **The receiver delays advertising an increase in window size until the window size advances to a significant amount**
- **Significant amount = min(receiver's buffer size/2, max segment size)**
- **Prevents small window advertisements for receivers which extracts data octets slowly.**

The operation of heuristic in Figure 9.7

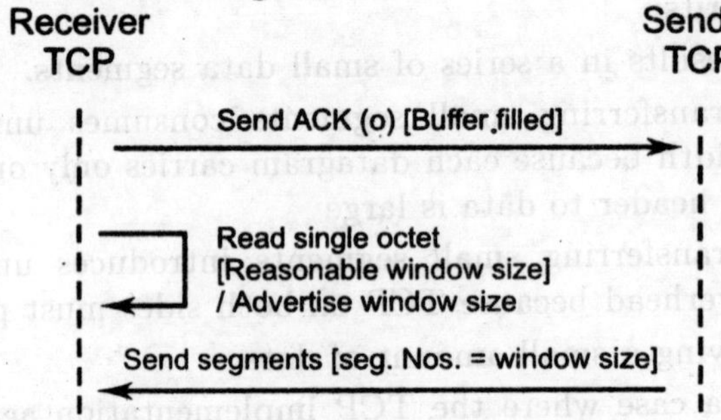

Fig. 9.8. *Operation of heuristic.*

Implementation of silly window avoidance

Follows two approaches

- Postponed advertisement
  - o **TCP acknowledges each segments that arrives, but does not advertise window size until the window reaches the limit specified by silly window avoidance heuristic.**
- **Delayed acknowledgement**
  - o **TCP delays sending an acknowledgement when window size is not up to the limit specified by silly window avoidance heurisitic.**
  - o **Advantages**
  - o **decreases the traffic thereby increasing the throughput *i.e.*,**
    - (*i*) **If additional data arrives during delay period, a single acknowledgement can be used to acknowledge all data received.**
    - (*ii*) **If the receiving application responds immediately, a short delay may support piggypacking.**
  - o Disadvantages
    - (*i*) **Too long delay will cause the sending TCP to make unnecessary retransmission thereby reducing throughput because of wastage of network bandwidth.**

(*ii*) Unnecessary retransmission introduces computational overhead on both sides of connection.

(*iii*) Estimation of RTT was based on arrival of acknowledgements, delayed acknowledgements can confuse the estimate and make retransmission timeout too long.

- Remedy

  To avoid potential problems, the TCP standards state that TCP cannot delay an acknowledgement for more than 500 milliseconds.

Sender-side Silly Window Avoidance

Heuristic

When a sending application generates additional data to be sent over a connection for which previous data has been transmitted but not acknowledged, place the new data in the output buffer as usual, but do not send additional segments until there is sufficient data to fill a maximum-sized segment. If still waiting to send when an acknowledgement arrives, send all data that has accumulated in the buffer. Apply the rule even when the user requests a push operation.

Explanation

- The sender delays sending a segment until it can accumulate a reasonable amount of data.
- Since TCP does not know whether to wait because it cannot know whether an application will generate data in the near future, it does not compute delay , instead uses the arrival of acknowledgement to trigger the transmission of additional segments and hence called as self-clocking.
- Otherwise known as Nagle algorithm.
- The operation of heuristic is shown in Figure 9.9.

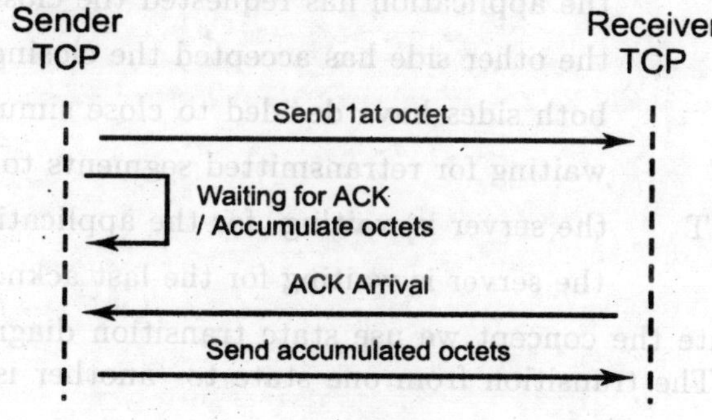

Fig. 9.9

- Advantages
  - (*i*) Since there is no need for the sender to compute the delay for transmission of additional segments, no additional computational overhead.
  - (*ii*) Even though the technique adapts to arbitrary combinations of network delay, maximum segment size and application speed, it does not lower throughput in conventional cases.

9.11 THE STATE/TRANSITION DIAGRAM

The state/transition diagram for the TCP protocol is given in Figure 9.8. The states are in round-ended boxes, and the transitions are the labelled arrows. The transitions show how program can make TCP move from one state to another. It also shows how the remote peer can make your stack change TCP states. To keep track of all the different events happing during connection establishment ,connection termination and data transfer the TCP software is implemented as a finite state machine. A finite state machine is a machine that goes through a limited number of states. At any moment the machine is in one of the states. It remains in that state until an event happens. The event can take the machine to a new state or the event can also make the machine perform some action. In other words the event is an input applied to a state.

It can change the state and can also create an output table

CLOSED	there is no connection
LISTEN	the server is waiting for calls from the client
SYN-SENT	a connection request is sent waiting for acknowledgement
SYN-RCVD	a connection request is received
ESTABLISHED	connection is established
FIN-WAIT 1	the application has requested the closing of the connection
FIN-WAIT 2	the other side has accepted the closing of the connection
CLOSING	both sides have decided to close simultaneously
TIME-WAIT	waiting for retransmitted segments to die
CLOSE WAIT	the server is waiting for the application to close.
LAST-ACK	the server is waiting for the last acknowledgement

To illustrate the concept we use state transition diagram. The states are shown using ovals. The transition from one state to another is shown using the directed lines.

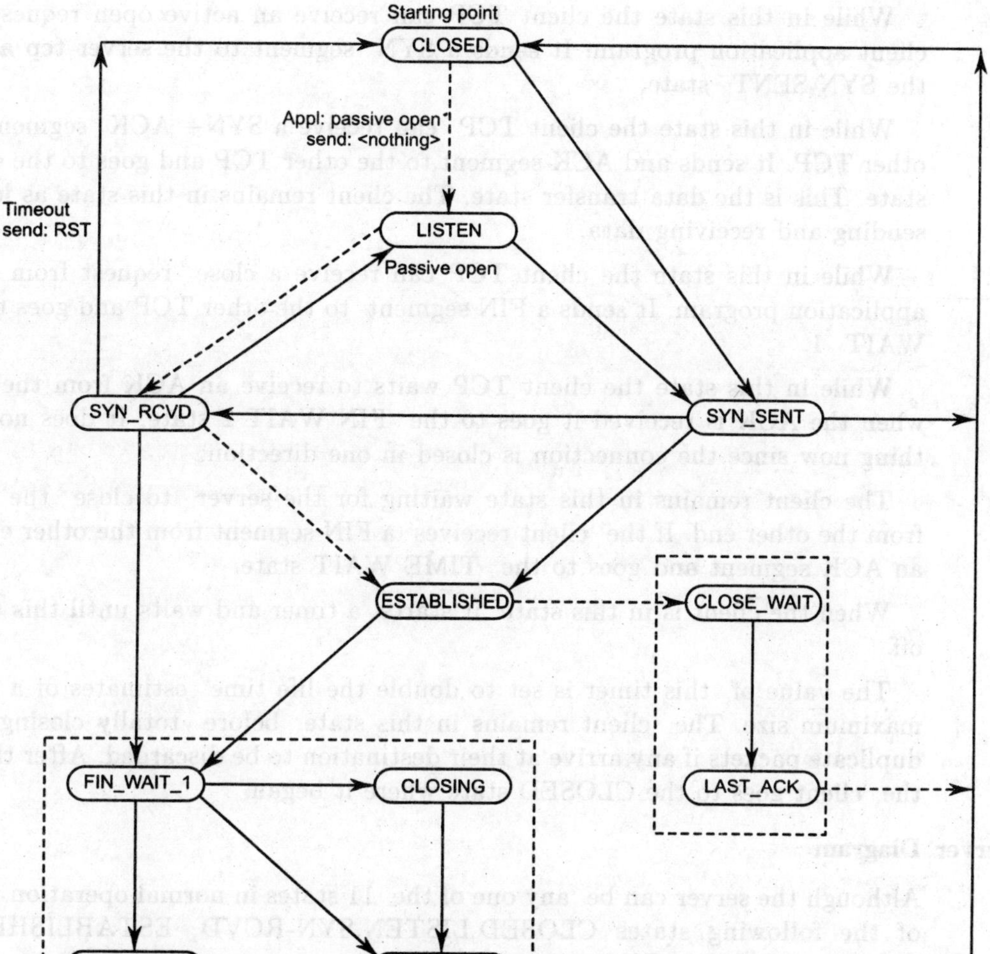

Fig. 9.10. *The state/transition diagram.*

Each line has two strings separted by a slash. The first string is the input what TCP receives. The second is the output what sends Figure. 9.8 shows the state transition diagram for both client and server. The dotted lines of the figure represent the server. The solid lines represent the client and the thin lines are for unusual situations.

Client Diagram

The client can be in one of the following states.

CLOSED, SYNN-SENT, ESTABLISHED,FIN-WAIT1,FIN-WAIT 2 AND TIME WAIT

The client TCP states in the closed state

While in this state the client TCP can receive an active open request from the client application program. It sends a SYN segment to the server tcp and goes to the SYN-SENT state.

While in this state the client TCP can receive a SYN+ ACK segment from the other TCP. It sends and ACK segment to the other TCP and goes to the established state. This is the data transfer state. The client remains in this state as long as it is sending and receiving data.

While in this state the client TCP can receive a close request from the client application program. It sends a FIN segment to the other TCP and goes to the FIN-WAIT 1.

While in this state the client TCP waits to receive an ACK from the server tcp when the ACK is received it goes to the FIN WAIT 2 state. It does not send any thing now since the connection is closed in one direction.

The client remains in this state waiting for the server to close the connection from the other end. If the client receives a FIN segment from the other end it sends an ACK segment and goes to the TIME WAIT state.

When the client is in this state it starts a timer and waits until this timer goes off.

The value of this timer is set to double the life time estimates of a segment of maximum size. The client remains in this state before totally closing tolet all duplicate packets if any arrive at their destination to be discarded. After the time out the client goes to the CLOSED state where it began.

Server Diagram

Although the server can be any one of the 11 states in normal operation it is in one of the following states CLOSED,LISTEN,SYN-RCVD, ESTABLISHED,CLOSE WAIT and LAST ACK

The server TCP starts in the closed state.

While in this state the server TCP can receive a passive open request from the server application program it goes to the listen state.

While in this state the server TCP can receive a SYN segment from the client tcp it sends an SYN + ACK segment to the client tcp and then goes to the SYN-RCVD state.

While in this state the server TCP can receive an ACK segment from the client tcp it goes to the ESTABLISHED state. This is the data transfer state. The server remains in this state as long as it is receiving and sending data.

While in this state the server tcp can receive a FIN segment from the client which means that the client wishes to close the connection. It can send an ACK segment to the client and go to the CLOSE WAIT state.

While in this state the server waits until it receives a close request from the server program it then sends a FIN segment to the client and goes to the LAST ACK state.

While in this state the server waits for the last ACK segment. It then goes to the ÇLOSED state.

State Transition Diagram

Step by step implementation

Closed

Step1: *If passive open message from application received*

Change the state to listen

Step2: *If active open message from application received*

Send a syn segment.

Change the state to syn-sent.

Step3: *If any segment received*

Send an rst segment

Step4: *If any other message received*

Issue an error message

Return

Listen

Step1: *If send data message from application received*

Send a syn segment

Change the state to syn-sent

Step2: *If syn segment received*

Send a syn +ack segment

Change the state to syn+rcvd

Step3: *If any other segment or message received*

Issue an error message

Return

Syn-sent

Step1: *If time out*

Change the state to closed

Step2: *If syn segment received*

Send a syn+ack segment

Change the statae to syn-rcvd

Step3: *If syn+ack segment received*

Send an ack segment

Change the state to established

Step4: *If any other segment or message received*

Issue an error message

Return

Syn-rcvd

Step1: *If ack segment received*

Change the state tok established

Step2: *If time out*

Send an rst segment

Change the state to closed

Step3: *If close message from application received*

Send a fin segment

Change the state to fin-wait-1

Step4: *If rst segment received*

Change the state to listen

If any other segment or message received

Issue an error message

Return

Established

Step1: *If fin segment received*

Send an ack segment

Change the state to close-wait

Step2: *If close message from application received*

Send a fin segment

Change the state to fin-wait-1

Step3: *If rst or syn segment received*

Issue an error message

Step4: *If date or ack segment is received*

Call the input module

Step5: *If send message from application received*

Call the output module

Return

Fin-wait-1

Step1: *If fin segment received*

Send an ack segment

Change the state to closing

Step2: *If fin +ACK segment received*

Send an ack segment

Change the state to time-wait

Step3: *If ack segment received*

Change the state to fin-wait-2.

Step4: *If any other segment or message received*

Issue an error message

Return

Fin-wait-2

Step1: *If fin segment received*

Send an ack segment

Change the state to time-wait

Closing

Step2: *If ack segment received*

Change the state to time-wait

Step3: *If any other segment or message received*

Issue an error message

Return

Time-wait

Step1: *If time out*

Change the state to closed

Step2: *If any other segment or message received*

Issue an error message

Return

Close-wait

Step1: *If close message from application received*

Send a fin segment

Change the state to last-ack

Step2: *If any other segment or message received*

Issue an error message

Return

Last-ack:

Step1: *If ack segment received*

Change the state to closed

Step2: *If any other segment or message received*

Issue an error message

Return.

9.12 FRAGMENTATION AND REASSEMBLE

Package

IP package involves eight components namely a header-adding module, a processing module, a routing module ,a fragmentation module, a reassembly module, a routing table an MTU table and a reassembly table. In addition the package includes input an output queues.

The package receives a packet either from the data link layer or from a higher-level protocol. If the packet comes from an upper-layer protocol it is delivered to the data link layer for transmission (unless it has a loopback address of 127.A.B.C). If the packet comes from the data link layer it is either delivered to the data link layer for forwarding(in a router) or it is delivered to a higher-layer protocol if the destination IP address of the packet is the same as the station address.

Header-Adding Module

The header adding module receives data from an upper-layer protocol along the destination IP address. It encapsulates the data in datagram by adding the IP header.

Processing Module

The processing module is the heart of the IP package. The processing module receives a datagram from an interface or from the header-adding module. It treats both cases the same. A datagram must be processed and routed regardless of where it comes from.

The processing module first checks to see if the datagram is a loopback packet (with the destination address of 127.A.B.C) or a packet that has reached its final destination. In either case the packet is sent to the reassembly module.

If the node is a router it decrements the time-to-live(TTL) field by one if this value is less than or equal to zero the datagram is discarded and an ICMP message is sent to the original sender. If the value of TTL is greater than zero after decrement processing module sends the datagram to the routing module.

Queues

Our package uses two types of queues input queues and output queues. The input queues store the datagram coming from the data link layer or the upper-layer protocols.

The outputs queues store the datagrams going to the data link layer or the upper-layer

Protocols. The processing module dequeues (removes) the datagrams from the input queues. The fragmentation and reassembly modules enqueue (add) the datagrams into the out put queues.

Routing Table

The routing table is used by the routing module to determine the next-hop address of the packet.

Routing Module

The routing module receives an IP packet from the processing module. If the packet is to be forwarded it is passed to this module. The module finds the IP address of the next station along with the interface number to which the packet should be sent. It then sends the packet with this information to the fragmentation module.

MTU Table

The MTU table is used by the fragmentation module to find the maximum transfer unit of a particular interface.

Fragmentation Module

The fragmentation module receives an IP datagram from the routing module. The routing module gives the IP datagram the IP address of the next station (either the final destination in a direct delivery or the next router in an indirect delivery) and the interface number through which the datagram is sent out.

The fragmentation module consults the MTU table to find the MTU for the specific interface number. If the length of the datagram is larger than the MTU the fragmentation module fragments the datagram adds a header to each fragment and sends them to the ARP package for address resolution and delivery.

Reassembly Table

The reassembly table is used by the reassembly module. The reassembly table has five fields namely state source IP address datagram ID time-out and fragments.

The value of the state field can be either FREE or IN-USE. The IP address field defines the source IP address of the datagram. The datagram ID is a number that uniquely defines a datagram and all of the fragments belonging to that datagram. The time-out is a predetermined amount of time in which all fragments must arrive. Finally the fragments field is pointer to a linked list of fragments.

Reassembly Module

The reassembly module receives from the processing module those datagram fragments that have arrived at their final destinations . In our package the reassembly module treats an unfragmented datagram as a fragment belonging to a datagram with only one fragment.

Because the IP protocol is a connectionless protocol there is no guarantee that the fragments arrive in order besides the fragments from one datagram can be intermixed with fragments from another datagram. To keep track of these situation the module uses a reassembly table with associated linked lists.

The job of the reassembly module is to find the datagram to which a fragment belongs to order the fragments belonging to the same datagram and reassemble all fragments of a datagram when all have arrived. If the established time-out has expired and any fragment is missing the module discards the fragments.

9.13 FRAGMENTATION

Step by step implementation

Header-Adding Module

receive: data, destination address

Step1: *encapsulate the data in an ip datagram*

Step2: *calculate the checksum and insert it in the checksum field*

Step3: *send the data to the corresponding input queue*

Step4: *return*

Processing Module

Step1: *remove one datagram from one of the input queues*

Step2: *if destination address is 127.A.B.C or matches one of the local address*

Step2.1: *send the datagram to the reassembly module*

Step2.2: *return*

Step3: *if machine is a router*

Step3.1: *decrement ttl*

Step4: *if ttl less than or equal to zero*

Step4.1: *discard the datagram*

Step4.2: *send an icmp error message*

Step4.3: *return*

Step5: *send the datagram to the routing module*

Step6: *return*

Fragmentation Module

receive: an ip packet from routing module

Step1: *extract the size of the datagram*

Step2: *if size>mtu of the corresponding network*

Step2.1: *if D do not fragment bit is set*

Step2.1.1: *discard the datagram*

Step2.1.2: *send an icmp error message*

Step2.1.3: *return*

Step2.2: *else*

Step2.2.1: *calculate the maximum size*

Step2.2.2: *divide the datagram into fragments*

Step2.2.3: *add header to each fragment*

Step2.2.4: *add required options to each fragment*

Step2.2.5: *send the datagrams*

Step2.2.6: *return*

Step3: *else*

Step3.1: *send the datagram*

Step4: *return*

Reassembly module

Receive: an ip datagram from the processing module

Step1: *if offset value is zero an the M bit is 0*

Step1.1: *send the datagram to the appropriate queue*

Step1.2: *return*

Step2: *search the reassembly table for the corresponding entry*

Step3: *if not found*

Step3.1: *create a new entry*

Step4: *insert the fragment at the appropriate place in the linked list*

Step 4.1: *if all fragments have arrived*

Step4.1.1: *reassemble the fragments*

Step4.1.2: *deliver the datagram to the corresponding upper layer protocol*

Step4.1.3: *return*

Step4.2: *else*

Step4.2.1: *check the time-out*

Step4.2.2: *if time-out expired*

Step4.2.2.1: *discard all fragments*

Step4.2.2.2: *send an icmp error message*

Step 5: *return*

CHAPTER 10

SOCKET PROGRAMMING

10.1 INTRODUCTION TO NETWORK

What we usually call a computer network is composed of a number of "network layers", each providing a different restriction and/or guarantee about the data at that layer. The protocols at each network layer generally have their own packet formats, headers, and layout. Figure 10.1 shows the socket interfaces.

The seven traditional layers of a network are divided into two groups: upper layers and lower layers. The sockets interface provides a uniform API to the lower layers of a networks, and allows you to implement upper layers within your sockets application. Further, application data formats may themselves constitute further layers, *e.g.*, SOAP is built on top of XML, XML may itself utilize SOAP. In any case, anything past layer 4 is outside the scope of this tutorial.

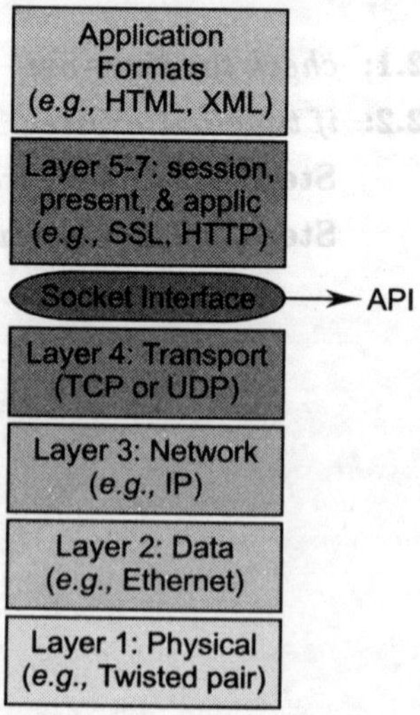

Fig. 10.1. *The socket interfaces.*

Definition of Socket

While the sockets interface theoretically allows access to protocol families other than IP, in practice, every network layer you use in your sockets application will use IP. We only look at IPV4; IPV6 will become important also, but the principles are the same. At the transport layer, sockets support two specific protocols: TCP (transmission control protocol) and UDP (user datagram protocol).

Sockets cannot be used to access lower (or higher) network layers; for example, a socket application does not know whether it is running over ethernet, token ring, or a dialup connection. Nor does the sockets pseudo-layer know anything about higher-level protocols like NFS, HTTP, FTP.

At times, the sockets interface is not your best choice for a network programming API. Specifically, many excellent libraries exist (in various languages) to use higher-level protocols directly.

The primary function of the TCP/IP is to provide a point to point communication mechanism. One process on one machine communicates with the another process on another machine or within the same machine. This communication appears as two streams of data. One stream carries data from one process to the other, while the other carries data in the other direction. Each process can read the data that have been written by the other, and in normal conditions, the data received are the same, and in the same order, as when they are sent.

In order to tell one machine from another machine and to make sure that you are connected with the machine you want, there must be some way of uniquely identifying machines on a network. Early networks were satisfied to provide unique names for machines within the local network. However, Java works within the Internet, which requires a way to uniquely identify a machine from all the others in the world. This is accomplished with the IP (Internet Protocol) address, a 32 bit number.

What are Sockets?

- A socket is an abstraction that represents an endpoint of communication.
- creating a socket of the appropriate type and then performing a series of operations on that socket.
- the operations that can be performed on a socket
- control operations
- associating a port number with the socket,
- initiating or accepting a connection on the socket,
- destroying the socket
- data transfer operations
- writing data through the socket to some other application,
- reading data from some other application through the socket and
- status operations
- finding the IP address associated with the socket.
- sockets are one way of doing inter-process communication (IPC) between processes on the same or on different machines in Unix.

- sockets are one way of doing inter-process communication (IPC) between processes on the same or on different machines in Unix.

Socket Protocol Families

- PF_UNIX Local communication
- PF_INET Internet (TCP/IP)
- PF_NS Xerox Network System (XNS) architecture
- PF_NDD The operating system NDD
- The /usr/include/sys/socket.h file contains a list of socket protocol families
- Major protocols in the suite of Internet Network Protocols include:
- TCP
- UDP
- IIP
- Internet Control Message Protocol (ICMP)

IP Address in Two Forms:

1. The DNS (Domain Name Service) form. Suppose, if my domain name is gsr.com and if I have a computer called rathinam in my domain. Its domain name would be rathinam.gsr.com.
2. Alternatively, we can use dotted quad form, which is four numbers separated by dots, such as 197.2.23.245

In addition to the machine addresses provided by the Internet Protocol part of the network system, TCP/IP has a mechanism for identifying individual processes on a machine, analogous to an office block. The building has phone number , but each room inside is also identified by an extension number. When a call arrives at the building, it must be connected to the correct room for handling. Payment requests go to accounts payable, orders to sales, and so forth. In the TCP/IP system, the extension numbers are called ports, and they are represented by a 16-bit binary number. To communicate with the correct port of a particular computer, the sending machine must know both the machine address and the port number to which the message should be sent. Many common services have a dedicated port. Because some ports are reserved for common services, the programmer cannot use any port. Ports numbered under 1024 are often referred to as reserved ports, many of which are reserved for a specific program. It is important that you only attempt to use ports over number 1024.

10.2 TYPES OF NETWORK PROGRAMMING

Two general types are:

1. Connection-oriented programming
2. Connectionless Programming

Connection-Oriented Networking

The client and server have a communication link that is open and active from the time the application is executed until it is closed. Using Internet jargon, the Transmission control protocol is a connection oriented protocol. It is reliable connection packets are guaranteed to arrive in the order they are sent.

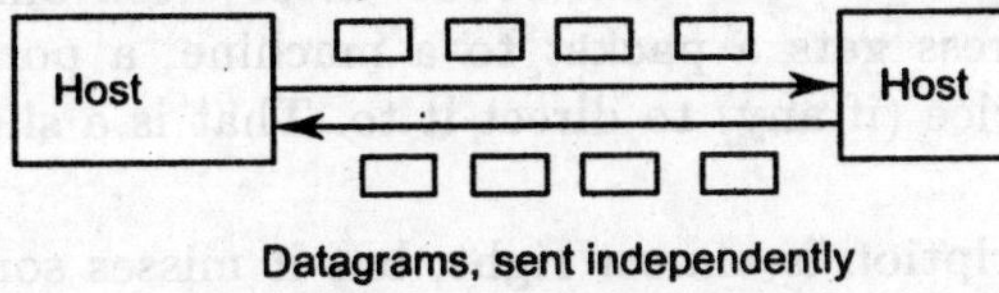

Fig. 10.2. *Telephone system.*

Connection-Less Networking

In each instance the packets are sent, they are transmitted individually. No link to the receiver is maintained after the packets arrive. The Internet equivalent is the User Datagram Protocol (UDP). Connectionless communication is faster but not reliable. Datagrams are used to implement a connectionless protocol, such as UDP.

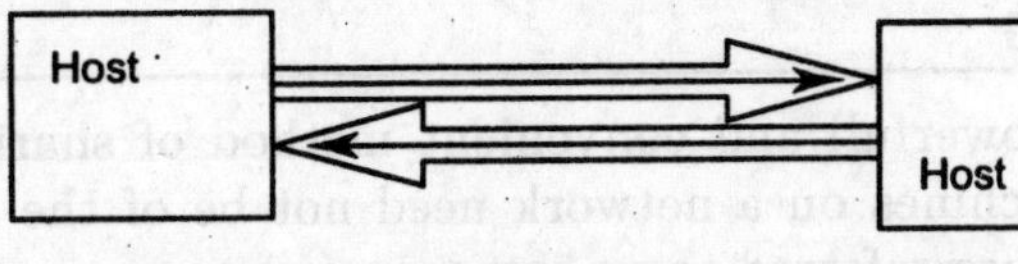

Fig. 10.3. *Connection item networking.*

Client-Server Programming

The most common model of network programming is referred to as client-server programming. The concept is simple: A client machine makes a request for information or sends a command to a server; in return, the server passes back the data or results of the command. Most often, the server only responds to clients; it does not initiate communication.

So the job of the server is to listen for a connection, and that's performed by the special server object that we create. The job of the client is to try to make a connection to the server, and this is performed by the special client object we create. Once the connection is made, you will see that at the server and client ends, the connection is magically just turned into the IO Stream object, and from then onwards you can treat the connection as if you were reading and writing into the file.

Common Services Port Number

Port Number	*Service*
21	FTP
23	Telnet
25	SMTP(mail)
80	HTTP(Web)
119	NNTP(News)

Peers, ports, names, and addresses

Beyond the protocol--TCP or UDP--there are two things a peer (a client or server) needs to know about the machine it communicates with: An IP address and a port. An IP address is a 32-bit data value, usually represented for humans in "dotted quad" notation, *e.g.,* 63.42.63.173 . A port is a 16-bit data value, usually simply represented as a number less than 65536--most often one in the tens or hundreds range. An IP address gets a packet to a machine, a port lets the machine decide which process/service (if any) to direct it to. That is a slight simplification, but the idea is correct.

The above description is almost right, but it misses something. Most of the time when humans think about an internet host (peer), we do not remember a number like 63.42.63.173, but instead a name like rathinam . To find the IP address associated with a particular host name, usually you use a Domain Name Server, but sometimes local lookups are used first (often via the contents of /etc/hosts). We will generally just assume an IP address is available, but the next panel discusses coding name/address lookups.

10.3 BYTE ORDERING

Networking is a powerfull and convenient method of sharing data between various machines. The machines on a network need not be of the same architecture. These kinds of networks are referred to as hetrogeneus.

The architecture of a machine (mainly the addressable word size) defines how data is represented in a systems memory. There are two conventional storage methods for data larger than the addressable word size (which is usually a byte - 8 bits). Little Endian and Big Endian. Figure 10.4 shows big Endian and little Endian

Little Endian is used by Intel and a few other CPU manufacturers. Little Endian simply means the least significant byte comes first in memory.

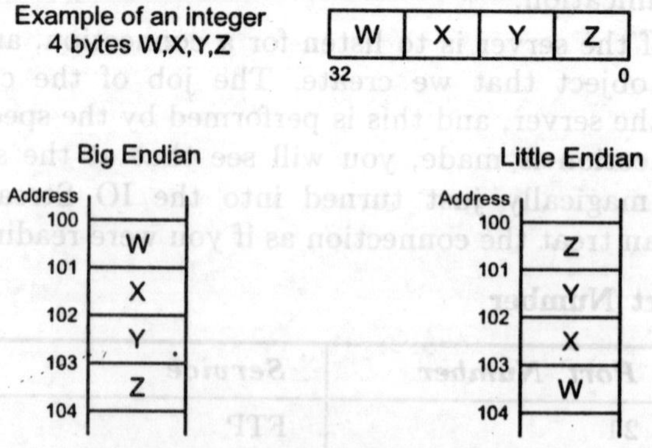

Fig. 10.4. *Big/little indian.*

Big Endian is used by MIPS, Motoralla and the rest of the world. Big Endian is opposite to that of Little Endian, namely, the most significant byte comes first in memory. The above diagram illustrates an integer and the how it would appear in the 2 different representation.

Network byte order is actually Big Endian. When righting code however we don't want to have to worry about what the architecture of the underling machine and to this end macros and routines have been defined to convert from network byte order to the machines byte order.

If the machines native byte order is Big Endian the routines do nothing to the data, but if the architecture is of Little Endian it swaps the byte ordering.

The routines to do the conversions are

ntohl() - network to host long integer conversion

ntohs() - network to host short integer conversion

htonl() - host to network long integer conversion

htons() - host to network short integer conversion

To make use of these routines you will need to #include <netinet/in.h>

Any data structure made up only of bytes (*i.e.*, char's) need not be converted, but if data structure contains any integers, longs or shorts the integers, etc. need to be converted to network byte order before sending and converted back into host byte order on receipt.

Specifying End Point Address

- Before using a socket, we Must specify one or both addresses.
- A communication end point consists of IP address and protocol port number.
- Generic Address structure
  (address family, end point address in that family)

Socket Options

- In addition to binding a socket to a local address or connecting it to a destination address, application programs need a method to control the socket. For example, when using protocols that use time out and retransmission, the application program may want to obtain or set the time-out parameters. An application program may also want to control the allocation of buffer space, determine if the socket allows transmission of broadcast, or control processing of out-of-band data.
- The getsockopt subroutine allows an application program to request information about socket options.
- int getsockopt (int socfd, int level, int optname, char *optval, int *optlen)
- socfd ® open socket descriptor.
- level ® who is to interpret (general socket code, TCP/IP code, XNS code)optname ® Name of the option.optval ® pointer to a user variable to return the value of the optname. (to set in setsockopt)optlen ® size of the optval set before the call.
- The setsockopt subroutine allows an application program to set a socket option using the same set of values obtained with the getsockopt subroutine.
- int setsockopt (int socfd, int level, int optname, char *optval, int *optlen)

Using Sockets

In order for sockets to be addressed, they must be named. There are several different methods of naming a socket. These methods are known as address families. This project requires the use of the internet domain addressing scheme in which the sockets "name" consists of two parts:

- 32-bit IP address of the host where the socket resides
- 16-bit port number

10.4 THE SOCKET ABSTRACTION

The basis for network I/O in BSD UNIX centers on an abstraction known as the socket. We think of a socket as a generalization of the UNIX file access mechanism that provides an endpoint for communications. As with file access, application programs request the operating system to create a socket when one is needed. The main difference between file descriptors and socket descriptors is that the operating system binds a file descriptor to a specific file or device when the application calls open, but it can create sockets without binding them to specific destination addresses

- bind
- listen
- connect
- accept
- recv
- send

we will also use a socket address structure, a sockaddr_in. It is an IPv4 socket address structure, also known as an "Internet socket address structure".

The socket function gets a socket descriptor , which is like a handle and similar to a file descriptor. It is the first function we will call in the networking part of your programs. A socket is an endpoint of communication through which applications can talk to each other.

Socket family:

The socket function is prototyped like this:

```
#include <sys/socket.h>
Int socket(int family, int type, int protocol);
```

The header file shown here is of course where it is prototyped. On success, socket returns a small nonnegative socket descriptor. When it fails, it returns -1.

The protocol family parameter is normally the constant AF_INET (IPV4). For IPV6 we'd use AF_INET6. For UNIX domain protocols it is AF_LOCAL (also known as. AF_UNIX), for routing sockets AF_ROUTE, and for key sockets

AF_KEY. We will be using only AF_INET and AF_INET6 in this series of articles.

The protocol type parameter is normally SOCK_STREAM. We might also encounter SOCK_DGRAM (datagram socket) and SOCK_RAW (raw socket), but we won't be using these.

The protocol parameter is almost always set to 0 (zero, not the capital letter O), except for raw sockets, which as mentioned we won't be using.

Bind function:

The bind function is prototyped as follows:

```
#include <sys/socket.h>

Int bind(int socket_fd, const struct sockaddr *myaddress, socklen_t address_length);
```

On success, bind returns 0. When it fails, it returns -1.

The bind function exists to assign a local protocol address to a socket, which is a combination of an IPv4 or v6 address and a port number. It is dependent upon the protocol used.

The first parameter is the socket descriptor that the call to the socket function would have returned, if it succeeded. The second parameter is a pointer to a protocol-specific address structure, it is the struct sockaddr_in for IPv4. (we can specify to bind just an address, just a port number, or neither, passing this job to the kernel. Since TCP has well known port numbers, we'll be specifying the port.) The third and last parameter is the size of the address structure, which we give by passing size of(whatever-its-name-is).

Listen function:

```
#include<sys/socket.h>
Intlisten(intsocket_fd,intbacklog);
```

The listen function returns 0 (zero) on success or -1 on error.

The first parameter is our socket descriptor. Listen is normally called after socket and bind but must be called before accept. The function causes the program to put its ear on the network, so to speak, and listen for incoming requests from clients that wish to establish a connection. Clients can and do call listen as well.

The second parameter -- backlog

Connect function:

```
#include<sys/socket.h>

Intconnect(intsocket_fd,conststructsockaddr*server_address,
socklen_taddress_length);
```

Connect is used by a TCP client to establish a connection with a TCP server. It returns 0 if OK or -1 on error. The first parameter, socket_fd, is the socket descriptor that was returned by the call to socket in the client. The second argument is a pointer to an address structure containing information on the server address that the client wants to connect to. Because it is constant and so cannot be modified in the function, we must specify the IP address of the server and the port it is listening on the third and final argument is where we give size of(the-server-address-structure).

Accept function:

```
#include<sys/socket.h>

Intaccept(intsocket_fd, structsockaddr*client_address, socklen_t address_length);
```

Accept accepts incoming client requests as its name suggests. It returns a nonnegative client socket descriptor if OK, or -1 on error.

The first parameter is the server's socket descriptor, the second is a pointer to an address structure containing details about the client, and the third is the size of the client address structure, again using size of(whatever-we-call-it-in-our-code).

Recv is function:

```
#include<sys/socket.h>

Ssize_trecv(intsocket_fd, void*buffer, size_tbuffer_size, intflags);
```

It returns the number of bytes actually read if OK, or -1 on error. The first argument is the socket descriptor, which will the descriptor returned by the accept function (the client's socket, so we can tell recv where we will be receiving data from). The second is a void pointer to a buffer, where we will stick all the data when we read it in. The third argument is the size of the buffer, theoretically so the function doesn't overwrite the bounds of the buffer. The fourth allows us to specify some flags which we can OR together. We will specify 0 as the flags for now, since we aren't interested in them at the moment. The possible flags are: MSG_DONTROUTE, MSG_DONTWAIT, MSG_OOB, MSG_PEEK and MSG_WAITALL. We'll talk about them later in this series.

Send is function:

```
#include <sys/socket.h>

size_t send(int socket_fd, const void *buffer, size_t buffer_size, int flags);
```

Send returns the number of bytes actually sent, or -1 on error. The first argument is the socket descriptor, which is the client's socket so send knows how to get the data we want to send, to the client. The second is a constant pointer to a void buffer area which is where the data is stored. The third argument is the size of the buffer. The fourth is the flags, just like recv. We'll ignore the flags and use 0 for now.

Finally, in the source we use the bzero function. (You could also use memset). Bzero sets the specified number of bytes to zero. It is not essential, but we do it anyway. I think it's good programming practice not to take short cuts, especially when you'd only save a line or two of typing anyway.

Write function:

Once an application program has established a socket, it can use the socket to transmit data. There are five possible operating system calls from which to choose: send, sendto, sendmsg, write, and writev. Send, write, and writev only work with connected sockets. Write takes arguments:

write (socket, buffer, length)

Writev function:

Writev function has the form:

writev (socket, iovector, vectorlen)

Argument iovector gives the address of an array of type iovec that contains a sequence of pointers to the blocks of bytes that form the message (a length accompanies each pointer). Argument vectorlen specifies the number of entries in iovector.

Read function:

BSD UNIX offers five system calls that a process can use to receive data through a socket: read, readv, recv, recvform, and recvmsg. The conventional UNIX input operation, read, can only be used when the socket is connected. It has the form:

readv (descriptor, buffer, length)

where descriptor gives the integer descriptor of a socket or file descriptor from which to read data, buffer, specifies the address in memory at which to store the data, and length specifies the maximum number of bytes to read.

An alternative form readv, allows the caller to use a "scatter read" style of interface that places the incoming data in noncontiguous locations. Readv has the form:

readv (descriptor, iovector, vectorlen)

Argument iovector gives the address of a structure of type iovec that contains a sequence of pointers to blocks of memory into which the incoming data should be stored. Argument vectorlen specifies the number of entries in iovector. There are three additional system calls for network message input. Processes call recv to receive data from a connected socket.

Argument socket specifies a socket descriptor from which data should be received. Argument buffer specifies the address in memory into which the message should be placed, and argument length specifies the length of the buffer area. Finally argument flags allows the caller to control the reception.

Recvfrom function:

The system call recvfrom allows the caller to specify input from an unconnected socket. The form is:

```
recvfrom (socket, buffer, length, flags, fromaddr, addrlen)
```

The two additional arguments fromaddr and addrlen are pointers to a socket address structure and an integer. The operating system uses fromaddr to record the address of the message sender and uses fromlen to record the length of the sender's address. Notice that the output operation sendto, discussed above, takes an address in exactly the same form as recvfrom generates. Thus, sending replies is easy.

Close function:

When a process finishes using a socket it calls close. Close has the form:

```
close (socket)
```

where the argument socket specifies the descriptor of a socket to close. When a process terminates for any reason, the system closes all sockets that remain open. Internally, a call to close decrements the reference count for a socket and destroys the socket if the count reaches zero.

IP, TCP and UDP

TCP is a stream protocol, while UDP is a datagram protocol. That is to say, TCP establishes a continuous open connection between a client and a server, over which bytes may be written--and correct order guaranteed--for the life of the connection. However, bytes written over TCP have no built-in structure, so higher-level protocols are required to delimit any data records and fields within the transmitted bytestream.

UDP, on the other hand, does not require that any connection be established between client and server, it simply transmits a message between addresses. A nice feature of UDP is that its packets are self-delimiting--each datagram indicates exactly where it begins and ends. A possible disadvantage of UDP, however, is that it provides no guarantee that packets will arrive in-order, or even at all. Higher-level protocols built on top of UDP may, of course, provide handshaking and acknowledgements.

A useful analogy for understanding the difference between TCP and UDP is the difference between a telephone call and posted letters. The telephone call is not active until the caller "rings" the receiver and the receiver picks up. The telephone channel remains alive as long as the parties stay on the call--but they are free to say as much or as little as they wish to during the call. All remarks from either party occur in temporal order. On the other hand, when you send a letter, the post office starts delivery without any assurance the recipient exists, nor any strong guarantee about how long delivery will take. The recipient may receive various letters in a different order than they were sent, and the sender may receive mail interspersed in time with those she sends. Unlike with the USPS, undeliverable mail always goes to the dead letter office, and is not returned to sender.

10.5 USING SOCKET CALLS IN PROGRAM

Connection Oriented (TCP)

Server

The server performs the following function

1. Opening a socket

   The server issues the socket call to ask the operating system to create a socket.

2. Binding

   The server issues the bind call to ask the operating system to enter information in the socket structure created in the previous step

3. Listening

   The server issues the listen call to convert a socket into a passive socket usually called the listening socket. It just waits for connection from the other end

4. Accepting

   The accept call creates a new socket called the accepting socket for actual communication and connects the next client in line

5. Reading

   To read as mush data as it can process in one shot from the incoming buffer assigned to the client

6. Processing

   The data read from the buffer is processed

7. write

   The write call is to write the result of processing to the outgoing buffer assigned to the client

Client

The client performs the following function

1. opening a socket.

   The client issues the socket call to ask the operating system to create a socket

2. connecting

   The client issues the connect call to ask the operating system to enter the socket address of the server structure this call also requests a connection with the TCP on the other side

3. Write

   The client issues the write call to write data into outgoing TCP buffer

4. Reading.

   The client issues the read call to get data from the incoming buffer

Iterative TCP Server Algorithm

Step1: *Create a socket and bind to the address for the service being offered.*

Step2: *Place the socket in passive mode, making it ready for use by the server.*

Step3: *Accept the next connection request from the socket, and obtain a new socket for the connection.*

Step4: *Repeatedly read a request from the client, formulate a response, and send reply back to the client according to the application protocol.*

Step5: *When finished with a particular client, close the connection and return to step 3 to accept a new connection.*

The TCP Client Algorithm

Step1: *Identify the IP address and protocol port number of the server to which communication is desired.*

Step2: *Allocate a socket.*

Step3: *Specify that the connection needs an unused protocol port on the local machine, and allow TCP to choose one. (side effect of connect call)*

Step4: *Connect the socket to the server.*

Step5: *Communicate with the server. (send & receive)*

Step6: *Close connection.*

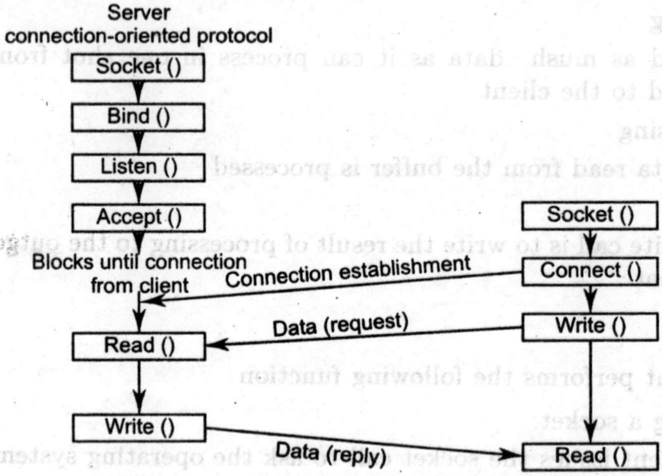

Fig. 10.5. *Connection-oriented protocol.*

Server Program

```
#defineMAXBUF 256
voidmain(void)
{
charbuf[MAXBUF]
intlistensocket;
intacceptsocket;
Socklen_tclientAddLen;
```

```
Struct sockaddress serverAddr;
Struct sockaddress clientAddr;
Litensocket=socket(AF_INET,SOCK_STREAM,0)
Memset(&serverAddr,0,sizeof(serverAddr));
ServerAddr.sin_family=AF_INET;
ServerAddr.sin_port = htons(awellknown-port);
ServerAddr.sin_addr.s_addr = htons(INADDR_ANY);
bind(listensocket,&serverAddr,sizeof(serverAddr));
acceptsocket=accept(listensocket&clientAddr,&clientAddrlen);
memset(buf,0,MAXBUF);
while(read(accept socket,buf,MAXBUF)>0)
{
process(..............)
memset(buf,0,MAXBUF);
write(acceptsocket,buf,MAXBUF);
memset(buf,0,MAXBUF);
}
close
```

TCP client program

```
#defineMAXBUF 256
voidmain(void)
{
charbuf[MAXBUF]
intactivesocket;
Struct sockaddress remoteAddr;
Struct sockaddress localAddr;
Structhostent *hptr;
activesocket=socket(AF_INET,SOCK_STREAM,0)
Memset(&serverAddr,0,sizeof(serverAddr));
remoteAddr.sin_family=AF_INET;
remoteAddr.sin_port = htons(awellknown-port);
hptr=gethostbyname("a-domain-name");
memcpy((char*)& remoteAddr.sin-addr.s_addr,
 hptr->h-addr_list[0],hptr->h-length);
```

```
connect(activesocket,remoteAddr,sizeofstruct sockaddress);
memset(buf,0,MAXBUF);
while(get(buf))
{
write(activesocket,buf,MAXBUF);
memset(buf,0,MAXBUF);
read(activesocket,buf,MAXBUF);
printf("%s/n",buf);
memset(buf,0,MAXBUF);
}
close
```

UDP

The server serves one request at a time .A server gets the request received in a datagram from UDP, processes the request and gives the responces to UDP to send to the client.

The server uses one single port for this purpose the well known port.All the datagram arriving at this port wait in line to be served.

Server

The server performs the following function:

1. **Opening a socket**

   The server issues the socket call to ask operating system to create a socket. The socket call create a new socket structure and the open call creates a new structure.

   The application program makes this call and passes three pieces of information family type and the protocol.

2. **Binding**

   The server issues the bind call to ask the operating system to enter information in the socket structure created

3. **Receiving**

   The server issues the recvfrom call to read from the incoming queue a datagram sent by a client

4. **Sending**

   After processing the datagram the server issues the sendto call to send the datagram that contain the result to the outgoing queue.

Client

The client performs the following functions:

1. **Opening a socket.**

   The client issues the socket call to ask the operating system to create a socket. The operating system enter the local IP address and the ephemeral port number in the local socket address field of the created socket

2. **Sending**

   After receiving the socket descriptor from the operating system the client issues the sendto calls to send its request to the server

3. **Receiving**

   The client issues the recvfrom to obtain the response of its request from the operating system

4. **Closing**

   when the client has no more request it issues to close call to destroy the socket

The UDP Client Algorithm

Step1: *Identify the IP address and protocol port number of the server to which communication is desired.*

Step2: *Allocate a socket.*

Step3: *Specify that the connection needs an unused protocol port on the local machine, and allow TCP to choose one. (side effect of connect call)*

Step4: *Specify the server to which the message must be sent.*

Step5: *Communicate with the server. (write & read)*

Step6: *Close connection.*

Iterative UDP Server Algorithm

Step1: *Create a socket and bind to the address for the service being offered.*

Step2: *Repeatedly read a request from the client, formulate a response, and send reply back to the client according to the application protocol.*

Step3: *An Iterative, connectionless server. A single process handles requests (datagrams) from clients one at a time.*

For a client-server using a connectionless protocol, the system calls are different Figures. The client does not establish a connection with the server. Instead, the client just sends a datagram to the server using the sendto system call, which requires the address of the destination (the server) as a parameter. Similarly, the server does not have to accept a connection from a client. Instead, the server just issues a recvfrom system calls that waits until data arrives from some client. Thus recvfrom returns the network address of the client process, along with the datagram, so the server can send its response to the correct process.

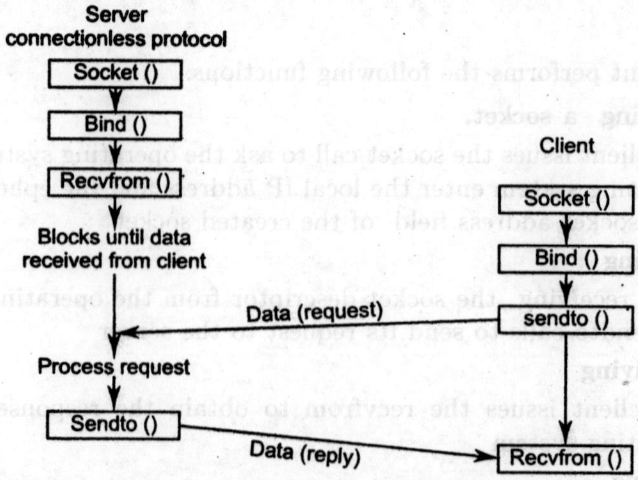

Fig.10.6. *Socket system calls for connectionless protocol.*

UDP server program

```
#defineMAXBUF 256
voidmain(void)
{
charbuf[MAXBUF]
intpassivesocket;
Socklen_tclientAddLen;
Structsockaddress serverAddr;
Structsockaddress clientAddr;
passivesocket=socket(AF_INET,SOCK_DGRAM,0)
Memset(&serverAddr,0,sizeof(serverAddr));
ServerAddr.sin_family=AF_INET;
ServerAddr.sin_port = htons(awellknown-port);
ServerAddr.sin_addr.s_addr= htons(INADDR_ANY);
bind(listensocket, &serverAddr,sizeof(serverAddr));
clientAddrlen=sizeof(serverAddr)
memset(buf,0,MAXBUF);
for(;)
{
while(recfrom(passivesocket,buf,MAXBUF,0,&clientAddr,
clientAddrlen)>0
{
```

```
process(...............)
sendto(passivesocket.buf.MAXBUF.0&clientaddrclientaddrlen);
memset(buf.0.MAXBUF);
}
close
```

UDPclientprogram

```
#defineMAXBUF 256
voidmain(void)
{
charbuf[MAXBUF]
intactivesocket;
Structsockaddress remoteAddr;
Structsockaddress localAddr;
Structhostent *hptr;
activesocket=socket(AF_INET.SOCK_DGRAM.0)
Memset(&serverAddr.0.sizeof(serverAddr));
remoteAddr.sin_family=AF_INET;
remoteAddr.sin_port = htons(awellknown-port);
hptr=gethostbyname("a-domain-name");
memcpy((char*)& remoteAddr.sin-addr.s_addr.
hptr->h-addr_list[0].hptr->h-length);
memset(buf.0.MAXBUF);
remoteAddrlen=sizeof(remoteAddr);
while(get(buf))
{
sendto(activesocket.buf.sizeof(buf).0.&remoteAddr.sizeof(remoteAddr));
memset(buf.0.MAXBUF);
recvfrom(activesocket.buf.0.&remoteAddr.&remoteAddrlen);
printf("%s/n".buf);
memset(buf.0.MAXBUF);
}
close
```

Program to determine host byte order

```
#include <stdio.h>
```

```
#include <stdlib.h>
#include <sys/types.h>
intmain(intargc, char**argv)
{
 union{
  short s;
 char c[sizeof(short)];
 }un;
 un.s=0x0102;
 if(sizeof(short)==2){
       if(un.c[0]==1&&un.c[1]==2)
              printf("big-endian\n");
       elseif(un.c[0]==2&&un.c[1]==1)
              printf("little-endian\n");
       else
              printf("unknown\n");
 }else
       printf("sizeof(short)=%d\n",sizeof(short));
 exit(0);
}
```

Conversion using inet_ntoa(struct in_addr)

```
#include   <stdio.h>
#include   <sys/types.h>
#include   <sys/socket.h>
#include   <netinet/in.h>
#include   <arpa/inet.h>
main(argc,argv)
int  argc;
char *argv[];
{
  int              sockfd;
  structsockaddr_in     serv_addr;
  structin_addrsrc;
  char*ptr;
```

```
if(argc<2){
  printf("Usage:Adrs_conv<ipaddressindotteddecimalnotation>n");
   exit(1);
   }
 /*
```

The conversion using inet_ntop

```
#include<stdio.h>
#include<sys/types.h>
#include<sys/socket.h>
#include<netinet/in.h>
#include<arpa/inet.h>
#defineINET_ADDRSTRLEN16    //forIPv4dotted-decimal
main(argc,argv)
int  argc;
char  *argv[];
{
    int                  sockfd;
    structsockaddr_in         serv_addr;
    structin_addr        src;
    charkkk[INET_ADDRSTRLEN];
   if(argc<2)      {
   printf("Usage:Add_con<IPAddress>\n");
   exit(1);
   }
 /*
    *Fillinthestructure"serv_addr"withtheaddressofthe
    *serverthatwewanttoconnectwith.
    */
serv_addr.sin_family  =AF_INET;
serv_addr.sin_addr.s_addr=inet_addr(argv[1]);
src.s_addr=serv_addr.sin_addr.s_addr;
printf("TheaddressconvertedtoHostaddressformUnsigned_long\n\n");
printf("TheaddressinHostaddressform:%ul\n",src.s_addr);
inet_ntop(AF_INET,&src,kkk,INET_ADDRSTRLEN);
```

```
    printf("Theconversionusinginet_ntop\n\n");
    printf("constchar*inet_ntop(intfamily,constvoid*addrptr,char*strptr,
size_tlen\n\n");
    printf("TheGivenIPinNetworkaddressform:%s\n",kkk);
}
```

An Example Server in VB

As a simple example we will develop an echo server that stores some per-connection state and can optionally shut down the connection in a variety of ways after echoing a certain number of data packets.

Our echo server consists of two forms. The first allows you to specify the port that the server should listen on and also set some parameters.

When a server is created the second form is displayed, this contains a list control and handles the events that the server fires. After creating a server you can switch back to the first form, change the port number and create another server. All servers can operate independently.

The code behind the first form is fairly simple and mostly consists of managing the user interface elements and passing parameters to the second form. The work required to create the socket server itself is very simple.

Option explicit

```
Private Sub Command1_Click()
 Dim server As JBSOCKETSERVERLib.server
 Set server = CreateSocketServer(CLng(Text1.Text))
 Dim frm As Form2
 Set frm = New Form2
 frm.SetServer server
 frm.ShowDataPackets.Value = ShowDataPackets.Value
 frm.DataIsBytes.Value = DataIsBytes.Value
 frm.DataIsString.Value = DataIsString.Value
 frm.SignOnAsUnicode.Value = SignOnAsUnicode.Value
 If ShutdownEnabled.Value Then
     If ShutdownAfterWrite.Value Then
          frm.ShutdownAfterWrite =
CLng(ShutdownAfter.Text)
     ElseIf ShutdownSocket.Value Then
```

```
            frm.ShutdownAfter = CLng(ShutdownAfter.Text)
        ElseIf CloseSocket.Value Then
            frm.CloseAfter = CLng(ShutdownAfter.Text)
        End If
    End If
    server.StartListening
    frm.Show , Me
End Sub
Private Sub ShowDataPackets_Click()
    DataIsFrame.Enabled = ShowDataPackets.Value
    DataIsBytes.Enabled = ShowDataPackets.Value
    DataIsString.Enabled = ShowDataPackets.Value
End Sub
Private Sub ShutdownEnabled_Click()
    ShutdownAfterWrite.Enabled = ShutdownEnabled.Value
    ShutdownSocket.Enabled = ShutdownEnabled.Value
    CloseSocket.Enabled = ShutdownEnabled.Value
    ShutdownAfter.Enabled = ShutdownEnabled.Value
End Sub
```

The second form is slightly more complex. The code that handles the socket server is as follows:

```
Option Explicit
Dim WithEvents m_server As JBSOCKETSERVERLib.server
Public ShutdownAfterWrite As Integer
Public ShutdownAfter As Integer
Public CloseAfter As Integer
Private ListWidth As Integer
Private ListHeight As Integer
Public Sub SetServer(server As JBSOCKETSERVERLib.server)
    Set m_server = server
```

```
    Caption = "Socket server listening on: " & server.LocalAddress.Port
End Sub
Private Sub m_server_OnConnectionClosed(ByVal Socket As
JBSOCKETSERVERLib.ISocket)
    If ShowDataPackets.Value Then
        AddToList "OnConnectionClosed : " & GetAddressAsString(Socket)
    End If
    Dim counter As Class1
    Set counter = Socket.UserData
    If ShowDataPackets.Value Then
        AddToList "User data = " & counter.GetCount()
    End If
    Socket.UserData = 0
End Sub
Private Sub m_server_OnConnectionEstablished(ByVal Socket As
JBSOCKETSERVERLib. ISocket)
    If ShowDataPackets.Value Then
        AddToList "OnConnectionEstablished : " & GetAddressAsString(Socket)
    End If
    Dim counter As Class1
    Set counter = New Class1
    Socket.UserData = counter
    Socket.WriteString "Welcome to VB echo server" & vbCrLf,
SignOnAsUnicode. Value
    Socket.RequestRead
End Sub
Private Sub m_server_OnDataReceived( _
    ByVal Socket As JBSOCKETSERVERLib.ISocket, _
    ByVal Data As JBSOCKETSERVERLib.IData)
    Dim counter As Class1
    Set counter = Socket.UserData
```

```
        counter.IncrementCount

        If DataIsBytes.Value Then

            OnReceivedBytes Socket, Data, counter.GetCount

        ElseIf DataIsString.Value Then

            OnReceivedString Socket, Data, counter.GetCount

        End If

        Socket.RequestRead

        If ShutdownAfter <> 0 And ShutdownAfter = counter.GetCount Then
            Socket.Shutdown ShutdownBoth
        End If

        If CloseAfter <> 0 And CloseAfter = counter.GetCount Then

            Socket.Close

        End If

End Sub
Private Sub OnReceivedBytes( _
    ByVal Socket As JBSOCKETSERVERLib.ISocket, _
    ByVal Data As JBSOCKETSERVERLib.IData, _
    counter As Integer)

    Dim Bytes() As Byte
    Bytes = Data.Read()

    If ShowDataPackets.Value Then

        Dim stringRep As String

        Dim i As Integer

        For i = LBound(Bytes) To UBound(Bytes)

            stringRep = stringRep & CLng(Bytes(i)) & " "

        Next i

        AddToList "OnDataReceived: "& GetAddressAsString(Socket) &" - "&
stringRep
```

```
    End If

    Dim thenShutdown As Boolean
    thenShutdown = False

    If ShutdownAfterWrite <> 0 And ShutdownAfterWrite = counter Then
        thenShutdown = True
    End If

    Socket.Write Bytes, thenShutdown

End Sub

Private Sub OnReceivedString( _
    ByVal Socket As JBSOCKETSERVERLib.ISocket, _
    ByVal Data As JBSOCKETSERVERLib.IData, _
    counter As Integer)

    Dim theData As String
    theData = Data.ReadString

    If ShowDataPackets.Value Then
        AddToList "OnDataReceived : " & GetAddressAsString(Socket) & " - " &
theData
    End If

    Dim thenShutdown As Boolean
    thenShutdown = False

    If ShutdownAfterWrite <> 0 And ShutdownAfterWrite = counter Then
        thenShutdown = True
    End If

    Socket.WriteString theData, False, thenShutdown

End Sub

Private Function GetAddressAsString(Socket As JBSOCKETSERVERLib.ISocket)
As String
    GetAddressAsString = Socket.RemoteAddress.Address & " : " &
Socket.Remote Address.Port
End Function
```

The code is made more complex by the fact that we can display and echo the data and shut down the connection in all of the possible ways. Notice how we initialise our user data in the m_server_OnConnectionEstablished event and store.

CHAPTER **11**

SOCKET PROGRAMMING APPLICATIONS

11.1 INTRODUCTION

Sockets

Everything in the unix world is a file. A socket is an abstraction of a communications channel. This abstraction allows the programmer to treat the communications channel as a standard file, from which (s)he can read and write directly.

Sockets are an endpoint to communications. It can be seen as the interface between the application and the transport provider.

Echo Server/Client Model

An echo client and server is useful mechanism to test communications. The function of each is quite simple, allowing the focus to be placed on the communications, rather than on protocols.

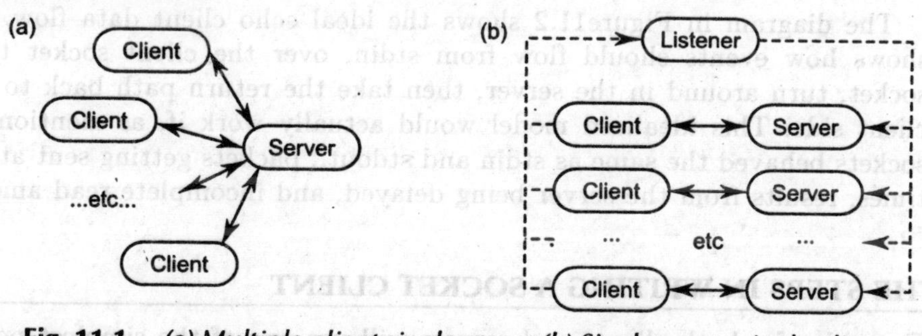

Fig. 11.1. *(a) Multiple-client single-server (b) Single-server single-client.*

There is usually only 1 server and several clients, but this depends on the exact architecture of the client/server. The clients sends data to the server, the data is either typed in by a user or is constant. The server recieves the data from one of the clients and then bouces it back. The client may then use the result to verify the communication has been successful.

This scheme allows us to check that the receive/transmit and connect/disconnect code works for both client and server. The sample code that follows will implementation various echo servers and clients

11.2 THE CLASSIC ECHO CLIENT/SERVER DATAFLOW

The simplest example that still demonstrates interaction is an echo client and server combination. An echo server has to deal with handling multiple clients, determining when to shutdown, gathering data and returning it to the client. It turns out that an echo server is actually easier to write than the client since it only needs to deal with one source of events (the client socket).

An echo client turns out to be very difficult to write correctly since it must deal with events from three sources, and then multi-plex them over three IO streams. A server basically just routes events and data from one side of the socket to the other. The client needs to be able to handle asynchronous events from standard input, standard output, the write side of the socket, and the read side of the socket, and do it all asynchronously. There's really no predictable way to do this, so our client will be implemented as two cooperating handlers.

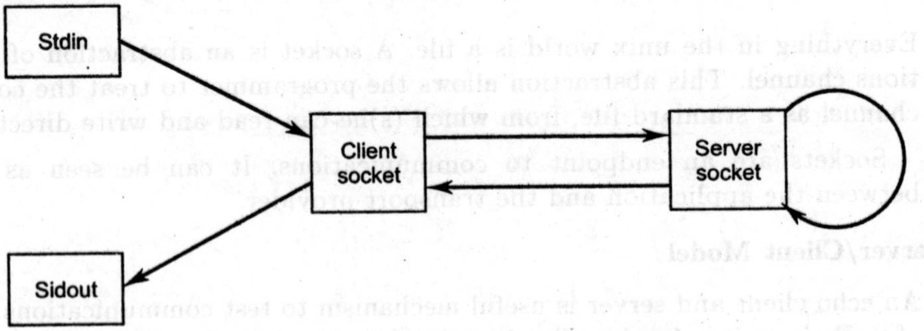

Fig.11.2. *Ideal echo client data flow.*

The diagram in Figure11.2 shows the ideal echo client data flow. This diagram shows how events should flow from stdin, over the client socket to the server's socket, turn around in the server, then take the return path back to stdout on the client side. This idealized model would actually work if, as mentioned previously, sockets behaved the same as stdin and stdout., packets getting sent at unpredictable times, results from the server being delayed, and incomplete read amounts.

11.3 THE STEPS IN WRITING A SOCKET CLIENT

Examples for both clients and servers will use one of the simplest possible applications: one that sends data and receives the exact same thing back. In fact, many machines run an "echo server" for debugging purposes; this is convenient for our initial client, since it can be used before we get to the server portion (assuming you have a machine with echo running).

The steps involved in writing a client application differ slightly between TCP and UDP clients. In both cases, you first create the socket; in the TCP case only, you next establish a connection to the server; next you send some data to the server; then receive data back; perhaps the sending and receiving alternates for a while; finally, in the TCP case, you close the connection.

A TCP echo client (client setup)

First we will look at a TCP client,Let's look at the first few lines--some includes, and creating the socket:

```
#include<stdio.h>
#include<sys/socket.h>
#include<arpa/inet.h>
#include<stdlib.h>
#include<string.h>
#include<unistd.h>
#include<netinet/in.h>
#defineBUFFSIZE32
voidDie(char*mess){perror(mess);exit(1);}
```

A particular buffer size is defined, which limits the amount of data echo'd at each pass (but we loop through multiple passes, if needed). A small error function is also defined.

A TCP echo client (creating the socket)

The arguments to the socket() call decide the type of socket: PF_INET just means it uses IP (which you always will); SOCK_STREAM and IPPROTO_TCP go together for a TCP socket.

```
intmain(intargc,char*argv[]){
  intsock;
  structsockaddr_inechoserver;
  charbuffer[BUFFSIZE];
  unsignedintecholen;
  intreceived=0;
  if(argc!=4){
    fprintf(stderr,"USAGE:TCPecho<server_ip><word><port>\n");
    exit(1);
  }
  /*CreatetheTCPsocket*/
```

```
if((sock=socket(PF_INET,SOCK_STREAM,IPPROTO_TCP))<0){
  Die("Failedtocreatesocket");
}
```

The value returned is a socket handle, which is similar to a file handle; specifically, if the socket creation fails, it will return -1 rather than a positive numbered handle.

A TCP echo client (establish connection)

Now that we have created a socket handle, we need to establish a connection with the server. A connection requires a sockaddr structure that describes the server. Specifically, we need to specify the server and port to connect to using echoserver.sin_addr.s_addr and echoserver.sin_port. The fact we are using an IP address is specified with echoserver.sin_family, but this will always be set to AF_INET.

```
/*Constructtheserversockaddr_instructure*/
memset(&echoserver,0,sizeof(echoserver));               /*Clearstruct*/
echoserver.sin_family=AF_INET;                          /*Internet/IP*/
echoserver.sin_addr.s_addr=inet_addr(argv[1]);          /*IPaddress*/
echoserver.sin_port=htons(atoi(argv[3]));               /*serverport*/
/*Establishconnection*/
if(connect(sock,
           (structsockaddr*)&echoserver,
           sizeof(echoserver))<0){
  Die("Failedtoconnectwithserver");
}
```

As with creating the socket, the attempt to establish a connection will return -1 if the attempt fails. Otherwise, the socket is now ready to accept sending and receiving data.

A TCP echo client (send/receive data)

Now that the connection is established, we are ready to send and receive data. A call to send() takes as arguments the socket handle itself, the string to send, the length of the sent string, and a flag argument. Normally the flag is the default value 0. The return value of the send() call is the number of bytes successfully sent.

```
/*Sendthewordtotheserver*/
echolen=strlen(argv[2]);
if(send(sock,argv[2],echolen,0)!=echolen){
  Die("Mismatchinnumberofsentbytes");
```

```
  }
  /*Receivethewordbackfromtheserver*/
  fprintf(stdout,"Received:");
  while(received<echolen){
    intbytes=0;
    if((bytes=recv(sock,buffer,BUFFSIZE-1,0))<1){
      Die("Failedtoreceivebytesfromserver");
    }
    received+=bytes;
    buffer[bytes]='\0';                        /*Assurenullterminatedstring*/
    fprintf(stdout,buffer);
  }
```

The rcv() call is not guaranteed to get everything in-transit on a particular call--it simply blocks until it gets *something*. Therefore, we loop until we have gotten back as many bytes as were sent, writing each partial string as we get it. Obviously, a different protocol might decide when to terminate receiving bytes in a different manner (perhaps a delimiter within the bytestream).

A TCP echo client (wrapup)

Calls to both send() and recv() block by default, but it is possible to change socket options to allow non-blocking sockets. However, this tutorial will not cover details of creating non-blocking sockets, nor such other details used in production servers as forking, threading, or general asynchronous processing (built on non-blocking sockets).

At the end of the process, we want to call close() on the socket, much as we would with a file handle

```
fprintf(stdout,"\n");
close(sock);
exit(0);
}
```

11.4 THE STEPS IN WRITING A SOCKET SERVER

A socket server is a bit more complicated than is a client, mostly because a server usually needs to be able to handle multiple client requests. Basically, there are two aspects to a server: handling each established connection, and listening for connections to establish.

In our example, and in most cases, you can split the handling of a particular connection into support function--which looks quite a bit like a TCP client application does. We name that function HandleClient().

Listening for new connections is a bit different from client code. The trick is that the socket you initially create and bind to an address and port is not the actually connected socket. This initial socket acts more like a socket factory, producing new connected sockets as needed. This arrangement has an advantage in enabling fork'd, threaded, or asynchronously dispatched handlers (using select()); however, for this first tutorial we will only handle pending connected sockets in synchronous order.

A TCP echo server (application setup)

Our echo server starts out with pretty much the same few #includes as the client did, and defines some constants and an error handling function:

```
#include<stdio.h>
#include<sys/socket.h>
#include<arpa/inet.h>
#include<stdlib.h>
#include<string.h>
#include<unistd.h>
#include<netinet/in.h>
#defineMAXPENDING5 /                    *Maxconnectionrequests*/
#defineBUFFSIZE32
voidDie(char*mess){perror(mess);exit(1);}
```

The BUFFSIZE constant limits the data sent per loop. The MAXPENDING constant limits the number of connections that will be queued at a time (only one will be *serviced* at a time in our simple server). The Die() function is the same as in our client.

A TCP echo server (the connection handler)

The handler for echo connections is straightforward. All it does is receive any initial bytes available, then cycle through sending back data and receiving more data. For short echo strings (particularly if less than BUFFSIZE) and typical connections, only one pass through the while loop will occur. But the underlying sockets interface (and TCP/IP) does not make any guarantees about how the bytestream will be split between calls to recv().

```
voidHandleClient(intsock){
charbuffer[BUFFSIZE];
intreceived=-1;
/*Receivemessage*/
if((received=recv(sock,buffer,BUFFSIZE,0))<0){
  Die("Failedtoreceiveinitialbytesfromclient");
}
```

```
    /*Sendbytesandcheckformoreincomingdatainloop*/
    while(received>0){
      /*Sendbackreceiveddata*/
      if(send(sock,buffer,received,0)!=received){
        Die("Failedtosendbytestoclient");
      }
      /*Checkformoredata*/
      if((received=recv(sock,buffer,BUFFSIZE,0))<0){
        Die("Failedtoreceiveadditionalbytesfromclient");
      }
    }
    close(sock);
  }
```

The socket that is passed in to the handler function is one that already connected to the requesting client. Once we are done with echoing all the data, we should close this socket; the parent server socket stays around to spawn new children, like the one just closed.

A TCP echo server (configuring the server socket)

As we outlined before, creating a socket has a bit different purpose for a server than for a client. Creating the socket has the same syntax it did in the client; but the structure echoserver is setup with information about the server itself, rather than about the peer it wants to connect to. You usually want to use the special constant INADDR_ANY to enable receiving client request on any IP address the server supplies; in principle, such as in a multi-hosting server, you could specify a particular IP address instead.

```
intmain(intargc,char*argv[]){
  intserversock,clientsock;
  structsockaddr_inechoserver,echoclient;
  if(argc!=2){
    fprintf(stderr,"USAGE:echoserver<port>\n");
    Exit(1);
  }
  /*CreatetheTCPsocket*/
  If((serversock=socket(PF_INET,SOCK_STREAM,IPPROTO_TCP))<0){
    Die("Failedtocreatesocket");
  }
```

```
/*Constructtheserversockaddr_instructure*/
memset(&echoserver,0,sizeof(echoserver));    /*Clearstruct*/
echoserver.sin_family=AF_INET;               /*Internet/IP*/
echoserver.sin_addr.s_addr=htonl(INADDR_ANY);   /*Incomingaddr*/
echoserver.sin_port=htons(atoi(argv[1]));    /*serverport*/
```

Notice that both IP address and port are converted to network byte order for the sockaddr_in structure. The reverse functions to return to native byte order are ntohs() and ntohl() . These functions are no-ops on some platforms, but it is still wise to use them for cross-platform compatibility.

A TCP echo server (binding and listening)

Whereas the client application connect() 'd to a server's IP address and port, the server bind() 's to its own address and port:

```
/*Bindtheserversocket*/
if(bind(serversock,(structsockaddr*)&echoserver, sizeof(echoserver))<
0){
  Die("Failedtobindtheserversocket");
}
/*Listenontheserversocket*/
if(listen(serversock,MAXPENDING)<0){
Die("Failedtolistenonserversocket");
}
```

Once the server socket is bound, it is ready to listen(). As with most socket functions, both bind() and listen() return -1 if they have a problem. Once a server socket is listening, it is ready to accept() client connections, acting as a factory for sockets on each connection.

A TCP echo server (socket factory)

Creating new sockets for client connections is the crux of a server. The function accept() does two important things: it returns a socket pointer for the new socket; and it populates the sockaddr_in structure pointed to, in our case, by echoclient.

```
/*Rununtilcancelled*/
while(1){
  unsignedintclientlen=sizeof(echoclient);
  /*Waitforclientconnection*/
  if((clientsock=
        accept(serversock,(structsockaddr*)&echoclient, &clientlen))<
0){
```

```
        Die("Failedtoacceptclientconnection");
    }
    fprintf(stdout,"Clientconnected:%s\n", inet_ntoa(echoclient.sin_addr));
    HandleClient(clientsock);
  }
}
```

We can see the populated structure in echoclient with the fprintf() call that accesses the client IP address. The client socket pointer is passed to HandleClient().

The Socket and Socket Server Module

Python's standard module socket provides almost exactly the same range of capabilities we find in C sockets. However, the interface is generally more flexible, largely because of the benefits of dynamic typing. Moreover, an object-oriented style is also used. For example, once you create a socket object, methods like .bind(), .connect(), and .send() are methods of that object, rather than global functions operating on a socket pointer.

At a higher level than socket, the module SocketServer provides a framework for writing servers. This is still relatively low level, and higher-level interfaces are available for server of higher-level protocols, *e.g.*, SimpleHTTPServer, DocXMLRPCServer, or CGIHTTPServer.

A TCP echo client

Let us just look at the complete client, then make a few remarks:

```
#!/usr/bin/envpython
"USAGE:echoclient.py<server><word><port>"
fromsocketimport* #import*,butwe'llavoidnameconflict
importsys
iflen(sys.argv)!=4:
    print__doc__
    sys.exit(0)
sock=socket(AF_INET,SOCK_STREAM)
sock.connect((sys.argv[1],int(sys.argv[3])))
message=sys.argv[2]
messlen,received=sock.send(message),0
ifmesslen!=len(message):
    print"Failedtosendcompletemessage"
print"Received:",
whilereceived<messlen:
```

```
        data=sock.recv(32)
        sys.stdout.write(data)
        received+=len(data)
    print
    sock.close()
```

At first brush, we seem to have left out some of the error catching code from the C version. But since Python raises descriptive errors for every situation that we checked for in the C echo client, we can let the built-in exceptions do our work for us. Of course, if we wanted the precise wording of errors that we had before, we would have to add a few try / except clauses around the calls to methods of the socket object.

A TCP echo client, continued

While shorter, the Python client is somewhat more powerful. Specifically, the address we feed to a .connect() call can be either a dotted-quad IP address or a symbolic name, without need for extra lookup work, *e.g.*, :

```
$ ./echoclient.py 192.168.2.103 foobar 7
Received: foobar
$ ./echoclient.py fury.gnosis.lan foobar 7
Received: foobar
```

We also have a choice between the methods .send() and .sendall(). The former sends as many bytes as it can at once, the latter sends the whole message (or raises an exception if it cannot). For this client, we indicate if the whole message was not sent, but proceed with getting back as much as actually was sent.

A TCP echo server (socket server)

The simplest way to write a echo server in Python is using the SocketServer module. In later panels, we will spell out the lower-level version, that follows the C implementation. For now, let us see just how quick it can be:

```
#!/usr/bin/env python
"USAGE: echoserver.py <port>"
from SocketServer import BaseRequestHandler, TCPServer
import sys, socket

class EchoHandler(BaseRequestHandler):
    def handle(self):
        print "Client connected:", self.client_address
        self.request.sendall(self.request.recv(2**16))
        self.request.close()
```

```
iflen(sys.argv)!=2:
    print__doc__
else:
    TCPServer(('',int(sys.argv[1])),EchoHandler).serve_forever()
```

The only thing we need to provide is a child of SocketServer.BaseRequestHandler that has a .handle() method. The self instance has some useful attributes, such as .client_address, and .request which is itself a connected socket object.

A TCP echo server (socket)

we can write almost exactly our C echo server in Python (but in fewer lines):

```
#!/usr/bin/envpython
"USAGE:echoserver.py<port>"
fromsocketimport*  #import*,butwe'llavoidnameconflict
importsys

defhandleClient(sock):
    data=sock.recv(32)
    whiledata:
        sock.sendall(data)
        data=sock.recv(32)
    sock.close()
iflen(sys.argv)!=2:
    print__doc__
else:
    sock=socket(AF_INET,SOCK_STREAM)
    sock.bind(('',int(sys.argv[1])))
    sock.listen(5)
    while1:  #Rununtilcancelled
        newsock,client_addr=sock.accept()
        print"Clientconnected:",client_addr
        handleClient(newsock)
```

But as in the C implementation, we manufacture new connected sockets using .listen(), and call our handler for each such connection.

A UDP Echo Client in C

Client setup

The first few lines of our UDP client are identical to those for the TCP client. Mostly we just use some includes for socket functions, or other basic I/O functions.

```
#include<stdio.h>
#include<sys/socket.h>
#include<arpa/inet.h>
#include<stdlib.h>
#include<string.h>
#include<unistd.h>
#include<netinet/in.h>

#defineBUFFSIZE255
voidDie(char*mess){perror(mess);exit(1);}
```

There is not too much to the setup. It is worth noticing that the buffer size we allocate is much larger than it was in the TCP version (but still finite in size). TCP can loop through the pending data, sending a bit more over an open socket on each loop. For this UDP version, we want a buffer that is large enough to hold the entire message, which we send in a single datagram (it can be smaller than 255, but not any larger). A small error function is also defined.

Declarations and Usage Message

At the very start of the main() function we allocate two sockaddr_in structures, a few integers to hold string sizes, another int for the socket handle, and a buffer to hold the returned string. After that, we check that the command-line arguments look mostly correct.

```
intmain(intargc,char*argv[]){
intsock;
structsockaddr_inechoserver;
structsockaddr_inechoclient;
charbuffer[BUFFSIZE];
unsignedintecholen,clientlen;
intreceived=0;
if(argc!=4){
  fprintf(stderr,"USAGE:%s<server_ip><word><port>\n",argv[0]);
exit(1);
}
```

A contrast with the Python code comes up already here. For this C client, you *must* use a dotted-quad IP address. In Python, all the socket module functions handle name resolution behind the scenes. If you wanted to do a lookup in the C client, you would need to program a DNS function.

In fact, it would not be a terrible idea to check that the IP address passed in as the server IP address really looks like a dotted-quad address. If you forgetfully pass in a named address, we will probably receive the somewhat misleading error: "Mismatch in number of sent bytes: No route to host" (see below for where this message is produced). Any named address amounts to the same thing as an unused or reserved IP address (which a simple pattern check could not rule out, of course).

Create the Socket and Configure the Server Structure

The arguments to the socket() call decide the type of socket: PF_INET just means it uses IP (which you always will); SOCK_DGRAM and IPPROTO_UDP go together for a UDP socket. In preparation for sending the message to echo, we populate the intended server's structure, using the command-line arguments.

```
/*CreatetheUDPsocket*/
if((sock=socket(PF_INET,SOCK_DGRAM,IPPROTO_UDP))<0){
  Die("Failedtocreatesocket");
}
/*Constructtheserversockaddr_instructure*/
memset(&echoserver,0,sizeof(echoserver));          /*Clearstruct*/
echoserver.sin_family=AF_INET;                     /*Internet/IP*/
echoserver.sin_addr.s_addr=inet_addr(argv[1]);      /*IPaddress*/
echoserver.sin_port=htons(atoi(argv[3]));          /*serverport*/
```

The value returned in the call to socket() is a socket handle is similar to a file handle; specifically, if the socket creation fails, it will return -1 rather than a positive numbered handle. Support functions inet_addr() and htons() (and atoi()) are used to convert the string arguments into appropriate data structures.

Send the Message to the Server

For what it does, this UDP client is a bit simpler than was the similar TCP echo client presented in the first part of this tutorial series. As we saw with the Python versions, sending a message is not based on first establishing a connection. we simply send it to a specified address using sendto(), rather than with send() on an established connection. Of course, this requires an extra couple arguments to indicate the intended server address.

```
/*Sendthewordtotheserver*/
echolen=strlen(argv[2]);
if(sendto(sock,argv[2],echolen,0,
        (structsockaddr*)&echoserver,
        sizeof(echoserver))!=echolen){
Die("Mismatchinnumberofsentbytes");
}
```

The error checking in this call usually establishes that a route to the server exists. This is the message raised if a named address is used by mistake, but it also occurs for valid-looking but unreachable IP addresses.

Receive the Message back from the Server

Receiving the data back works pretty much the same way as it did in the TCP echo client. The only real change is a substitute a call to recvfrom() for the TCP call to recv().

```
/*Receivethewordbackfromtheserver*/
fprintf(stdout,"Received:");
clientlen=sizeof(echoclient);
if((received=recvfrom(sock,buffer,BUFFSIZE,0,

    (structsockaddr*)&echoclient,

    &clientlen))!=echolen){
  Die("Mismatchinnumberofreceivedbytes");
}
/*Checkthatclientandserverareusingsamesocket*/
if(echoserver.sin_addr.s_addr!=echoclient.sin_addr.s_addr){
  Die("Receivedapacketfromanunexpectedserver");
}
buffer[received]='\0';                /*Assurenullterminatedstring*/
fprintf(stdout,buffer);
fprintf(stdout,"\n");
close(sock);
exit(0);
}
```

The structure echoserver had been configured with an *ad hoc* port during the call to sendto() ; in turn, the echoclient structure gets similarly filled in with the call to recvfrom(). This lets us compare the two addresses--if some other server or port sends a datagram while we are waiting to receive the echo. We guard at least minimally against stray datagrams that do not interest us (we might have checked the .sin_port members also, to be completely certain).

At the end of the process, we print out the datagram that came back, and close the socket.

11.5 A UDP ECHO SERVER IN C

Server Setup

Even more than with TCP applications, UDP clients and servers are quite similar to each other. In essence, either one consists mainly of some sendto() and recvfrom() calls mixed together. The main difference for a server is simply that it usually puts its main body in an indefinite loop to keep serving.

Let us start out with the usual includes and error function:

```
#include<stdio.h>
#include<sys/socket.h>
#include<arpa/inet.h>
#include<stdlib.h>
#include<string.h>
#include<unistd.h>
#include<netinet/in.h>
#define BUFFSIZE 255
void Die(char *mess) { perror(mess); exit(1); }
```

Declarations and Usage Message

Again, not much is new in the UDP echo server's declarations and usage message. We need a socket structure for the server and client, and a few variables that will be used to verify transmission sizes; and, of course, the buffer to read and write the message.

```
int main(int argc, char *argv[]) {
  int sock;
    struct sockaddr_in echoserver;
    struct sockaddr_in echoclient;
    char buffer[BUFFSIZE];
unsigned int echolen, clientlen, serverlen;
int received = 0;

if (argc != 2) {
  fprintf(stderr, "USAGE: %s <port>\n", argv[0]);
  exit(1);
}
```

Create, Configure, and Bind the Server Socket

The first real difference between UDP client and server comes in the need to bind the socket on the server side. We saw this already with the Python example, and the situation is the same here. The server socket is not the actual socket the message is transmitted over; rather, it acts as a factory for an *ad hoc* socket which is configured in the recvfrom() call we will see soon.

```
/*CreatetheUDPsocket*/
if((sock=socket(PF_INET,SOCK_DGRAM,IPPROTO_UDP))<0){
  Die("Failedtocreatesocket");
}
/*Constructtheserversockaddr_instructure*/
memset(&echoserver,0,sizeof(echoserver));                /*Clearstruct*/
echoserver.sin_family=AF_INET;                            /*Internet/IP*/
echoserver.sin_addr.s_addr=htonl(INADDR_ANY);          /*AnyIPaddress*/
echoserver.sin_port=htons(atoi(argv[1]));                 /*serverport*/

/*Bindthesocket*/
serverlen=sizeof(echoserver);
if(bind(sock,(structsockaddr*)&echoserver,serverlen)<0){
  Die("Failedtobindserversocket");
}
```

Readers will also notice that the echoserver structure is configured a bit differently. In order to allow connection on any IP address the server hosts, we use the special constant INADDR_ANY for the member .s_addr.

The Receive/Send Loop

The heavy lifting--such as it is--in the UDP sever is its main loop. Basically, we perpetually wait to receive a message in a recvfrom() call. When this happens, the echoclient structure is populated with relevant members for the connecting socket. We then use that structure in the subsequent sendto() call.

```
/*Rununtilcancelled*/
  while(1){
   /*Receiveamessagefromtheclient*/
   clientlen=sizeof(echoclient);
   if((received=recvfrom(sock,buffer,BUFFSIZE,0,(structsockaddr*)
&echoclient,&clientlen))<0){
     Die("Failedtoreceivemessage");
   }
   fprintf(stderr,
             "Clientconnected:%s\n",inet_ntoa(echoclient.sin_addr));
   /*Sendthemessagebacktoclient*/
```

```
        if(sendto(sock,buffer,received,0,
                (structsockaddr*)&echoclient,
                  sizeof(echoclient))!=received){
          Die("Mismatchinnumberofecho'dbytes");
        }
      }
    }
```

And that's it! We can receive and send messages forever, reporting connections to the console as we go along. Which might be a problem for a server handling many clients (probably not for this simple echo server, but something more complicated might introduce poor latencies).

Program of tcp Echo Server-Client

Tcpechoserver

Tcpserv01.c

```
#include"unp.h"

int
main(intargc,char**argv)
{
int                                    listenfd,connfd;
pid_t                                  childpid;
socklen_t                              clilen;
structsockaddr_in                      cliaddr,servaddr;
listenfd=Socket(AF_INET,SOCK_STREAM,0);
bzero(&servaddr,sizeof(servaddr));
servaddr.sin_family=AF_INET;
servaddr.sin_addr.s_addr=htonl(INADDR_ANY);
servaddr.sin_port=htons(SERV_PORT);
Bind(listenfd,(SA*)&servaddr,sizeof(servaddr));
Listen(listenfd,LISTENQ);
for(;;){
```

```
        clilen=sizeof(cliaddr);
        connfd=Accept(listenfd,(SA*)
        &cliaddr,&clilen);
        if((childpid=Fork())==0){    /*childprocess*/
          Close(listenfd);           /*closelisteningsocket*/
          str_echo(connfd);          /*processtherequest*/
          exit(0);
        }
        Close(connfd);               /*parentclosesconnectedsocket
      */
    }
}
```

Tr_echo.c

```
#include"unp.h"
void
str_echo(intsockfd)
{
ssize_t n;
char line[MAXLINE];
for(;;){
    if((n=Readline(sockfd,line,MAXLINE))==0)
      return; /*connectionclosedbyotherend*/
    Writen(sockfd,line,n);
}
}
```

Tcpecho client

Tcpcli.c

```
#include"unp.h"
int
main(intargc,char**argv)
{
int  sockfd;
structlinger ling;
```

```
struct sockaddr_in servaddr;
if(argc!=2)
    err_quit("usage:tcpcli<IPaddress>");
sockfd=Socket(AF_INET,SOCK_STREAM,0);
bzero(&servaddr,sizeof(servaddr));
servaddr.sin_family=AF_INET;
servaddr.sin_port=htons(SERV_PORT);
Inet_pton(AF_INET,argv[1],&servaddr.sin_addr);
Connect(sockfd,(SA*)&servaddr,sizeof(servaddr));
str_cli(stdin,sockfd); /*doitall*/
ling.l_onoff=1;
ling.l_linger=0;
Setsockopt(sockfd,SOL_SOCKET,SO_LINGER,&ling,sizeof(ling));
exit(0);
}
```

str_cli.c

```
#include"unp.h"
void
str_cli(FILE*fp,int sockfd)
{
char sendline[MAXLINE],recvline[MAXLINE];
while(Fgets(sendline,MAXLINE,fp)!=NULL){
Writen(sockfd,sendline,strlen(sendline));
if(Readline(sockfd,recvline,MAXLINE)==0)
err_quit("str_cli:serverterminatedprematurely");
Fputs(recvline,stdout);
}
}
```

UDP Echo server

```
/*
ExampleofserverusingUDPprotocol.
```

```
*/
#include"inet.h"
main(argc,argv)
intargc;
char*argv[];
{
int sockfd;
structsockaddr_inserv_addr,cli_addr;
pname=argv[0];
/*
Opena UDPsocket(anInternetdatagramsocket).
*/
if((sockfd=socket(AF_INET,SOCK_DGRAM,0))<0)
err_dump("server:can'topendatagramsocket");
/*
Bindourlocaladdresssothattheclientcansendtous.
*/
bzero((char*)&serv_addr,sizeof(serv_addr));
serv_addr.sin_family   =AF_INET;
serv_addr.sin_addr.s_addr=htonl(INADDR_ANY);
serv_addr.sin_port    =htons(SERV_UDP_PORT);
if(bind(sockfd,(structsockaddr*)&serv_addr,sizeof(serv_addr))<
0)
err_dump("server:can'tbindlocaladdress");
dg_echo(sockfd,(structsockaddr*)&cli_addr,sizeof(cli_addr));
/*NOTREACHED*/
}
```

UDP echo client

```
/*
 * ExampleofclientusingUDPprotocol.
*/
```

```
1. #include"inet.h"

2. main(argc, argv)
3. intargc;
4. char*argv[];
5. {
6. int sockfd;
7. structsockaddr_incli_addr, serv_addr;

8. pname=argv[0];
9. /*
a. Fillinthestructure"serv_addr"withtheaddressofthe
b. serverthatwewanttosendto.
c. */

10. bzero((char*)&serv_addr, sizeof(serv_addr));
11. serv_addr.sin_family   =AF_INET;
12. serv_addr.sin_addr.s_addr=inet_addr(SERV_HOST_ADDR);
13. serv_addr.sin_port     =htons(SERV_UDP_PORT);

14. /*
a. OpenaUDPsocket(anInternetdatagramsocket).
b. */

15. if((sockfd=socket(AF_INET, SOCK_DGRAM, 0))<0)
    i. err_dump("client:can'topendatagramsocket");

16. /*
a. Bindanylocaladdressforus.
b. */

17. bzero((char*)&cli_addr, sizeof(cli_addr));/*zeroout*/
18. cli_addr.sin_family   =AF_INET;
19. cli_addr.sin_addr.s_addr=htonl(INADDR_ANY);
20. cli_addr.sin_port     =htons(0);
21. if(bind(sockfd, (structsockaddr*)&cli_addr, sizeof(cli_addr))<0)
    i. err_dump("client:can'tbindlocaladdress");

22. dg_cli(stdin, sockfd, (struct sockaddr *) &serv_addr,
    sizeof(serv_addr));

23. close(sockfd);
```

```
exit(0);
}
```

Dg_cli.c

```
/*
ReadthecontentsoftheFILE*fp,writeeachlinetothe
datagramsocket,thenreadalinebackfromthedatagram
socketandwriteittothestandardoutput.
*
ReturntocallerwhenanEOFisencounteredontheinputfile.
*/
#include<stdio.h>
#include<sys/types.h>
#include<sys/socket.h>
#defineMAXLINE512
dg_cli(fp,sockfd,pserv_addr,servlen)
FILE *fp;
int sockfd;
structsockaddr*pserv_addr;/*ptrtoappropriatesockaddr_XXstruc-
ture*/
int servlen;/*actualsizeof(*pserv_addr)*/
{
intn;
charsendline[MAXLINE],recvline[MAXLINE+1];
while(fgets(sendline,MAXLINE,fp)!=NULL){
n=strlen(sendline);
if(sendto(sockfd,sendline,n,0,pserv_addr,servlen)!=n)
err_dump("dg_cli:sendtoerroronsocket");
/*
Nowreadamessagefromthesocketandwriteitto
ourstandardoutput.
*/
n=recvfrom(sockfd,recvline,MAXLINE,0,
(structsockaddr*)0,(int*)0);
if(n<0)
```

```
err_dump("dg_cli:recvfromerror");
recvline[n]=0;/*nullterminate*/
fputs(recvline,stdout);
}
if(ferror(fp))
err_dump("dg_cli:errorreadingfile");
}
```

Dg_echo.c

```
/*
Readadatagramfromaconnectionlesssocketandwriteitbackto
thesender.
*
Weneverreturn,asweneverknowwhenadatagramclientisdone.
*/
#include<sys/types.h>
#include<sys/socket.h>
#defineMAXMESG2048
dg_echo(sockfd,pcli_addr,maxclilen)
int sockfd;
structsockaddr*pcli_addr;/*ptrtoappropriatesockaddr_XXstructure
*/
int maxclilen;/*sizeof(*pcli_addr)*/
{
intn,clilen;
charmesg[MAXMESG];
for(;;){
clilen=maxclilen;
n=recvfrom(sockfd,mesg,MAXMESG,0,pcli_addr,&clilen);
if(n<0)
err_dump("dg_echo:recvfromerror");
if(sendto(sockfd,mesg,n,0,pcli_addr,clilen)!=n)
err_dump("dg_echo:sendtoerror");
}
}
```

11.6 FTP

Introduction

The File Transfer Protocol (FTP) is a TCP protocol that is described by RFC (Request for Comment) 959.The File Transfer Protocol (FTP) process is the method by which you move files from a personal computer to a Web server so that those files may be shared across the Internet. FTP requires specialized software, generally available free of charge.Not so long ago, this was the easiest and simplest way to transfer files from one desktop computer to another. Later, modems and serial connections made it possible to transfer files between two computers using telephone lines. Setting up both computers for serial connections requires some preparation and timing considerations. Although not as simple and as easy as diskettes, transfers using serial connections are convenient and can more easily handle large amounts of data and longer distances.

Once more modern computer networks made their debut, transferring files became as simple as retrieving or saving a file. All of the disk and file operations over the network act exactly as they would on a disk drive. Network software often depicts a remote computer as simply another disk drive. Communications within such networks are done over high-speed network cables. The only real limitation is the scope of the network. Accessing computers that are not on the high-speed network still requires a modem or some other communication method.

With the introduction of the Internet came a new and extensive network system, packed with features. Communications and file transfers are simpler and easier than ever before. The Internet indirectly connects any computer on the Internet to every other computer on the Internet. Access is immediately possible to growing millions of computers and files. The administrator of each computer on the Internet grants permission to access their computer.

Client/Server Environment

The computing environment of the Internet is based on the client/server model. A client/server network has two roles for computers: clients and servers. The server is a computer that responds to requests for its services. The client is a computer that requests a service from a server. In a client/server network, the server can be considered the host and the client can be considered the guest. When the guest asks for something, the host tries to fill the request.

Internet servers need to be powerhouse computers, handling high volumes and concurrent requests. Depending on the type of client requests and their volume, a server's performance might slow to a crawl, or it could even crash. System administrators work to maintain a reliable server and sometimes apply restrictions to the services. The administrators can do such things as restrict some services to off-peak hours, restrict some services to only local users, and restrict the number of concurrent client requests.

The services provided by most servers on the Internet include electronic mail, participating in newsgroups, connections to other computers, transferring files, browsing World Wide Web pages, and joining chat groups. An Internet server site may have one server that provides all of the Internet services for the site, or the site may have several servers, each dedicated to providing one specific service.

IP Addresses and Domain Names

Administrators assign every computer on the Internet an Internet Protocol or IP address. They create an IP address with four numbers, each between 1 and 255. Periods separate each number in the address, as in 189.247.63.5. This arrangement provides for more than four billion different addresses. A central administrative body oversees the distribution of IP addresses.

Along with an IP address, administrators can optionally assign a domain name to their computer. Domain names are more user-friendly and recognizable in that they can contain real words and abbreviations. An administrator has more flexibility in creating domain names than in assigning IP addresses. Within the Internet, the Domain Name System manages and matches domain names to their IP addresses.

Most Internet sites conform to a standard naming convention. The first part of a domain name often represents the type of computer. For instance, "www" represents a web server, "ftp" is a file transfer server, and "news" is a news server. The last part of the domain name often represents the country where the computer is located, as in "ca" for Canada. Site administrators in the United States have their own convention for ending their domain names. For educational institutions, they use "edu." Commercial organizations use "com." These are only conventions. Administrators are free to use whatever they want in their site name, provided the whole name is unique and not offensive.

The IP address and domain name each uniquely identify every Internet computer, client or server. Connecting to a server on the Internet requires you to know either its IP address or domain name. The Internet has more than three million servers to browse through, so aimlessly walking about them will not work. In essence, we cannot easily connect to an Internet server unless we have its IP address or domain name.

File Transfer Protocol

One of the most useful services of the Internet is FTP, or File Transfer Protocol. FTP is a network protocol. It also refers to the method by which we transfer data and program files between computers on the Internet. We refer to computers configured to accept FTP requests as FTP servers. These servers store a tremendous amount of information, and it is available to anyone on the Internet using FTP.

In an FTP client/server connection, the user's computer is called the client or local computer. The FTP server is called the host or remote computer. Downloading refers to transferring files from the FTP server to the client computer. Uploading refers to transferring files to the FTP server from the client computer.

Anonymous FTP

Having a computer hooked onto the Internet does not mean that everyone else on the Internet has access to its files. Similarly, having an FTP server on the Internet does not mean everyone can access it. Some system administrators may choose to restrict access to their files to a local or selected group of users. Others administrators may choose to make all of their files available to everyone.

When an FTP server has an access restriction, it requires a user identification code and password before allowing access to its files. If it has no access restriction, the FTP server allows any and every user to access its files; we call these servers anonymous FTP servers.

Although the anonymous FTP server has unrestricted access, it usually still has a logon procedure. Most anonymous FTP servers are set up to accept "anonymous" as the user identification. For the password, they accept, and sometimes require, the user's e-mail address. Entering your e-mail address is a courtesy to the site's owners and gives them an idea of who is accessing their files. Very rarely is this information used for any other purpose.

Site administrators can restrict anonymous FTP services to a specific number of concurrent users to reduce the drain on their server's overall performance. For instance, they can limit the number of users connected at one time to 25, 250, or whatever they want. Administrators may also restrict access to certain times of the day, often outside their regular business hours.

Mirror Sites

Some FTP servers and the files they store are very popular with many users. Reaching a site that is too busy to accept new client requests is common. It is like getting a busy signal during the rush to buy concert tickets by phone. Administrators establish mirror sites as a solution to this problem.

Mirror sites are FTP servers that maintain an exact copy of the files from one or more FTP servers. For example, an FTP server at the University of Toronto may mirror the files of a University of Michigan FTP server. All of the files on the Michigan server are available from the Toronto server. Administrators usually set aside a separate section in their file storage area for the files of the mirrored sites. The administrators refresh the contents of the mirrored files periodically.

Accessing a mirror site that is closer or less busy than the original site can be advantageous to a user. By being closer, the file transfer may involve fewer network connections and less network traffic. This can help to make the file transfer faster. A less busy server ensures a better chance of connecting.

Directories and Files

Most FTP servers run under the UNIX operating system. UNIX uses hierarchical file storage similar to both PC and Macintosh computers. What is called a directory on a PC or a folder on a Macintosh is called a directory in UNIX. Directories can hold both files and subdirectories. Accessing a specific file involves knowing all of the directories in the path from the top or root directory down to the file.

Some directory and file names on an FTP server may look strange or obscure. Often this is due to UNIX, since it allows long directory and file names. A user may also see directories and files that are a part of the server's operating system. UNIX system directories include bin, etc, and usr. Usually these directories have nothing of interest to the user and are often restricted anyway.

Common FTP-related directory names include pub, mirrors, uploads, and incoming. The most commonly used directory for files on an FTP server is the pub directory. Under it are stored the many subdirectories and files for public use. The mirrors directory holds the copies of files from mirrored sites. Depending on how many files the server has stored, it may have many subdirectories to traverse to get to the desired file. Most FTP programs make navigating through the server's directories as easy as it is on a hard drive.

FTP Client Software

To transfer files between an FTP server and a desktop computer, the local computer needs to be running FTP client software. All these client programs orchestrate the file transfer communications between the client computer and the FTP server. Such programs include WS_FTP for the PC and Fetch for the Macintosh. Many of today's popular Web browsers also have FTP download capabilities, but they do not have upload capabilities or the additional features found in most FTP programs.

Each FTP program has its own interface, some more intuitive and user-friendly than others. Whatever the program, they all work the same way. After starting, the first thing they require is an FTP server with which the file transfer is to occur. The IP address or domain name identify the server to the program. Depending on the server, it might also require a user identification code and password. Some programs can store a list of regular or favorite servers, including the user identification code and password required for server access.

After the user enters a specific FTP server name or address, the FTP program attempts to connect to the server. Most FTP programs display the responses they receive from the server when they are communicating with it. If the server is too busy to accept any new clients, it may return such a message. It may also list some of its mirror sites. Until the program establishes a connection with the FTP server, file transfers cannot take place. When the connection is successful, the FTP program displays its main file transfer screen.

Web Browsers and FTP

Most Web browsers can do FTP downloads. In a HyperText Markup Language (HTML) document, a mouse-clickable FTP link is written as follows:

<A HREF="ftp://ftp.npgsr.net/pub/win3/ws_ftp.zip">Winsock FTP Program</a>

When the user clicks on the link text, "Winsock FTP Program", the Web browser initiates an FTP file transfer session. If the link does not include a specific file, most browsers display the contents of the last directory in the path. This allows the user to see the entire contents of the directory and choose one or more files for transfer.

Communicating FTP Pathnames

To receive a file from an FTP server, we need the server's IP address or domain name, the name of the directory in which the file is located, and the name of the file itself. This information can be sent to others in an electronic mail message or a word processor document in the following format:

ftp.npgsr.net/pub/win3/ws_ftp.zip

This line of text specifies all of the necessary information for a user to find a file on an FTP server: the server's name (ftp.npgsrnet), the directory path (/pub/win3), and the filename (ws_ftp.zip). The reference can also use the server's IP address, as in:

204.71.8.21/pub/win3/ws_ftp.zip

Program

Server code

Server:

```
Importjava.io.*;
Importjava.net.*;
Classfileser
{
publicstaticvoidmain(stringa[]throwsexception
{
charch[]=newchar[35];
stringstr;
intI=0.j;
//createaserversocketandestablishtheconnection
serversocketss=newserversocket(2000);
sockets=ss.accept();
bufferedreaderin=newbuffereReader(new
inputstreamReader(s.getinputStream()));
PrintWriterout=newPrintWriter(newBufferedWriter(newoutputstream
writer
(s.getOutputStream()),true);
stringframe=in.readLine();
FileinputStreamfin=newFileinputstream("chumma.java");
//readthecontentoffileandsendittootheruser.
While(true)
{
for(I=0;I<30;I++)
{
```

```
j=fin.read();
ch[I]=(char)j;
if(j==_1)
break;
}
str=newstring(ch,0,I);
out.println(str);
if(I!=30)
break;
}
out.println("EFO");
in.close();
out.close();
s.close();
ss.close();
}
}
```

Client:

```
import.java.io.*;
import.java.net.*;
classfcli
{
publicstaticvoidmain(stringa[]throwsexception
{
bufferedreader in 1=new buffered reader (new input stream reader
(sustem.in);
system.out.println(enterthehostnameyouwanttoconnect");
//connectthesocket
sockets \=newsokclet(inetaddress.getbyname(in1.readline()),2000);
inputstreamreader(s.getinputstream()));
printwriterout=newprintwriter(newbufferedwriter(new
outputstreamwriter(s.getoutputstream())),true);
system.out.println("enterthesourcefilename");
out.println(in1.readline()));
system.out.println("enterthedestinationfilename");
fileoutputstreamo=newfileoutputstream(in1.readline());
```

```
stringdata;
intI=0;
while(true)
{
//readthefilecontentandwriteitinafile
data=in2.readline();
if(data.equals("EFO"))
break;
charch[]=newchar[35];
data.getcharas(0,data.length(),ch,o);
for(I=0;I<data.length();I++)
o.write(int)ch[I];
}
o.close();
in1.close();
in2.close();
out.close();
s.close();
}
}
```

11.7 PING

Testing Your TCP/IP LAN

Once we have set up at least two PCs with TCP/IP support it is best to start testing it as you go along. The basic way of doing this is by using the PING tool which comes with all versions of Windows. PING basically sends a short message (a 'ping') from one machine to another, the target machine responds, and the first machine tells you that it has got a response and how long the message took.

Example 1: if we just set up machines with IP addresses 192.168.0.1 and 192.168.0.2, you would type 'PING 192.168.0.1' in a DOS box on the machine with address 192.168.0.2. You should get a response something like:

```
Pinging192.168.0.1with32bytesofdata:

Replyfrom192.168.0.1:bytes=32time<10msTTL=32

Replyfrom192.168.0.1:bytes=32time<10msTTL=32

Replyfrom192.168.0.1:bytes=32time<10msTTL=32
```

```
Replyfrom192.168.0.1:bytes=32time<10msTTL=32
```

If we do get a response like this, then all is well. Any other response means that something is wrong. Check physical network connections first, then panic...

Every time you configure a new machine, we should check that we can PING the same machine - so always check that we can PING the first machine we set up. This way, if all machines can PING a single machine, it is very likely that all machines can PING each other as well. (Note that to be extra safe you should ping 'back' to the new machine as well, as some network configuration problems can mean that a ping will work in one direction but not the other).

Ping is a protocol that verifies whether a host is reachable by the local computer. Ping is usually used in a diagnostic capacity.

Windows has a command-line utility to perform a Ping. Its usage is:

```
ping <host name or IP>
```

Example 2:The following is sample output of a successful Ping:

```
D:\>ping127.0.0.1
Pinging127.0.0.1with32bytesofdata:

Replyfrom127.0.0.1:bytes=32time<10msTTL=128
Replyfrom127.0.0.1:bytes=32time<10msTTL=128
Replyfrom127.0.0.1:bytes=32time<10msTTL=128
Replyfrom127.0.0.1:bytes=32time<10msTTL=128

Pingstatisticsfor127.0.0.1:
   Packets:Sent=4,Received=4,Lost=0(0%loss),
Approximateroundtriptimesinmilli-seconds:
   Minimum=0ms,Maximum= 0ms,Average= 0ms
```

If a host cannot be reached, the output will look similar to this:

```
D:\>pingCAESAR

Pinging192.168.0.4with32bytesofdata:

Destinationhostunreachable.
Destinationhostunreachable.
Destinationhostunreachable.
Destinationhostunreachable.

Pingstatisticsfor192.168.0.4:
   Packets:Sent=4,Received=0,Lost=4(100%loss),
```

```
Approximateroundtriptimesinmilli-seconds:
    Minimum=0ms,Maximum= 0ms,Average= 0ms

Pingstatisticsfor127.0.0.1:
    Packets:Sent=4,Received=4,Lost=0(0%loss),
Approximateroundtriptimesinmilli-seconds:
    Minimum=0ms,Maximum=0ms,Average=0ms
```

pingisusedtodiagnoseconnection-relatedfailures.Byexecutingtheping command,youcandeterminewhetheraparticularTCP/IP-basedhostisavailable andrespondinginanondysfunctionalmanner.

Technically,thepingcommandistransmittingInternetControlMessageProtocol(ICMP)packetsbetweentwoTCP/IP-basedhosts.RememberthatICMPrelates tosessionmanagementandspecialcommunicationsbetweenhosts.WithICMP, messagesanderrorsregardingpacketdeliveryarereported.Greatstuff!

Thepingcommandhasseveralcommandlineswitchesthatincreaseitsfunctionality.Theseswitches,listedhere,maybeobservedbytypingping/?atthe commandline:

```
Usage:ping[-t][-a][-ncount][-lsize][-f][-iTTL][-vTOS]
                [-rcount][-scount][[-jhost-list]|[-khost-list]]
                [-wtimeout]destination-list
```

Options:

```
 1 -t             Pingthespecifiedhostuntilstopped.
                      Toseestatisticsandcontinue-typeControl-Break;
                      Tostop-typeControl-C.
 2 -aResolveaddressestohostnames.
   -ncount Numberofechorequeststosend.
   -lsize          Sendbuffersize.
 3 -f              SetDon'tFragmentflaginpacket.
 4 -iTTL               TimeToLive.
 5 -vTOS               T ypeOfService.
 6 -rcount         Recordrouteforcounthops.
 7 -scount         Timestampforcounthops.
 8 -jhost-list     Loosesourceroutealonghost-list.
 9 -khost-list     Strictsourceroutealonghost-list.
10 -wtimeout       Timeoutinmillisecondstowaitforeachreply.
```

follow the traditional six-step ping command food chain and its relationship to IPConfig (we call this phenomenon of IPConfig and ping working together as being reunited!

To Use the IPConfig and PING Commands

1. Run the IPConfig command on the local workstation and observe the TCP/IP configuration information.

2. Ping the internal loopback address to verify that TCP/IP is installed and configured correctly on the local host computer. This address is 127.0.0.1, a reserved address that can't be used as a real IP address on a network.

3. Ping the address of the local host computer to ensure that TCP/IP is working correctly. Here we are typically pinging the network adapter card(s).

4. Ping the IP address of the router or default gateway so that you know and may verify that the router/default gateway are functioning correctly. This also ensures that you have a functional infrastructure in place to communicate with a local host on the local network or subnet.

5. Ping the distant router across a WAN link if appropriate. Often you can ping a remote router yet are unable to ping the desired remote host. That's because something as simple as a return route may not be programmed.

6. Ping the IP address of the remote host. Success at this stage establishes that you can communicate through the remote router and that the remote host is functional.

A Few General Steps to Consider when the Ping Command doesn't Work Include:

- Reboot the computer after TCP/IP was installed or modified
- Check that the local host's address is valid as displayed in Internet Protocol (TCP/IP) Properties tab sheet under the Local Area Connection Properties, found under Network Connections if it is a static IP address
- If necessary, make sure Windows NT Server-based routing is operational and a link exists between routers. In other words, perhaps you're having a Telco-related communications problem.

Ping server

```
//headerfiles
#include<stdio.h>
#include<unistd.h>
#include<sys/types.h>
#include<netinet/in.h>
#include<string.h>
```

```
#include<sys/socket.h>
intmain()
{
//variabledeclarations
intsd,I=0,len;
structsockaddr_inser,cli;
chatarr[30]="";
//socketcreationandchecking
if(sd=socket(AF_INET,SOCK_DGRAM,0))<0)
{printf("/nERROR::SOCKETCREATIONPROBLEM\n");
return();
}
//initializethestructurestozero
bzero(&ser,sizeof(ser));
bzero(&cli,sizeof(cli));
//Assignthevaluestothestructures
ser.sin_family=cli.sin_family=AF_INET;
ser.sin_port=htons(2000);
ser.sin_addr.s_addr=cli.sin_addr.s_addr=hton(INADDR_ANY);
cli.sin_port=htons(3000);
//bindingandchecking
if(bind(sd,(structsockaddr*)&ser,sizesizeof(ser))<0)
{
printf("\nERROR::BINDINGPROBLEM\n");
return0;
}
len=sizeof(ser);
for(I=0;<4;++)
{
//receivethemessageandsendreplytotheclient
recvfrom(sd,&arr,30,0,(structsockaddr*)&cli,&len);
sendto(sd,"received",10,0,(structsockaddr*)&cli,len);
}
//closethesocket
close(sd);
return0;
}
```

ping client:

```
//headerfiles
#include<stdio.h>
#include<unistd.h>
#include<sys/types.h>
#include<netinet/in.h>
#include<string.h>
#include<sys/socket.h.
intmain()
{
//variabledeclarations
intsd,I=0,len;
longsec,msec;
structsockaddr-inser,cli;
structtimevaltp;
structtimezonep;
chararr[30]="";
//socketcreation& checking
if((sd=socket(AF_INET,SOCK_DGRAM,0))==_1)
{
printf("nERROR::SOCKETCREATIONPROBLEM\n");
return0;
}
//initializesthestructurestozero
bzero(&ser,sizeof(ser));
bzero(&cli,sizeof(cli));
//Assignthevaluestothestructures
ser.sin_family=cli.sin_family=AF_INET;
ser.sin_port=htons(2000);
ser.sin_adddr.s_addr.s_addr=htonl(INADDR_ANY);
cly.sin_port=htons(3000);
//Binding& checking
if(bind(structsockaddr*)&cli,sizeof(cli)==_1)
{.
printf("nERROR::BINDINGPROBLEM\n");
return0;
```

```
}
//readthedata
while(I<30)
{
scanf("%c",&arr[i]);
if(arr[I++]=='\n')
{
arr[I-1]='\0';
break;
}
}
len=sizeof(ser);
for(I=0;I<4;I++)
{
//getthetimebeforesendingthedata
gettimeofday(&tp,&p);
sec=tp.tv_sec;
msec=tp.tv_usec;
//sendthedatatotheserver
sendto(sd,"ping",5,0,(structsockaddr*)&ser,sizeof(ser));
//receivethereplymessagefromserver
recvfrom(sd,arr,10.0.(structsockaddr*)&ser,&len);
//getthetimeaftersending
gettimeofday(&tp,&p);
//timecalculationforsendingandreceiving
sec=tp.tv_sec-sec;
msec=tp.tv_usec-msec;
msec+=sec*1000000;
//printthemessage
if(!strcmp(arr,"received"))
printf("64bytesfrom127.0.0.1:icmp_seeq_no:!d)
time=!ldmicrosecs\n".i.msec);
}
//closethesocket
close(sd);
return0;
}
```

Question and Answer

Choose the best answer

1. A diskless client is not configured for DHCP. The client boots from a JumpStart server. How does the client obtain an IP address?
   (a) It does a DNS lookup
   (b) It issues an ARP request
   (c) It issues an RARP request
   (d) It reads the /etc/hosts file
   (e) It reads the /etc/nsswitch.conf file.

   Answer: c

2. Which LAN component forwards a packet between two separate networks based on the software protocol address?
   (a) Bridge
   (b) Router
   (c) Switch
   (d) Gateway
   (e) Repeater.

   Answer: b

3. In the five-layer TCP/IP model, which protocol is part of the same layer as IP?
   (a) TCP
   (b) UDP
   (c) PPP
   (d) ARP
   (e) ICMP.

   Answer: e

4. In the five-layer TCP/IP model, which two functions does the network interface layer provide? (Choose two)
   (a) Packet framing
   (b) Connections between applications
   (c) Data addressing between networks
   (d) Cyclical Redundancy Checking (CRC).

   Answer: a, d

5. Which is an automatically configured IPv6 address?
   (a) fe80::a00:20ff:fe8e:4f1c/10
   (b) fec0::a00:20ff:fe8e:4flc/10
   (c) ff00::a00:20ff:fe8e:4flc/10
   (d) fe80::a00:20fg:fe8e:4flc/10
   (e) fec0::a00:20fg:fe8e:4flc/10.

   Answer: a

6. What is the purpose of RARP?
   (a) It maps a 32-bit IP address to a 48-bit Ethernet address
   (b) It maps a 48-bit IP address to a 32-bit Ethernet address
   (c) It maps a 48-bit Ethernet address to a 32-bit IP address
   (d) It maps a 128-bit IP address to a 48-bit Ethernet address
   (e) It maps a 32-bit Ethernet address to a 128-bit IP address.

   Answer: c

7. The interface hme0 has the wrong IP address. Which command will re-establish the correct address of 192.168.20.118, broadcast of 192.168.20.127, and netmask of 255.255.255.192?
   (a) ifconfig hme0 192.168.20.118 netmask 255.255.255.0 + broadcast
   (b) ifconfig hme0 192.168.20.118 netmask 192.168.20.127 broadcast +
   (c) ifconfig hme0 192.168.20.118 netmask 255.255.255.127 broadcast +
   (d) ifconfig hme0 192.168.20.118 netmask 255.255.255.192 broadcast +
   (e) ifconfig hme0 192.168.20.118 netmask 255.255.255.192 + broadcast.

   Answer: d

8. You are not sure if you have received an Ethernet frame from a workstation you are trying to reach by Telnet, which is on the same logical network. You may have a cabling fault. Which command should you use to verify that you have recently received the MAC addresses of the workstation?
   (a) arp *-a*
   (b) arp *-n*
   (c) arp *-d*
   (d) arp *-f*
   (e) arp *-k*.

   Answer: a

9. What is the full pathname of the file which contains the clock type of an NTP server?

   Answer: /etc/inet/ntp.conf

   What is stored in DNS zone files?
   (a) The zones SOA record
   (b) The root name servers
   (c) The process ID of in.named file.
   (d) The name of the DNS cache dump.

   Answer: a

10. What does the following command do?

    Router(config)#ip default-network 172.68.0.0
    (a) No routing updates are sent on interface E0
    (b) If there is no route in the table, send the packet to the default Route 172.68.0.0
    (c) This would enter an administrative route in the routing table
    (d) This begins the configuration for the routing interface to use an access list.

    Answer: b

    This command tells the router to send the packet to the default route 172.68.0.0 if there is no route in the routing table for the packet.

11. Which of the following methods can be used on a router to control route update traffic? Choose four.
    (a) Passive interface
    (b) Default routes
    (c) Static routes
    (d) Active interface
    (e) Route update filtering.

    Answer: a, b, c, and e

    A passive interface, default routes, static routes, and route update filtering can all be used to control route update traffic.

12. What is the purpose of the "default-information originate always" command in OSPF?
    (a) Causes OSPF to accept routing protocol as it was originally provided
    (b) This is not a valid OSPF command
    (c) OSPF will always advertise a default route
    (d) Is applicable only on ASBR's for Internet default routes.

Answer: c

The purpose of the "default-information originate always" command in OSPF is to make sure that OSPF will always advertise a default route. This command ensures that the default route will get advertised into OSPF, even if the path to the default route goes down.

13. What command would you use to view the active/passive states of EIGRP routes?
    (a) show ip eigrp neighbors
    (b) show ip protocols state
    (c) show route eigrp
    (d) show ip eigrp topology.

Answer: d

You would use the "show ip eigrp topology" command to view the active/passive states of EIGRP routes, view the topology table, the number of successors, and the feasible distance to the destination.

14. Which of the following routing protocols sends a subnet mask along with the address? Choose three.
    (a) RIP v2
    (b) IGRP
    (c) EIGRP
    (d) RIP1
    (e) OSPF.

Answer: a, c, and e

RIP v2, EIGRP, and OSPF support VLSM, which sends a subnet mask along with the address.

15. Which addresses could you use if you had no need to connect to the Internet?
    (a) 10.0.0.0 to 10.255.255.255
    (b) 172.16.0.0 to 172.16.255.255
    (c) 192.168.0.0 to 192.168.255.255
    (d) 172.168.0.0 to 172.168.255.255
    (e) 20.0.0.0 to 20.155.255.255.

Answer: a, b, and c

16. If you had no need to connect to the Internet, you could use private addresses. These are 10.0.0.0 to 10.255.255.255, 172.16.0.0 to 172.16.255.255, and 192.168.0.0 to 192.168.255.255.

    You have two different routes in a routing table to destination

17. Write out the addresses in binary:

    10101100.00010000.00100000.01000000

    10101100.00010000.00100000.10000000

    ans The address match up to a certain point (in bold). This address would be 172.16.32.0 using the subnet mask of 255.255.255.0, which is 172.16.32.0/24.

18. You are given the address 192.168.49.32/27. How many subnets and hosts are available?
    (a) 6 subnets (b) 62 hosts
    (c) 30 hosts (d) 62 subnets.

Answer: a and c

19. Writing out the subnet mask /27 (255.255.255.224) in binary gives you: 11111111.11111111.11111111.11100000
    Looking at the last octet since this is the octet you use when subnetting on a class C address, you have three "on" bits (1's) and five "off" bits (0's). The number of subnets is 2n-2 where n is the number of "on" bits. So, 23-2=6 subnets. The number of hosts is 2y-2 where y is the number of "off" bits. So, 25-2=30 hosts
20. If you have an IP address of 172.16.1.10/25, what is the broadcast address that the host will use?
    (a) 172.16.255.255 (b) 172.16.1.255
    (c) 172.16.1.0 (d) 172.16.1.127.

Answer: d

With 25 bits of subnetting, we have the last seven bits to use as the host address. If we set each of these last seven bits to 1 (the definition of a broadcast address), then we get 172.16.1.127.

21. How many hosts will the 255.255.255.224 subnet mask support?
    (a) 6 (b) 14
    (c) 30 (d) 62.

Answer: c

If you convert 224 to binary, you get 11100000. With five host bits (i.e., bits set to 0 in the subnet mask), you can support 30 host addresses (25 – 2 = 30, where 5 is the number of host bits).

22. In what type of topology do all routers have a virtual connection to all other routers?
    (a) Full-mesh (b) Star
    (c) Hub-and-spoke (d) Bus.

Answer: a

In a full-mesh topology, all routers have a virtual connection to all other routers. The configuration of a fully meshed network can quickly become administratively prohibitive, because as the number of full-meshed routers grows, the number of required virtual links grows exponentially.

23. What is involved in peer-to-peer communication?
    (a) The sequential layer on another machine.
    (b) The sequential layer on the same machine.
    (c) The sequential protocol on the same machine.
    (d) The sequential protocol on another machine.
    (e) The corresponding layer on another machine.
    (f) The corresponding layer on the same machine.

Answer: e

24. In the five-layer TCP/IP model, which function does the transport layer provoide?
(a) Data routing
(b) Data formatting
(c) Physical connections
(d) End-to-end data transfer.

Answer: d

25. What is a link local address?
(a) A class D IPv4 address
(b) An IPv4 compatible IPv6 address
(c) An IPv6 address that will not be forwarded by a router
(d) An IPv6 address that will not be forwarded onto the Internet
(e) An IPv4 address given by a DHCP server on the same subnetwork.

Answer: c

26. The ping command uses which protocol?
(a) TCP encapsulated in IP
(b) UDP encapsulated in IP
(c) ICMP encapsulated in IP
(d) ICMP encapsulated in UDP.

Answer: c

27. What is the purpose of NTP?
(a) To register clock differences within a network.
(b) To synchronize clocks within a global network.
(c) To provide an accurate network clock transmitter.
(d) To synchronize clocks within a timezone network.

Answer: b

28. Which of the following layers provides end-to-end connections?
(a) Application Layer 7
(b) Presentation Layer 6
(c) Session Layer 5
(d) Transport Layer 4
(e) Network Layer 3
(f) Data Link Layer 2
(g) Physical Layer 1.

Answer: d

29. Which of the following layers would most likely provide connection oriented sei vice.
(a) Application Layer 7
(b) Presentation Layer 6
(c) Session Layer 5
(d) Transport Layer 4
(e) Network Layer 3
(f) Data Link Layer 2
(g) Physical Layer 1.

Answer: d

30. Which of the following layers defines network addressing and determines the best path?
(a) Application Layer 7
(b) Presentation Layer 6
(c) Session Layer 5
(d) Transport Layer 4
(e) Network Layer 3
(f) Data Link Layer 2
(g) Physical Layer 1.

Answer: e

31. Raw data is converted to segments at which layer?
    (a) Application Layer 7
    (b) Presentation Layer 6
    (c) Session Layer 5
    (d) Transport Layer 4
    (e) Network Layer 3
    (f) Data Link Layer 2
    (g) Physical Layer 1.

Answer: d

32. Segments are converted to Datagrams at which layer?
    (a) Application Layer 7
    (b) Presentation Layer 6
    (c) Session Layer 5
    (d) Transport Layer 4
    (e) Network Layer 3
    (f) Data Link Layer 2
    (g) Physical Layer 1.

Answer: e

33. Datagrams are converted to frames at which layer?
    (a) Application Layer 7
    (b) Presentation Layer 6
    (c) Session Layer 5
    (d) Transport Layer 4
    (e) Network Layer 3
    (f) Data Link Layer 2
    (g) Physical Layer 1.

Answer: f

34. Which of the following could be a feature of a connection-oriented service?
    (a) Flow Control
    (b) "Three-Way" hand shake
    (c) Error checking
    (d) Windowing
    (e) All of the above.

Answer: e

35. With a connection-oriented service a host will ACK (Acknowledge) with: (Answer all that apply)
    (a) The last (SEQ) sequence number received from the remote host
    (b) The next expected (SEQ) sequence number from the remote host
    (c) The last ACK number from the remote host
    (d) The current SEQ number from the remote "plus" 1
    (e) None of the above.

Answer: a, d

36. Simple Network Management Protocol uses what numeric value, in decimal, of the destination port field of the User Datagram Protocol (UDP) header?
    (a) 20
    (b) 21
    (c) 23
    (d) 69
    (e) 161.

Answer: e

37. The first segment of the "Three-Way Handshake" will most likely carry an ACK of (Choose the best answer):
    (a) 1
    (b) The SEQ number of the remote host "plus" 1

(c) 0 (d) There is no ACK.

(e) A randomly generated number.

Answer: c

38. Which one of the following describes the process of a TCP/IP host learning a remote host MAC address?
    (a) ARP (Address Resolution Protocol)
    (b) SLARP (Serial Line Address Resolution Protocol)
    (c) RARP (Reverse Address Resolution Protocol)
    (d) IARP (Inverse Address Resolution Protocol)
    (e) MOP (Maintenance Operation Protocol).

Answer: a

39. If mask 255.255.255.128 were used with a class B network, how many subnets could exits, with how many hosts per subnet respectively ?
    (a) 254 and 256 (b) 62 and 78
    (c) 54 and 1022 (d) 510 and 126.

Answer: d

40. Which of the following IP address are not in the same subnet as 190.4.80.80, mask 255.255.255.0
    (a) 190.4.80.1 (b) 190.4.90.1
    (c) 190.4.80.200 (d) 190.1.1.1.

Answer: b

41. when configuring a network card to communicate using TCP/IP which two entries are mandatory
    (a) IP address (b) Gateway
    (c) Wins server (d) Socket.

Answer: a

42. TCP/IP protocol properties are found as part of which control panel selection ?
    (a) modems (b) network
    (c) devices (d) tcp/ip protocol.

Answer: d

43. you find that your workstation has an IP address of 129.16.15.24 with subnet mask of 255.255.255.0.0 what is the network portion of that address
    (a) 129.0.0.0 (b) 129.16.0.0
    (c) 129.16.15.0 (d) 129.16.15.6.

Answer: b

44. The Inter NIC has assigned you an IP address of 205.46.15.0 what is the default subnet mask for this address?
    (a) 255.0.0.0 (b) 255.255.0.0
    (c) 255.255.255.0 (d) 255.255.255.255.

Answer: c

45. what happens to the TTL when a packet a crosses a router
   (a) the router adds 1 to the TTL
   (b) nothing happens to the TTL
   (c) the router subtracts 1 from the TTL
   (d) the router adds a number equal to the metric to the TTl.

Answer: c

46. An API is a set of
   (a) declarations (b) definitions
   (c) procedures (d) all of the above.

Answer: a

47. The structure to define an IPV4 address is called _____ and contains a field called _____
   (a) unit 8_t ; s_addr (b) s_addr;in_addr
   (c) in addr.; s addr (d) in_addr ; unit8_t.

Answer: unit 8_t ; s_addr

48. The _____ field in the socket structure is usually set 0 for a process using the services of TCP or UDP
   (a) family (b) type
   (c) protocol (d) local socket address.

Answer: protocol

49. The _____ field in the socket structure defines the protocol group
   (a) family (b) type
   (c) protocol (d) local socket address.

Answer: family

50. The _____ socket is used with a connection _oriented protocol
   (a) stream (b) datagram
   (c) raw (d) remote.

Answer: stream

51. The _____ socket is used with a connectionless protocol
   (a) stream (b) datagram
   (c) raw (d) remote.

Answer: datagram

52. The _____ socket is used with a connectionless protocol
   (a) stream (b) datagram
   (c) raw (d) remote.

Answer: raw

53. In network programming the _____ function set a specified number of bytes
   (a) memset (b) memcpy
   (c) memcmp (d) memstr.

Answer: memcpy

54. The _____ function provides information about the remote host

(a) hostent (b) hostname

(c) gethostbyname (d) getnameofhost.

Answer: hostent

55. A connectionless process issues the _____ system call to receive from the incoming queue the datagram sent by a remote process

(a) listen (b) receive

(c) bind (d) recfrom.

Answer: recfrom

56. A connection oriented process issues the _____ system call to send datagram to remote process

(a) sendto (b) bind

(c) accept (d) write.

Answer: sendto

57. The _____ system call adds the local socket address to an already created socket

(a) address (b) create

(c) bind (d) socket.

Answer: socket

58. The _____ system call creates a socket

(a) create (b) socket

(c) open (d) bind.

Answer: bind

59. The _____ system call converts a socket into passive socket

(a) convert (b) listen

(c) socket (d) bind.

Answer: convert

60. tcp lies between the _____ and the _____ layer of the tcp/ip protocol suite

(a) application; UDP (b) application; transport

(c) application; network (d) network; datalink.

Answer: application ; transport

61. IP is responsible for _____ communication while TCP is responsible for _____ communication

(a) host to host ;process to process

(b) process to process; host to host

(c) process to process; network to network

(d) network to network; process to process.

Answer: host to host ;process to process

62. A host can be identified by _____ while a program running on the host can be identified by _____

(a) an ip address; aport number
(b) a port number; a ip address
(c) an ip address; a host address
(d) an ip address; a well known port

Answer: an ip address ; aport number

63. The _____ address uniquely identifies a running application program
(a) ip address
(b) host
(c) NIC
(d) socket.

64. If a segment carries data along with an acknowledgement this is called _____
(a) backpacking
(b) piggybacking
(c) piggypacking
(d) mother helper.

Answer: piggybacking

65. The ___________field is used to order packet of message
(a) urgent pointer
(b) checksum
(c) sequence number
(d) acknowledgement number.

Answer: sequence number

66. The _____ field is used for error detection
(a) urgent pointer
(b) checksum
(c) sequence number
(d) acknowledgement number.

Answer: checksum

67. Multiply the header length field by _____ to find the total number of bytes in the tcp header
(a) 2
(b) 4
(c) 6
(d) 8.

Answer: 4

68. Urgent data requires the urgent pointer field as well as the URG bit in the _____ field
(a) control
(b) offset
(c) sequences number
(d) reserved.

Answer: control

69. The option field of the tcp header from 0 to _____ bytes
(a) 10
(b) 20
(c) 40
(d) 80.

Answer:

70. What is the maximum number of no operation options in one 32 bit word ?
(a) one
(b) two
(c) three
(d) four.

Answer: three

71. What is the maximum number of the end of option options in entire tcp header
(a) 30
(b) 10
(c) 9
(d) 1.

Answer: 1

72. Which option defines the maximum number of bytes in a tcp segment?
    (a) maximum segment size (b) window scale factor
    (c) time stamp (d) no operation.

Answer: maximum segment size

73. In _____ data are sent or processed at very in efficient rate such as 1 byte at a time
    (a) Nagle syndrome (b) silly window syndrome
    (c) sliding window syndrome (d) delayed acknowledgement.

Answer: silly window syndrome

74. To prevent silly window syndrome created by receiver that processes data at a very slow rate _____ can be used
    (a) clark solution (b) nagle algorithm
    (c) karns algorithm (d) all above answer.

Answer: clark solution

75. To prevent silly window syndrome created by sender that sends data at a very slow rate _____ can be used
    (a) clark solution (b) nagle algorithm
    (c) karns algorithm (d) all above answer.

Answer: Nagle algorithm

76. The tcp uses __________ for error detection
    (a) checksum (b) acknowledgement
    (c) time out (d) all above answer.

Answer: checksum

77. The _____ timer prevents a long idle connection between two TCPs
    (a) retransmission (b) persistences
    (c) Keepalive (d) time waited.

Answer: keepalive

78. The _____ timer is needed to handle the zero window size advertisement
    (a) retransmission (b) persistences
    (c) Keepalive (d) time waited.

Answer: persistences

79. Karns algorithm is used in calculation by the _____ timer
    (a) retransmission (b) persistences
    (c) Keepalive (d) time waited.

Answer: retransmission

80. The _____ timer is used in the termination phase
    (a) retransmission (b) persistences
    (c) Keepalive (d) time waited.

Answer: time waited

81. The timer _____ keeps track of the time between the sending of segment and the receipt of an acknowledgement
(a) retransmission
(b) persistences
(c) Keepalive
(d) time waited.

Answer: retransmission

82. The server issues _____ open while a client issues _____ open
(a) apassive active
(b) an active passive
(c) an ephemeral a wellknown
(d) a well known an ephemeral.

Answer: apassive active

83. Connection established involves. a _____ handshake, connection termination involves a _____ handshake
(a) one way two way
(b) two way three way
(c) three way three way
(d) three way four way.

Answer: three way four way

84. In the _____ state the server is waiting for the application to close
(a) closed
(b) established
(c) close wait
(d) last-ack.

Answer: close wait

TWO MARKS

1. What is IP?
   Internet Protocol (IP) is an unreliable, best effort delivery, connection-less protocol used for transmitting and receiving data between hosts in a TCP/IP network.
2. To which OSI layer does IP belong?
   IP belongs to the Network Layer (layer 3) in the OSI model.
3. Which RFC discusses IP?
   RFC 791 discusses about the IP protocol version 4.
4. Which version of IP is discussed in this document?
   IP version 4 (IPv4) is discussed in this document.
5. What do you mean by IP is an unreliable protocol?
   IP is a unreliable protocol because it does not guarantee the delivery of a datagram to its destination. The reliability must be provided by the upper layer protocols like TCP. IP does not support flow control, retransmission, acknowledgement and error recovery.
6. What do you mean by IP is a best-effort protocol?
   IP is a best-effort protocol, because it will make every effort to always transmit a datagram and also datagrams will not be just discarded. However, the delivery of the datagram to the destination is not guaranteed.
7. What do you mean by IP is a connection-less protocol?
   IP is a connection-less protocol because it does not maintain state information about the connection to a destination host. Each datagram is handled independent of other datagrams and also each datagram may reach the destination through different network routes.
8. What is the role of IP in the TCP/IP protocol suite?
   IP is used for
   (*i*) Transmitting data from higher-level protocols like TCP, UDP in IP datagrams, from one host to another host in the network.
   (*ii*) Identifying individual hosts in a network using an IP address.
   (*iii*) Routing datagrams through gateways and
   (*iv*) Fragmenting and reassembling datagrams based on the MTU of the underlying network.
9. What is an IP Datagram?
   An IP datagram is a basic unit of information used by the IP layer to exchange data between two hosts. A IP datagram consists of an IP header and data.
10. How higher-level data is carried by IP to a destination host?
    The data from higher-level protocols like TCP, UDP is encapsulated in an IP datagram and transmitted to the destination host. IP will not modify the higher-level data.
11. What is the minimum and maximum size of an IP datagram?

The minimum size of an IP datagram is 576 bytes and the maximum size is 65535 bytes.

12. What is the minimum and maximum size of an IP datagram header?
    The minimum size of an IP datagram header is 20 bytes. The maximum IP datagram header size is 60 bytes.
13. Is there a limitation on the minimum size of a IP datagram a network can handle?
    Yes. All IP networks must be able to handle datagrams of at least 576 bytes in length.
14. What is the byte order used for transmitting datagram headers in the TCP/IP protocol suite?
    All the datagram headers in the TCP/IP protocol suite are transmitted in the "big endian" byte order. *i.e.*, The most significant byte is transmitted first. This is also called as "network byte order"
15. Why there are two length fields (IP header length, IP datagram length) in the IP header?
    The size of the IP header is not fixed. Depending on the IP options present, the size of the IP header will vary. A separate field for the IP header length is added, so that the destination system can separate the IP datagram header from the payload.
16. How is the value for datagram identifier calculated?
    The IP datagram identifier is just a sequence number assigned by the transmitting host. The algorithm for assigning value to this field is not specified by the IP protocol.
17. What is the use of datagram identifier field?
    The IP datagram identifier field is used to uniquely identify and assemble the different fragments of an IP datagram.
18. Is the datagram identifier field unique for each IP datagram?
    Yes. The IP datagram identifier field is different for each IP datagram transmitted. The fragments of an IP datagram will have the same identifier value.
19. What is the use of Type Of Service field in the IP header?
    The Type Of Service (TOS) field is used TCP to describe the desired quality of service for an IP datagram by upper layer protocols like TCP. This field can be used to specify the nature and priority of a IP datagram (like Network Control, Immediate, Critical, etc) and the criteria for selecting a path for forwarding a datagram by a gateway.
20. What are the different types of criteria can be specified using the TOS field?
    The different types of criteria that can be specified by the TOS field in an IP datagram are:
    (*i*) Minimize delay, (*ii*) Maximize throughput
    (*iii*) Maximize reliability (*iv*) Minimize cost and
    (*v*) Normal service
21. Which RFC discusses the Type Of Service (TOS) field?
    RFC 1349 discusses the Type Of Service (TOS) field.

22. What is the use of the Time To Live (TTL) field in the IP header?

    The TTL field is used to limit the lifetime of a IP datagram and to prevent indefinite looping of IP datagrams.

23. How is the TTL field used to prevent indefinite looping of IP datagrams?

    The TTL field contains a counter value set by the source host. Each gateway that processes this datagram, decreases the TTL value by one. When the TTL value reaches zero, the datagram is discarded.

24. What is the typical value for the TTL field?

    The typical value for a TTL field is 32 or 64.

25. When is a datagram considered undeliverable?

    If a datagram cannot be delivered to the destination host due to some reason, it is considered an undeliverable datagram.

26. How a datagram becomes an undeliverable datagram?

    A datagram may become undeliverable, if

    (*i*) The destination host is down.

    (*ii*) The route for the destination host is not found.

    (*iii*) A network in the route to the destination host is down.

    (*iv*) The Time To Live (TTL) value of the datagram becomes zero.

27. What happens to an undeliverable datagram?

    An undeliverable datagram is discarded and an ICMP error message is sent to the source host.

28. Is it possible for an IP datagram to be duplicated?

    Yes. A host may receive the same copy of an IP datagram twice. It is upto the higher layer protocols to discard the duplicate copy of the datagram.

29. Which part of the IP datagram is used for calculating the checksum?

    The checksum field in the IP header covers only the IP header. The payload data is not used for calculating this checksum.

30. What the application wants from the transport layer ?

    (*i*) A reliable bit pipe to another application

    (*ii*) A unique address or addresses to be known by

31. What the transport layer gets from the network layer?

    (*i*) An unreliable bit pipe to another host

    (*ii*) Unique addresses for each host

    (*iii*) May be only one of connection-oriented and connectionless

    (*iv*) In TCP/IP, the network layer (IP) only provides an unreliable, connectionless protocol

    1. what does reliable mean?

32. Explain the Connection-Oriented vs. Connectionless ?

    (*i*) Connection-oriented must establish a connection between two hosts before sending data

    (*ii*) Connectionless just sends the data without establishing a connection

(*iii*) Connection-oriented must also terminate the connection after sending data
(*iv*) Connection-oriented usually means an ordered stream of bytes
(*v*) Connectionless usually means unordered pieces of data, usually called datagrams
(*vi*) TCP provides a reliable, connection-oriented service
1. reliable startup, sending, and shutdown
2. full-duplex (both directions simultaneously)
3. stream interface (continuous sequence of bytes -- no blocks or records)
(*vii*) But the TCP transport layer also provides applications access to an unreliable, connectionless service -- UDP, or "User Datagram Protocol", or just datagrams.

33. Transport layer may request the application to ask for ?
(*i*) Connection-oriented or connectionless service
(*ii*) Quality-of-service parameters
1. how much bandwidth can I get (or do I have)?

34. What are the Grouping data in all of the layers ?
(*i*) All network layers group data somehow
(*a*) we already saw that the data link layer uses frames
(*b*) we will use the word segment for TCP transport-layer groups,
(*c*) and packet for IP network-layer groups (datagram is also used).
(*ii*) So, TCP segments are contained in IP packets, which is contained in data-link layer frames
(*iii*) Though not one-to-one, of course.

35. The default CLOSED state, how does a client program normally get to the ESTABLISHED state?
The client calls the connect() function (or similar), which causes TCP to send an empty packet with the SYN control bit set (SYN_SENT). The remote peer's stack sees this "synchronize" request, and sends back an empty packet with the SYN and ACK bits set (*i.e.*, "I acknowledge your synchronize request"). When the client receives the SYN/ACK packet, it sends back an ACK packet, and reports a successful connection to the client program.

36. What is the normal TCP shutdown sequence?
The important thing to understand is that TCP is a bidirectional protocol. So, the connection is shut down in two identical stages, one for each "direction". One peer sends a packet with the FIN bit set, which the other end ACKnowledges; when the other end is also finished sending data, it sends out a FIN packet, which the other end ACKs, closing the connection.

37. What is the significance of the RST bit?
This is an abnormal close, also called "slamming the connection shut." It happens under several circumstances, but none of the common ones are documented in the Stevens diagram. Two of these cases you can cause from Winsock: the first method is to set SO_LINGER to 0 with setsockopt() and then call

closesocket(). The second method is to call shutdown() with how equal to 2, optionally followed by a closesocket() call.

38. Netstat shows lots of sockets in the TIME_WAIT state. What's wrong?

    Nothing's wrong. TIME_WAIT is absolutely normal. If you go through the state-transition diagram above, you see that every socket that gets closed normally goes through this state after it's closed. The TIME_WAIT state is a safety mechanism, to catch stray packets for that connection after the connection is "officially" closed. Since the maximum time that such stray packets can exist is 2 times the "maximum segment lifetime" (the time for a packet to go from your machine to the remote peer and for the response to come back), the TIME_WAIT state lasts for 2 * MSL. The only tricky bit is, there is no easy way to estimate MSL on the fly, so stacks traditionally hard-code a value for it, from 15 to 60 seconds. Thus, TIME_WAIT usually lasts 30-120 seconds.

39. My sockets keep getting into a FIN_WAIT_x state. What's wrong?

    Solution: Either your program or the remote peer is not closing the socket properly. If you walk through the state-transition diagram above, you can see that FIN_WAIT_1 usually happens when the local program calls shutdown() with the "how" parameter set to 1 or SD_SEND, but the remote peer doesn't respond. Likewise FIN_WAIT_2 happens when the remote peer shuts down its sending half of the connection, and your program doesn't respond. Since FIN_WAIT states often last up to 10 minutes, it's well worth the effort to fix the problem that's causing these FIN_WAIT states. (The exact length of the state depends on the stack and the circumstances that got it into that state.)

40. Often my calls to bind() fail when I try to re-bind to a port that I was just using. What's wrong?

    The socket is probably in one of the FIN_WAIT states or in the TIME_WAIT state. If it's a FIN_WAIT problem and you can't fix it, or if it's the normal TIME_WAIT state, the best thing to do is to redesign your program so that it doesn't need to keep re-binding. For example, a server program generally keeps its listener socket alive so that it doesn't have to keep re-binding it to the port; if you closesocket() the listener for some reason after each successful connection, your listener socket will go into the TIME_WAIT state for somewhere between 30 and 120 seconds, during which you won't be able to re-bind to that port. However, if you find that re-binding is absolutely necessary, setting the SOREUSEADDR option with setsockopt() will usually get you around the problem.

41. Why does the IP header have a Time to Live field?

    The easiest way to answer this is to consider what would happen without the field. A datagram with faulty information in the IP header could circulate around a network forever, forwarding from one gateway to another in search of a destination. With a Time to Live field, the number of bounces the datagram makes is limited. This has been proven to have an important effect on network traffic.

42. Give a one-sentence description of ICMP.

    A ICMP is an error-reporting system that communicates between different IP-based devices, providing information about status changes and failed devices.

43. What is a neighbor in the IP sense?

Neighbors are connected through a gateway. There is no physical restriction on the distance between neighbors. However, all neighbors share gateways.

44. How is an ICMP message datagram constructed?

The ICMP message, which can include part of the datagram that causes an ICMP message to be generated, has an ICMP header attached to the front of it. This is then passed to IP, which encapsulates it within an IP header. Finally, a network header is added when the datagram is sent over the network.

45. What are sockets?

A socket is a software interface that allows a program to link to another program in a physical IP communications network. Each TCP/IP-enabled computer has 65536 sockets available for TCP communications with other hosts. The sockets are really just logical ports, created by software, and all run over the same physical TCP/IP link. By agreement, certain socket numbers are assigned to services available on every TCP/IP host. Services such as FTP (File Transfer Protocol), which runs over socket 21, and telnet, which runs over socket 23. In general, sockets numbered 1 through 1023 are reserved for TCP/IP host services and should not be used for your applications.

46. What do you mean by "sockets programming"?

I mean creating a client/server application. That is, writing two programs -- one on a PC and one on the AS/400 -- that work together, pretty much like the AS/400 and a display file work together. The programs interact over a communications link such as Ethernet, Token Ring, the Internet, etc.

47. Why would using sockets programming be better than, say, using the ODBC driver or ADO?

It isn't always better - it depends on the application you're developing. For simple things you can usually get adequate results with the two-tier methods (ODBC/ADO). For more complex applications, using sockets gives you the ability to write the server program yourself, much like you would with a traditional green-screen program. Your server program can then access all of the 400's resources in the usual ways. It's not uncommon for a production-quality AS/400 server program to access 25 or 30 files. Applications like that are best written with a three-tier method such as sockets.

48. What about performance when using sockets?

Coding to the TCP/IP sockets support layer gives you the fastest possible response time and throughput because you're using the same communications support layer the TCP/IP utilities, such as FTP, are using.

49. What other utilities use sockets?

Many well-known TCP/IP utilities run over sockets, such as Telnet (5250 emulation runs over Telnet,) SMTP, POP, SNMP, etc. These common utilities run over ports 1-1024 (called "well-known" sockets). When you write a sockets application, you should avoid using sockets numbered under 1024.

Port names	Port Number	Service Descriptions
Echo	7	echoes whatever you send
discard	9	discards whatever you send
daytime	13	returns the destination machine's local time
qotd	17	returns the "quote of the day" for that machine
chargen	19	returns a test stream of characters
ftp	21	File Transfer Protocol port
smtp	25	Simple Mail Transfer Protocol port
finger	79	Finger protocol port
http	80	Web server port
pop3	110	POP version 3 port

50. How many sockets are there?

A socket is just a number used to identify a communications session. There are about 65,000 sockets for each of the two protocol groups - TCP (Transaction Communications Protocol) and UDP (User Datagram Protocol.) When you write sockets c/s applications you'll most likely be using TCP, which establishes a transactional link between the participants.

51. Under what jobs on the 400 do socket programs run?

Most of the TCP/IP sockets jobs are running in the QSYSWRK subsystem. There may also be some HTTP jobs running in their own subsystem, as well. You can tell what they are, generally, by the names (QTFTP... are FTP jobs, and you'll see Telnet there, etc.). If you create your own sockets server it will probably run in qsyswrk, as well...

52. How do I access the sockets support from within an RPG program?

Sockets support is accessed through IBM APIs. These APIs are intended to be used with the C programming language, but since the development of ILE they can be accessed from RPG. This makes it possible for a traditional AS/400 programmer to develop a production-quality client/server application in much the same manner as they would develop a green-screen program.

53. Why should I code a client/server application like a green-screen program?

All the best features of the PC are used (like the GUIs and access to the PC's other applications - Excel, Word, e-mail) while retaining the AS/400's best features (central data storage and management, security, processing power).

54. What do I have to code on the PC side?

You have to know enough about a client language (like Visual Basic) to put up the screens and collect the information from the user (again, much like a display file program.) The actual communications through sockets from the client side is relatively easy because there are custom controls available. A custom control is a wrapper for low-level communications processes.

55. What do I have to code on the AS/400 side?

The AS/400 side is not so easy. To code to the sockets support layer, you have to learn how to use a half-dozen or so sockets APIs. Here are some function names and their meanings: socket -- create a descriptor for use in network communication; connect -- connect to a remote peer; closesocket -- terminate communication and deallocate a descriptor; bind -- bind a local IP address and protocol port to a socket; listen -- place the socket in passive mode and set the number of incoming TCP connections the system will queue (server); accept -- accept the next incoming connection (server); recv -- acquire incoming data from a stream connection or the next incoming message; send -- send outgoing data or a message; setsockopt -- change the options for a socket.

56. How does the server handle multiple requestors?

On the 400, there's a main server program that "listens" over a well-known socket (at least well-known to your clients, but not in the 1-1024 range) for incoming service requests (like for customer inquiry). The main server program finds an available socket and submits a new server job that performs specific functions for your request.

57. What does "socket binding" mean?

"Binding" is the actual process of actually acquiring the logical socket resource used in communications.

58. Can more than one client connect to the same server port at the same time? Will the server serve the multiple clients?

No. You may specify that multiple incoming requests for processing be queued, but each process would be assigned it's own thread (or job).

59. Can I connect a sockets client to a port that was created by a socket server from a different application?

No. Normally, you use two sockets server program. A main server program that "listens" for incoming requests over a well-known socket. When a request is received, an available socket is found and a second server job is program is spawned (submitted.) The original connection to the main server program is ended, and the client is instructed to reconnect to the spawned server, under the assigned socket number. Typically, a production-quality c/s application will use a range of socket numbers, like 18201-18300. Port 18201 is the well-known port and 18202-18300 are for individual spawned jobs.

60. How do the sockets link one program to another?

Pretty much the same as a display file application. Sockets is the underlying communications support that allows two programs to pass data back and forth based on IP address and port number, much the same as a display file is controlled from a driver program through operating system support for interactive sessions. In sockets programming, you read and write to a sockets port, instead of a display file.

61. Are sockets strictly 'TCP' or can you use 'UDP'?

There are both (about 65000 of each.) When you establish your communications session, you tell TCP/IP support which "family" of protocols you'll be using -- TCP or UDP.

62. What environment & languages do we use to do sockets programming?

The main thrust of this occasion is to place the server program on the AS/400, written in an ILE language like RPG. On the client side (PC), a program is created to interact with the user and to perform communications with the server (just like a fancy display file program). This client program is written in VB, C, Java, PowerBuilder, VA -- anything that can get at TCP/IP communications support using Windows APIs or a custom control. VB's the easiest.

63. Does the server establish the port number?

 Yes. The server must be up and "listening" for an incoming connection request over a well-known port. (See prior answer regarding using a range of ports.)

64. How can I detect when a client has disconnected?

 The main server program will receive a transmission from the client, but the transmission data will be zero bytes. The server program will recognize this as a disconnect request from the client and end gracefully. svenkatr65399: How does the server do the session management for multiple simultaneous clients?

 Frequently asked questions about FTP

65. What is FTP?

 FTP is an Internet standard or protocol for transferring files between any two computers. Special software allows a computer to act as an FTP server, making files available to others across the network. Other computers can connect to the server using client software and either retrieve files that are there or put new files on the server.

66. What would I use FTP for?

 FTP has a variety of uses. You might want to make backup copies of files on your computer on a remote server. Or you might want to access files on your office computer from your computer at home, via a modem link. A colleague might leave files on an FTP server for you to collect later, or use FTP to share files between a number of users. All of these facilities are useful, but these days the most common use of FTP is to retrieve software to install on your personal computer.

67. Is FTP restricted to a particular type of computer?

 No, any type of computer that can connect to the Internet can act as either FTP client or server. One of the advantages of FTP is that files can be easily exchanged between different types of computer - say a Mac and a PC, or a PC and a Unix workstation. This is not always straightforward however

68. What is anonymous FTP?

 Normal FTP involves connecting to a server which you already have an account (username and password) on. For example, if you register you might use FTP to download datafiles created by your use of one of Gum's packages. But FTP is also a simple way of making files available to a wide range of people. For example, the C&IT Services have licensed certain packages for College use: the cheapest and most efficient way of making this available is via our own download site, so we do this whenever licence conditions permit. College members can log on to the server and quickly and easily retrieve the package, effectively at no cost. This saves on administration, the cost of copying software to floppy disks and distributing the disks and so on.

 Anonymous FTP servers can be accessed without having an account. Instead of a username, you will normally login under the username ftp or anonymous - all anonymous servers will accept one or both of these usernames. And instead of a password you should type your full e-mail address, . Anonymous login names and passwords can be preset in WS_FTP and Fetch to save you typing them in every time.

Access to our anonymous FTP server is limited to computers directly attached to the King's network (this includes computers which access the network via RAMS (Remote Access Modem Service). Students who use alternative Internet Service Providers (ISPs) at home can download software in the PAWS rooms and save them on floppy disks. But there are many hundreds of servers around the world which can be accessed anonymously and without restriction such as the UK Academic Mirror Service.

69. What are 'downloading' and 'uploading'?

Downloading is the process of retrieving files from a remote server and saving them on your local computer. Uploading is the reverse - sending files from your computer to the remote server. Another term in FTP for downloading is Get, and uploading is also referred to as an FTP Put.

70. What software can I use for FTP?

For Microsoft Windows 95/98/NT our recommended package is WS_FTP. For the Macintosh we recommend Fetch. When we connect PCs or Macs to the College network the appropriate FTP package is generally installed, and this is also the case for computers in the PAWS rooms. If you are a registered user of our general Unix server Gum, FTP software is provided as part of the operating system and is invoked by typing ftp at the system prompt. You can also use Netscape Navigator for anonymous FTP retrievals only by typing in the URL of the server, for example ftp://ftp.kcl.ac.uk, and see the section on viruses.

71. How do I initiate an FTP session?

Start up Fetch on the Mac or WS_FTP on the PC in the normal way. Type in the name of the host you want to connect to and the password. You can transfer files either by using Get or Put on the Mac, or on the PC, by selecting a file and clicking the arrow in the appropriate direction to move a specific file.

72. Can I transfer more than one file at a time?

Yes. Check the help files for WS_FTP and Fetch for instructions. On Unix FTP use the mget and mput commands.

Can I view the contents of a file within my FTP application?

Yes, provided that it is a text file. Check the help files for WS_FTP and Fetch for instructions.

73. What are software archives?

Software archives are anonymous FTP servers which can normally be used by anyone with Internet access. The software on these archives falls into three main types. Freeware or public domain software is software which you can obtain and install free of charge. Shareware is software which you can download and use for an initial period of evaluation. If you find the software useful then a small fee is payable to register the package and make yourself eligible for upgraded versions.

The third category is updates to software you already use - generally bug fixes or enhancements to packages. Companies such as Microsoft and Apple use anonymous FTP to make this kind of software available to registered users of their software.

Actually, another type of archive exists - these are collections of documents, such as literary texts or public records.

74. What do ASCII/text/binary/image/raw data mean?

Broadly speaking there are two types of FTP transfer - text transfer and binary transfer. One of the primary differences between an ASCII (American Standard Code for Information Interchange) or text and a binary transfer (in fact the only real one of note) is in the treatment of end-of-line. A binary transfer just copies the bytes with no conversion, an ASCII transfer copies bytes but also changes the end-of-line representation to that of the destination system (*e.g.*, it might convert CR/LF(Carriage Return/Line Feed) to LF. Other bytes can exist and are copied as is (even non-printing bytes). One other difference, which is a result of this end-of-line conversion, is that the destination system needs to buffer an incoming line in ascii mode in order to write out the whole line (you can't always write part lines in some systems). As a result, there may be a restriction on the maximum line length of an ASCII or text transfer, whereas there is never any such limit with a binary transfer.

On the whole, the transfer software will choose the right kind of transfer depending on the file but you can override it if necessary. Plain text will go as ASCII or text and Word files, images and PDF (Portable Document Format) as binary. On the Macintosh these last two go as Raw Data. There are also variations on binary, such as MacBinary.

75. What is file compression?

Compression is a way of improving the efficiency of FTP by making files smaller. Examples include ZIP on the PC, BinHex and Stuff It on the Mac and GZIP and TAR on Unix systems. Compressed files occupy less space on FTP servers, so that they can accommodate more files in total, and also minimise file transfer time. File transfers can be time-consuming, so the smaller the file the quicker the transfer. You can then expand the file once it is on your computer, see section on file formats.

Compression software works by analysing files and looking for duplicated information. The software then creates a smaller, compressed version of the file. In a compressed file recurring information appears once, and other occurrences are replaced with a pointer to this first occurrence. Very high levels of compression can be achieved with some files. More than one file can be included in an archive file, so it can also be a useful way to send collections of files via FTP or e-mail.

76. What is file encoding?

Different types of computer and operating system have different file structures. File encoding allows a file created on one type of computer to be converted into a convenient file format, so that it can safely be stored on another type of computer. Storing does not mean that the file can be executed or even opened successfully on a machine that can store it. If you want to retrieve the file and use it, it will need to be decoded in line with the system it is to be used on, see section on file formats. Some files are compressed and then encoded before being placed on FTP servers, some are just encoded and some are just compressed.

File formats

77. What is ZIP?

ZIP is a widely used standard for compressing datafiles. It is common on most platforms and is the preferred compression format for PC users. To encode and decode ZIP archives on the PC you need special software. Although ZIP is not common on the Mac, packages like Zip. It allow Mac users to encode and decode ZIP files. ZIP files usually have the file extension .zip.

78. What is BinHex?

BinHex is a standard adopted by the Macintosh early on for file encoding. It converts binary files into text files, so that they can be stored on any type of computer and passed between different computers. BinHex files are always bigger than the original data files, so it is common to compress the file first before using BinHex to encode it. Fetch (ftp package) on the Macintosh can be preset to decode BinHex files while downloading them. Standalone packages that understand BinHex include BinHex 4 and the very versatile Stuffit Expander.

NB - You should only use version 4 of BinHex - later versions produce files with an incompatible format which is not widely used on the Internet. BinHex files usually have the file extension .hqx.

79. What is StuffIt?

StuffIt is a widely used standard for compressing datafiles. It is mainly used on the Macintosh platform but Stuffit archives can also be understood by PCs with appropriate software. To decode Stuffit archives you need the package StuffIt Expander, which is available for Mac and PC (16-bit only). StuffIt Expander is freeware. To create Stuffit archives you need a package like StuffIt Lite (Macintosh only). Stuffit files usually have the file extension .sit.

80. What is StuffIt Expander?

Stuffit Expander is a versatile program for decoding and expanding archives and encoded files. The Mac version handles the most common type of Mac archives and encoded files - StuffIt, Compact Pro (.sit, .sea, and .cpt), BinHex (.hqx), and MacBinary (.bin). Stuffit Expander is freeware. A shareware add-on to the package called DropStuff with Expander Enhancer adds drag and drop facilities and the ability to deal with the following file types: Zip (.zip), ARC (.arc), gzip (.gz), Unix Compress (.Z), UUencoded (.uu), and Tar (.tar). Stuffit Expander for Macintosh is perhaps the simplest way for Mac users to decode the most common files, although other packages are available.

StuffIt Expander for Windows expands files in the following formats: Stuffit (.sit), Zip (.zip), BinHex (.hqx), MacBinary (.bin), ARC (.arc), Arj (.arj) and gzip (.gz). It is a 16-bit application which works under either Windows 3.x or Windows 95. It may be useful for PC users who regularly need to make use of Mac files and archives, but it is now something of an ageing package. Stuffit Expander for Windows cannot handle segmented Zip files.

81. What is Compact Pro?

Compact Pro is a standard for compressing datafiles on the Macintosh. It is less common than StuffIt files. To decode Compact Pro archives use the Compact Pro package itself or StuffIt Expander. To create Compact Pro archives you need a copy of Compact Pro. Compact Pro archives usually have the file extension .cpt.

82. What is BOO?

BOO is a PC standard for compressing data files. It is now rare and you are less and less likely to encounter it. Most PC archives are created in ZIP format.

83. What is GZIP?

GZIP (Gnu Zip) is a compression utility often used for compressing files on Unix FTP servers. It is broadly the same as ZIP except it circumvents the algorithm patents used in ZIP. GZIP archives usually have the file extension .gz.

84. What is Unix Compress?

Unix compress, sometimes just called compress, is an earlier version of LZW and is an alternative compression standard to GZIP. Compress files usually have the extension .Z.

85. What is TAR?

TAR is a Unix file encoding method, originally used for backing up to tape - the name is a contraction of Tape ARchiver. TAR files usually have the extension .tar.

86. What is MacBinary?

MacBinary is a particular type of binary encoding primarily used for Macintosh files. Many files on Macintosh archives are encoded with MacBinary. On the Macintosh Stuffit Expander can decode MacBinary, and Fetch can decode and encode MacBinary. Windows Stuffit Expander can also decode MacBinary files, which usually have the file extension .bin.

87. What is a self-extracting archive?

All of the encoding and compression types we have described so far require special PC or Mac software to be interpreted properly. Not everyone will have the right software, so sometimes it is preferable to create files which can expand themselves without the need of additional software.

On PC archives, these files will generally have the extension .exe, which is the standard DOS extension for any executable file. When you retrieve a .exe file from an archive to your PC and run it, it will expand the archive. Some .exe files will also then install the program you have retrieved for you. Others will create an installer application which you then need to run.

On Macintosh archives, self-extracting files will generally have the extension .sea. Double-clicking on the icon of a .sea file will cause it to expand. Some .sea files will also then install the program you have retrieved for you. Others will create another installer application which you need to run.

88. What's the difference between Web software archives and FTP software archives?

Many anonymous FTP archives are being changed into Web archives to make them easier to use. Anonymous FTP archives hold many different files, sometimes numbering in the thousands, so it can be difficult to locate a file you're interested in if you don't already know the directory structure well. Searching FTP server directory trees is often crude and difficult. As a result many of the popular archives are offering Web interfaces of various sophistication, as well as their FTP interface. This allows you to use Web search tools and hopefully locate what you need more quickly and easily. Some archives are now Web-only.

89. What are 'mirrors'?

There are many useful FTP sites overseas, particularly in North America, but connection can be a problem with these, more so than using e-mail or the World Wide Web. Sending mail messages or reading Web pages does not require a continuous connection between your computer and the remote computer. Mail messages quickly leave your computer and then are routed to their destination via a number of intermediate steps - once you have sent the message you can forget about it as it travels on its way. Similarly, once you have loaded up a Web page and associated graphics in your browser you break the connection with the Web server you got the page from. You only connect to it again if you request a further page, which is a relatively efficient use of the network.

FTP transfers require a continuous connection between the client machine and the server. If the file is a large one then you may need to be connected to the server for some time. If the server is thousands of miles away, this may be a problem: if the network between the two machines gets busier with other traffic, or if the server is dealing with a large number of connections, your file transfer may start to slow down unacceptably. In some cases your connection may even be broken. It is not uncommon to see estimated transfer times of two or three hours or even longer.

One way round this is to provide 'mirror' sites. These are essentially an identical copy of an FTP site at a nearer geographical location. For example, a US site may have mirrors in the UK, continental Europe and Australia. This means that you can connect to the mirror nearby and get the file you are after much more quickly and efficiently. Mirrors are regularly synchronised with the 'parent' site, so they are normally very up to date. Try the UK Academic Mirror site.

90. What support is available for software obtained from archives? -

Computing &IT Services agree the range of packages it supports with the College. These negotiations also determine the level of support. For example, our supported word processor for Windows and the Macintosh is Microsoft Word and our supported e-mail clients are Simeon and Eudora Light; we do not offer support for other word processing or mail packages. Computing &IT Services support is based on users adopting a standard desktop using officially supported products.

If you find a package on the Internet which you think may be useful and download and install it on your computer you do so at your own risk and we can offer you no support. We are not trying to discourage you from doing this; in many cases the software will be trouble-free. But we cannot be expected to support a package we may never have seen and whose effects on your system may be unpredictable.

On the other hand if you download bug fixes or enhancements for supported packages then we would generally support them, provided the software is not intended for a version of the software which we do not support. An example might be Internet Assistant, an add-on for Word 6 (Windows and Mac) which allows Word documents to be converted to Web pa.

91. What is a cache server or proxy server? Should I use it?

As mentioned earlier, long-distance Internet connections can be a problem. JANET, the UK academic network, has a dedicated undersea cable connection to the USA known as the Fat Pipe. All UK higher education institutions access American Internet sites via the Fat Pipe, and at certain times this makes connections slow down. To make matters worse, there is no direct JANET connection to the Pacific area (Australia, New Zealand, Japan etc): any connection requests to that part of the world first travel to the US via the Fat Pipe, then cross the USA and press on to their destination.

One way round this problem is to keep local copies of frequently accessed documents and files. One way to do this with archives is to set up mirror sites, but not all sites are mirrored. An alternative is to set up a proxy or cacheing server and send connection requests via the server rather than directly.

Essentially a cache is used for holding temporary copies of something; in the ftp context, the cache holds files retrieved from ftp servers. The sole purpose of a cache is to save time - and more importantly, bandwidth - if the file is requested a second time. Let's suppose that yesterday morning I downloaded some software from an archive in the USA, and later in the day you tried to retrieve the same package from the same location. It took me a while to retrieve the file, and it would probably take you even longer in the afternoon, as the transatlantic link tends to be busier then. If we had both configured our browsers to use the cache, a copy of the file would have been placed there at the same time as I retrieved it to my computer. When you tried to retrieve the file later, your browser would first check whether there was a copy of the file held on the cache, and discovering that there was, would retrieve it from there rather than from the original server. As you got the file from a machine on the King's network you would normally save a significant amount of time.

There are several levels of caching. Browsers usually have caches; Netscape, for example, sets aside disk space by default in order to save copies of the pages you download. A browser cache is only accessible to the user(s) of that browser, but servers can also have caches: they permit a large store of material to be held at the server site, for all local users to access. At a higher level, we can have national caches; the national cache at HENSA has a vast capacity and holds copies of pages downloaded by any user in the UK who chooses to make use of the cache. If a user configures their copy of Netscape (or other browser) to point to the local cache here at King's, and requests a file, the browser will first check its own cache, then the local server cache. If the page isn't found, the cache server will contact the parent and neighbours. If a parent or neighbour cache does not reply within 2 seconds, then the request will be forwarded to the default source.

For instructions on configuring Netscape, see Local Cache Configuration.

92. What is "ping"?

"Ping" is a protocol used to test whether another device on the network is reachable and active. Ping is essentially an echo service -- the server responds with a copy (or near copy) of the client's original packet. Ping is very lightweight, causing very little network or CPU overhead. However, ping tests a significant portion of overall network functionality.

Ping is much more powerful than the version found on typical Unix workstations. Ping can use ICMP, UDP, or SNMP as the underlying protocol (Most other versions only use ICMP.) gives the user control over a large number of operational parameters including the packet rate, the packet size, the data pattern included in the packet, the reporting interval, and the underlying protocol to use.

Ping also checks that the data which it receives from the server is a correct copy of that which was sent. (Many UNIX implementations do not do this.)

93. What is "ARP"?

ARP is the Address Resolution Protocol. ARP is typically used by TCP/IP hosts to ascertain the Ethernet address of a host on a LAN gives its user the ability to send an ARP request either to ascertain a device's Ethernet address or as a form of "reachability" test.

94. What is TCP/IP?

TCP/IP is a name given to the collection (or suite) of networking protocols that have been used to construct the global Internet. The protocols are also referred to as the DoD (dee-oh-dee) or Arpanet protocol suite because their early development was funded by the Advanced Research Projects Agency (ARPA) of the US Department of Defense (DoD).

The TCP/IP name is taken from two of the fundamental protocols in the collection, IP and TCP. Other core protocols in the suite are UDP and ICMP. These protocols work together to provide a basic networking framework that is used by many different application protocols, each tuned to achieving a particular goal.

TCP/IP protocols are not used only on the Internet. They are also widely used to build private networks, called internets (spelled with a small 'i'), that may or may not be connected to the global Internet (spelled with a capital 'I'). An internet that is used exclusively by one organization is sometimes called an intranet.

95. How is TCP/IP defined?

All of the protocols in the TCP/IP suite are defined by documents called Requests For Comments (RFC's). An important difference between TCP/IP RFC's and other (say, IEEE or ITU) networking standards is that RFC's are freely available online.

RFC's can be composed and submitted for approval by anyone. Standards RFC's are often the product of many weeks or months of discussion between interested parties designated as working groups, during which time drafts of the proposed RFC are continually updated and made available for comment. These discussions typically take place on open mailing lists which welcome input from all quarters. The RFC approval process is managed by the Internet Engineering Steering

Group (IESG) based on recommendations from the Internet Engineering Task Force (IETF) which is a prime mover in the formation of working groups focused on strategic TCP/IP issues. You can find out more about IESG and IETF activities from the IETF home page at <http://www.ietf.org/>.

Not all RFC's specify TCP/IP standards. Some RFC's contain background information, some provide hints for managing an internet, some document protocol weaknesses in the hope that they might be addressed by future standards, and some are entirely humorous.

96. Where can I find RFC's?

The Definitive RFC Repository

The official and definitive RFC repository is the anonymous FTP archive maintained by the Information Sciences Institute of the University of Southern California at <ftp://ftp.isi.edu/in-notes/>. It is reachable via the Web at <http://www.rfc-editor.org/>.

RFC Repository Mirror Sites

The RFC repository is mirrored at many sites on the Internet, and you may get a faster response from a local archive than you would from the often-overworked ISI site. Primary mirrors are updated at the same time as the ISI site. Secondary mirrors may lag by a few hours or days. The current primary mirror sites are:

97. How do I find the right RFC?

There are over 2500 RFC's. Each RFC is known by a number. For instance, RFC 1180 presents a tutorial on TCP/IP, RFC 1920 lists the current standards RFC's and explains the RFC standards process, and RFC 1941 is a FAQ list on the topic of Internet deployment in educational establishments. RFC numbers are assigned in ascending order as each RFC is approved.

The RFC files in the archive are named rfcNNNN.txt where NNNN is the number of the RFC. For instance, the text of RFC 822 is contained in the file named rfc822.txt. A small number of RFC's are also available in PostScript format, in which case a file named rfcNNNN.ps will exist in addition to the .txt file.

Basic information (number, title, author, publication date and so on) on all of the RFC's is contained in the RFC index document named rfc-index.txt which you can find alongside the RFC's at any of the RFC archive sites. If you don't know which RFC's you need, the index is a good place to start. The index also indicates the current status of each RFC. The content of an RFC does not change once the RFC has been published, but since TCP/IP is in a constant state of evolution the information in one RFC is often revised, extended, clarified and in some cases completely superseded by later RFC's. Annotations in the index indicate when this is the case.

98. What is IP?

Internet Protocol (IP) is the central, unifying protocol in the TCP/IP suite. It provides the basic delivery mechanism for packets of data sent between all systems on an internet, regardless of whether the systems are in the same room or on opposite sides of the world. All other protocols in the TCP/IP suite depend on

IP to carry out the fundamental function of moving packets across the internet. In terms of the OSI networking model, IP provides a Connectionless Unacknowledged Network Service, which means that its attitude to data packets can be characterised as "send and forget". IP does not guarantee to actually deliver the data to the destination, nor does it guarantee that the data will be delivered undamaged, nor does it guarantee that data packets will be delivered to the destination in the order in which they were sent by the source, nor does it guarantee that only one copy of the data will be delivered to the destination.

Because it makes so few guarantees, IP is a very simple protocol. This means that it can be implemented fairly easily and can run on systems that have modest processing power and small amounts of memory. It also means that IP demands only minimal functionality from the underlying medium (the physical network that carries packets on behalf of IP) and can be deployed on a wide variety of networking technologies.

The no-promises type of service offered by IP is not directly useful to many applications. Applications usually depend on TCP or UDP to provide assurances of data integrity and (in TCP's case) ordered and complete data delivery.

The fundamentals of IP are defined in RFC 791. RFC 1122 summarises the requirements that must be met by an IP implementation in an Internet host, and RFC 1812 summarises the IP requirements for an Internet router.

99. How Is IP Carried On A Network?

IP really isn't very fussy about how its packets are transported. The details of how an IP packet is carried over a particular kind of network are usually chosen to be convenient for the network itself. As long as the transmitter and receiver observe some convention that allows IP packets to be differentiated from any other data that might be seen by the receiver, then IP can be used to carry data between those stations.

On a LAN, IP is carried in the data portion of the LAN frame and the frame header contains additional information that identifies the frame an IP frame. Different LAN's have different conventions for carrying that additional information. On an Ethernet the Ethertype field is used; a value of 0x0800 identifies a frame that contains IP data FDDI and Token Ring use frames that conform to IEEE 802 Logical Link Control, and on those LAN's IP is carried in Unnumbered Information frames with Source and Destination LSAP's of 0xAA and a SNAP header of 00-00-00-08-00.

The only thing that IP cares strongly about is the maximum size of a frame that can be carried on the medium. This controls whether, and to what extent, IP must break down large data packets into a train of smaller packets before arranging for them to be transmitted on the medium. This activity is called "fragmentation" and the resulting smaller and incomplete packets are called "fragments". The final destination is responsible for rebuilding the original IP packet from its fragments, an activity called "fragment reassembly".

100. Does IP Protect Data On The Network?

IP itself does not guarantee to deliver data correctly. It leaves all issues of data protection to the transport protocol. Both TCP and UDP have mechanisms that guarantee that the data they deliver to an application is correct.

IP does try to protect the packet's IP header, the relatively small part of each packet that controls how the packet is moved through the network. It does this by calculating a checksum on the header fields and including that checksum in the transmitted packet. The receiver verifies the IP header checksum before processing the packet. Packets whose checksums no longer match have been damaged in some way and are simply discarded.

The IP checksum is discussed in detail in RFC 1071, which also includes sample code for calculating the checksum. RFC 1141 and RFC 1624 describe incremental modification of an existing checksum, which can be useful in machines such as routers which modify fields in the IP header while forwarding a packet and therefore need to compute a new header checksum.

The same checksum algorithm is used by TCP and UDP, although they include the data portion of the packet (not just the header) in their calculations.

101. What is ARP?

Address Resolution Protocol (ARP) is a mechanism that can be used by IP to find the link-layer station address that corresponds to a particular IP address. It defines a method that is used to ask, and answer, the question "what MAC address corresponds to a given IP address?". ARP sends broadcast frames to obtain this information dynamically, so it can only be used on media that support broadcast frames. Most LAN's (including Ethernet, FDDI, and Token Ring) have a broadcast capability and ARP is used when IP is running on those media. ARP is defined in RFC 826. That definition assumes an Ethernet LAN. Additional details fór ARP on networks that use IEEE 802.2 frame formats (IEEE 802.3 CSMA/CD, IEEE 802.4, IEEE 802.5 Token Ring) are in RFC 1042. ARP on FDDI is described in RFC 1390.

When IP is runnning over non-broadcast media (say, X.25 or ATM) some other mechanism is used to match IP addresses to media addresses. IP really doesn't care how the media address is obtained.

RFC 903 defines Reverse ARP (RARP) which lets a station ask the question "which IP address corresponds to a given MAC address?&quot. RARP is typically used to let a piece of diskless equipment discover its own IP address as part of its boot procedure. RARP is rarely used by modern equipment; it has been supplanted by the Boot Protocol (BOOTP) defined in RFC 1542. BOOTP in turn is being supplanted by the Dynamic Host Configuration Protocol (DHCP).

102. What is IPv6?

IP Version 6 (IPv6) is the newest version of IP, sometimes called IPng for "IP, Next Generation". IPv6 is fairly well defined but is not yet widely deployed. The main differences between IPv6 and the current widely-deployed version of IP (which is IPv4) are:

- o IPv6 uses larger addresses (128 bits instead of 32 bits in IPv4) and so can support many more devices on the network, and
- o IPv6 includes features like authentication and multicasting that had been bolted on to IPv4 in a piecemeal fashion over the years.

103. What happened to IPv5?

Or, &quot"Why are we skipping from IPv4 to IPv6?"

IPv5 never existed. The version number "5" in the IP header was assigned to identify packets carrying an experimental non-IP real-time stream protocol called ST. ST was never widely used, but since the version number 5 had already been allocated the new version of IP was given its own unique identifying number, 6. ST is described in RFC 1819.

104. What is the 6bone?

The 6bone is the experimental IPv6 backbone being developed using IPv6-in-IPv4 tunnels. This is intended for early experimentation with IPv6 and is not a production service.

105. What is the MBONE?

The Multicast backBONE (MBONE) is a multicast-capable portion of the Internet backbone. Multicast support over IP is provided by a protocol called IGMP (Internet Group Management Protocol) which is defined in RFC 1112. The MBONE is still a research prototype, but it extends through most of the core of the Internet (including North America, Europe, and Australia). It is typically used to relay multimedia (audio and low bandwidth video) presentations from a single source to multiple receiving sites dispersed over the Internet.

106. What is IPsec?

IPsec stands for "IP Security". The IPsec working group of the IETF is developing standards for cryptographic authentication and for encryption within IP. The base specifications are defined in RFC's 1825, 1826 and 1827. Products that implement these are beginning to appear.

107. What is TCP?

Transmission Control Protocol (TCP) provides a reliable byte-stream transfer service between two endpoints on an internet. TCP depends on IP to move packets around the network on its behalf. IP is inherently unreliable, so TCP protects against data loss, data corruption, packet reordering and data duplication by adding checksums and sequence numbers to transmitted data and, on the receiving side, sending back packets that acknowledge the receipt of data.

Before sending data across the network, TCP establishes a connection with the destination via an exchange of management packets. The connection is destroyed, again via an exchange of management packets, when the application that was using TCP indicates that no more data will be transferred. In OSI terms, TCP is a Connection-Oriented Acknowledged Transport protocol.

TCP has a multi-stage flow-control mechanism which continuously adjusts the sender's data rate in an attempt to achieve maximum data throughput while avoiding congestion and subsequent packet losses in the network. It also attempts to make the best use of network resources by packing as much data as possible into a single IP packet, although this behaviour can be overridden by applications that demand immediate data transfer and don't care about the inefficiencies of small network packets.

The fundamentals of TCP are defined in RFC 793, and later RFC's refine the protocol. RFC 1122 catalogues these refinements as of October 1989 and summarises the requirements that a TCP implementation must meet.

TCP is still being developed. For instance, RFC 1323 introduces a TCP option that can be useful when traffic is being carried over high-capacity links. It is important that such developments are backwards-compatible. That is, a TCP implementation that supports a new feature must continue to work with older TCP implementations that do not support that feature.

108. How does TCP try to avoid network meltdown?

TCP includes several mechanisms that attempt to sustain good data transfer rates while avoiding placing excessive load on the network. TCP's "Slow Start", "Congestion Avoidance", "Fast Retransmit" and "Fast Recovery" lgorithms are summarised in RFC 2001. TCP also mandates an algorithm that avoids "Silly Window Syndrome" (SWS), an undesirable condition that results in very small chunks of data being transferred between sender and receiver. SWS Avoidance is discussed in RFC 813. The "Nagle Algorithm", which prevents the sending side of TCP from flooding the network with a train of small frames, is described in RFC 896.

109. How do applications coexist over TCP and UDP?

Each application running over TCP or UDP distinguishes itself from other applications using the service by reserving and using a 16-bit port number. Destination and source port numbers are placed in the UDP and TCP headers by the originator of the packet before it is given to IP, and the destination port number allows the packet to be delivered to the intended recipient at the destination system.

So, a system may have a Telnet server listening for packets on TCP port 23 while an FTP server listens for packets on TCP port 21 and a DNS server listens for packets on port 53. TCP examines the port number in each received frame and uses it to figure out which server gets the data UDP has its own similar set of port numbers.

Many servers, like the ones in this example, always listen on the same well-known port number. The actual port number is arbitrary, but is fixed by tradition and by an official allocation or "assignment" of the number by the Internet Assigned Numbers Authority (IANA).

110. Where do I find assigned port numbers?

The IANA allocates and keeps track of all kinds of arbitrary numbers used by TCP/IP, including well-known port numbers. The entire collection is published periodically in an RFC called the Assigned Numbers RFC, each of which supersedes the previous one in the series. The current Assigned Numbers RFC is RFC 1700.

111. What is UDP?

User Datagram Protocol (UDP) provides an unreliable packetized data transfer service between endpoints on an internet. UDP depends on IP to move packets around the network on its behalf.

UDP does not guarantee to actually deliver the data to the destination, nor does it guarantee that data packets will be delivered to the destination in the order in which they were sent by the source, nor does it guarantee that only one copy of the data will be delivered to the destination. UDP does guarantee data integrity, and it does this by adding a checksum to the data before transmission. (Some machines run with UDP checksum generation disabled, in which case data corruption or truncation can go undetected. Very few people think this is a good idea.)

112. What is ICMP?

Internet Control Message Protocol (ICMP) defines a small number of messages used for diagnostic and management purposes. ICMP depends on IP to move packets around the network on its behalf.

The fundamentals of ICMP are defined in RFC 792. RFC 1122 summarises the requirements that must be met by an ICMP implementation in an Internet host, and RFC 1812 summarises the ICMP requirements for an Internet router.

ICMP is basically IP's internal network management protocol and is not intended for use by applications. Two well known exceptions are the ping and traceroute diagnostic utilities:

- ping sends and receives ICMP "ECHO" packets, where the response packet can be taken as evidence that the target host is at least minimally active on the network, and
- traceroute sends UDP packets and infers the route taken to the target from ICMP "TIME-TO-LIVE EXCEEDED" or "PORT UNREACHABLE" packets returned by the network. (Microsoft's TRACERT sends ICMP "ECHO" packets rather than UDP packets, and so receives ICMP "TIME-TO-LIVE EXCEEDED" or "ECHO RESPONSE" packets in return.)

113. How can I measure the performance of an IP link?

You can get a quick approximation by timing how long it takes to FTP or RCP a large file over the link, but bear in mind that measurement will be skewed by the time spent in dealing with the local and remote filesystems, not simply with the network itself. And remember to measure the time it takes to receive a file, not the time it takes to send it; the sender can report completion even though large amounts of data are still buffered locally by TCP and have not yet been delivered to the destination.

Two well-known open-source programs that measure and report throughput over an IP link without involving the filesystem are:

114. What IP addresses should I assign to machines on a private internet?

You shouldn't use IP addresses that have been assigned to some other organisation, because if knowledge of your network ever gets leaked onto the Internet they may disrupt that innocent organisation's activity. RFC 1918 provides a solution for this problem by allocating several IP address ranges specifically for use on private networks. These addresses will never be assigned to any organisation and are never supposed to appear on the Internet. The ranges are:

Class A: 10.0.0.0 through 10.255.255.255 Class B: 172.16.0.0 through 172.31.255.255 Class C: 192.168.0.0 through 192.168.255.255

115. Can I set up a gateway to the Internet that translates IP addresses, so that I don't have to change all our internal addresses to an official network?

This is called Network Address Translation, or NAT. In general it is a difficult thing to do properly because many applications embed IP addresses in the application-level data (FTP's "PORT" command is a notable example) so NAT isn't simply a matter of translating addresses in the IP header and recalculating header checksums. Also, if the network number(s) you're using match those assigned to another organisation, your gateway may not be able to communicate with that organisation. As noted above, RFC 1918 proposes network numbers that are reserved for private use, to avoid such conflicts, but if you're already using a different network number this won't help you.

However, there are several products that do attempt to provide this kind of on-the-fly NAT. Linux provides NAT through its "IP Masquerading" feature, and many firewall and router vendors offer NAT capabilities in their products -- look for "Network Address Translation" in your favourite Web search engine to get a list of vendors. Proxy servers developed for firewalls can also sometimes be used as a substitute for an address-translating gateway for particular application protocols.

116. Can I use a single bit subnet?

The answer used to be a straightforward "no", because a 1-bit subnet can only have a subnet part of all-ones or all-zeroes, both of which were assigned special meanings when the subnetting concept was originally defined. (All-ones meant "broadcast, all subnets of this net" and all-zeroes meant "this subnet, regardless of its actual subnet number".)

However, the old definition of subnetting has been superseded by the concept of Classless Inter-Domain Routing (CIDR, pronounced 'cider'). Under CIDR the subnet doesn't really have an existence of its own and the subnet mask simply provides the mechanism for isolating an arbitrarily-sized network portion of an IP address from the remaining host part. As CIDR-aware equipment is deployed it becomes increasingly like that you will be able to use a 1-bit subnet with at least some particular combinations of networking equipment. However, it's still not safe to assume that a 1-bit subnet will work properly with all kinds of equipment.

EXERCISES

1. change the following IP addresses from dotted—decimal notation to binary notation:
   (a) 112.32.1.7 (b) 128.13.7.9 (c) 207.35.55.12 (d) 221.30.1.7.
2. change the following IP address from dotted-decimal notation to hexadecimal notation:
   (a) 113.33.2.7 (b) 128.14.6.8 (c) 207.33.55.127.
3. find the class of the following IP address:
   (a) 207.33.55.11 (b) 233.13.2.8 (c) 113.54.3.97.
4. find the netid and the hosted of the following IP address
   (a) 123.13.7.8 (b) 13.33.20.4 (c) 22.56.11.17.
5. In a class A subnet we know the IP address of one of the hosts and the mask as given IP Address:23.33.11.52 mask: 255.255.0.0 what is the first address and the last address in this subnet?

6. In a class B subnet we know the IP address of one of the hosts and the mask as given IP Address:123.133.111.52 mask: 255.255.223.0 what is the first address and the last address in this subnet.
7. In a class C subnet we know the IP address of one of the hosts and the mask as given IP Address:178.33.16.12 mask: 255.255.225.192 what is the first address and the last address in this subnet.
8. Find the range of address in the following blocks
   (a) 126.54.66.23 (b) 200.16.22.123 (c) 16.33.11.227.
9. A host with IP address 136.22.35.33 sends a packet to a host with IP address 136.22.32. 22 Is the delivery direct or indirect?
10. Arouter with IP address 102.33.55.7 sends a packet to a host with IP address 200.33.2.5 Is the delivery direct or indirect.

INDEX